Bibliografische Information der Deutschen Nationalbibliothek
Die Deutsche Nationalbibliothek verzeichnet diese Publikation in der
Deutschen Nationalbibliografie; detaillierte bibliografische Daten
sind im Internet über http://dnb.d-nb.de abrufbar.

Neil Deane
Modern Germany
An outsider's view from the inside

Berlin: Pro BUSINESS 2014

ISBN 978-3-86386-713-3

1. Auflage 2014

Cover Design & Layout
Judith Damen
University of Duisburg-Essen
Contact: judith.damen@stud.uni-due.de

Modern Germany – an outsider's view from the inside

by Neil Deane

For L....

I hope you gain some
useful insight.

Best wishes,

Neil Deane

Essen 1st July 2014

Modern Germany – an outsider's view from the inside

7   The state of the nation at the start of the 21st century

> *"The "Economic Giant, Political Dwarf" role fits like the proverbial comfy shoe and nobody is in any great hurry to try on any other."*

8   The final verdict

> *"German hygiene is wonderful, but man does not live on hygiene alone."*

Introduction

The British seem more eager than most to circulate the myth that Germans are humourless creatures, efficient robots who swill beer from stone mugs while slapping their *Lederhosen*-clad thighs to the loud and angry melody of "*Deutschland über alles*". I would like to be the Brit that doesn't and this book gives me the chance to do just that. Clichés, admittedly, don't appear out of thin air, but it may well be time to state categorically that Germans *do* mention the war, *do not* fall into severe bouts of depression if they don't get their favourite sunbed by the pool and *do* sometimes miss penalties (except when playing against England, of course). Renouncing those and the many other clichés and prejudices that abound regarding Germany and the Germans is, therefore, one of the main aims of this book. If you are at this very moment standing in a bookshop and you wish to read something which earnestly attempts to offer a balanced, informative and entertaining look at Germany today, you could do worse than to take this book over to the sales assistant and say: "I'll have this, please." If you're German, just say: "*Ich hätte gern dieses Buch.*" (This is of course assuming that you are actually one of those rare specimens of the human race that still buy their books in old-fashioned bookshops. If you aren't, just click the usual options).

A German student friend of mine went onto the streets of Liverpool, GB at the end of the seventies, armed with a microphone, a tape recorder and the simple question: "What comes to mind when you hear the word GERMANY?" Most answers were predictable in the extreme: the War; Franz Beckenbauer; Beer (and the Munich beer festival); Volkswagen cars and yes, of course, Hitler. Perhaps the answers said more about the intelligence and parochialism of the interviewees than anything else. When prompted to talk more about Germany, however, they articulated a grudging respect, bordering on mild affection. This gave me hope that Anglo-German relations could still be rescued; this book is also attempting to continue that tenuous trend, well over thirty years on. This account of life in Germany is by a British German specialist who feels the need to try and put the record straight about the place and the people who live in it. Simply put, I have done my level best to give a balanced and comprehensive survey of what modern

Germany is, has been and is in the process of becoming since I ventured off those Liverpool streets all those years ago and ultimately made Germany what I now tentatively call (and with a nagging, guilty conscience) "home".

The book consists of eight chapters answering the main questions I believe an intelligent human being might have when their thoughts turn to modern Germany. The first chapter turns to recent history for some preliminary answers. Based on the common sense assumption that to understand today's Germany means understanding yesterday's Germany, Chapter 1 starts the proceedings by describing how Germany was moulded in the crucial years after the end of the Second World War. Chapter 2 tries to answer the fundamental question which many Brits ask me: "What's it actually like to live in Germany?" For those readers who want to go a few profound steps further and ask such questions as "What makes the Germans tick?", Chapter 3 is my brave dig into the German soul to answer that very question. An impossible task, but I felt I owed it to myself to get the spade working on that challenging project. The auto-biographical chapter 4 relates my own personal journey through (I'm showing my age now) 35 years of life in Germany, warts and all. Living in Germany as a Brit is not always plain sailing and Chapter 5 looks into the challenges a Brit (or other foreigners for that matter) might face. People from other cultures (primarily from the Anglo-Saxon world, I suppose) will derive some degree of glee reading about my painful, amusing and baffling cultural learning process in Germany over the course of 30 years or more. The subject of the two Germanys since reunification is another challenge I wanted to face head-on - see Chapter 6 for some personal insights. Germans, ever willing to improve themselves and discover what other nations think about them, should also find much to interest them on those pages. Chapter 7 focuses on what I regard as being the burning issues of Germany today and the final chapter 8 does the usual summarizing and looking-into-the-future job.

There have been a number of highly entertaining books recently written by hapless Brits and Americans relating thigh-slapping, hilarious scenes of confusion and mirth, brought upon by their lack of cultural knowledge about their new foreign homes. I am attempting to write a book which, however, does not restrict itself to relating such scenarios. *A year in the merde* by Stephen Clarke and

A year in the Scheiße by Roger Boyes, to name but two, are highly anecdotal and personalized accounts which look at life in France and Germany respectively over a short period of time. Bill Bryson wrote, I suppose, the mother of such books in the form of *Notes from a small island* in 1995, when he expressed American bewilderment at the British way of life. While my book also constantly refers to the good *and* bad experiences, it also aims to get away from the rather churlish tendency to "have a go at the Germans". The main aim throughout is to inform, referring to facts, figures and statistics where necessary and entertain, in the laugh-out-loud style of the books mentioned above when humour is the only antidote to the tricky business of surviving in a foreign culture.

Anybody living much of their life in a foreign country eventually feels the overwhelming urge to talk about it and what you hold in your hands is the accumulated version of that foreign experience. Life in a foreign culture is a continuous series of learning processes, some uplifting, some annoying, but always interesting. As a man reaches a certain age in life, he (or at least I) feels the even more overwhelming need to get it in print before memories and faculties fade and there is nobody left to relate them to. That man, therefore, has decided to act.

The starting point for this book is still that of an Englishman who has his roots in a town on the River Mersey, called Liverpool. Despite the fact that I have now spent more time living in Germany than England, I am still a Scouser. But I am also often reminded of John Lennon's words: "I grew up in Liverpool, but became a man in Hamburg". In my case it wasn't Hamburg but a number of different towns the length and breadth of Germany. I still spend much of my life comparing my own culture with the German one and come to the rather unsurprising conclusion that Germany is totally different from Britain. The rather peculiar fact is, however, that I have now accepted this and am happy with my lot here. A fully integrated, happy outsider. Confused? Well, read on and you might achieve enlightenment.

1   Creating a new Germany – a post-war historical survey

"THE DESIRE TO FORGET WAS GREAT, KEEPING THE POPULATION IN ITS FIRM GRIP IN THE IMMEDIATE POST-WAR CHAOS, YET FREEING THE MIND TO DEAL WITH MORE PRESSING MATTERS."

The Second World War in Europe came to an end on May 8, 1945 and the situation in the country that started it all truly beggared description. Which is why the Germans called it *"Stunde Null"*- zero hour. Time had stood still. They had nothing. They could see nothing but destruction all around them. An estimated 20 million people were homeless, further millions searched desperately to find anything worth eating and burning in rubble-strewn urban landscapes which had little in common with the orderly well-kept cities of pre-1939 Germany. Even in that catastrophic and hopeless situation we can observe the Germans' desire to somehow bring forth order from chaos in the form of *"Trümmerfrauen"* (literally, women of the rubble) forming columns to clear away the worst of that rubble and place it in neat orderly lines along the streets and roads. The only males left were men over the age of 60, disabled veterans from six years of fighting on various fronts and boys under the age of 16. The rest of the German male population were dead, wounded, or in (or on the way to) prisoner of war camps all over Europe, Siberia and North America. Germany had lost approximately five million men in the war. Tony Judt chillingly reminds us in *Post War: a history of Europe since 1945* (2005: 19) that "two out of three (German) men born in 1918 did not survive the war".

Anything of up to two million civilians lost their lives and to make matters worse, approximately 13 million refugees had already started their exodus from Eastern provinces (primarily from present day Poland and the former Soviet Union) to start a new life in the four allied military sectors of zero-hour Germany. Quite what they expected to find in their new home was difficult to imagine, but the forced expulsion from a Germany which was no longer Germany according to directives laid down by the Allied powers gave them no option. Parts of Germany became Poland or the Soviet Union and further hundreds of thousands expellees came from Czechoslovakia, Romania and Hungary. The grandfather of a former girlfriend of mine committed suicide when he and his family were forced out of Breslau (now called Wroclaw in Poland) in 1945. His widow and her two sons and daughter spent 18 months drifting in a westerly direction before getting to a refugee camp in Stahnsdorf near Berlin in the Soviet Zone, sometime in 1946. The widow had lost one of her sons on that treacherous journey, burying him in an unnamed, shallow grave by the roadside. My girlfriend's mother survived, never talked about these 18 months again and remained visibly marked by the nightmare for the rest of her life. The grandmother, apparently, talked more, arguing that there were certain things you have to do in matters of survival. What these "things" were remained a grisly secret. She re-married in the fifties, survived her second husband, the GDR (German Democratic Republic), two strokes and died well into her nineties.

Other women with more fragile constitutions fared less well as the Red Army surged westward in the first months of 1945. It is a sad fact that the soldiers of that brave army had carte blanche in those desperate months and widespread rape seemed to be almost the norm. I knew an elderly woman in Berlin who was 18 at the end of the war. She worked at a chemist's and her illegally-obtained cyanide tablets were her constant companion as Berlin crumbled. Violent rape or suicide? She had already made her decision. Thankfully she never had to take the cyanide or the decision. Such horrific stories abounded in the twisted chaos and bedlam in the eastern provinces of the fast disintegrating Third Reich at the beginning of 1945.

Germany had just emerged from six years of war, three years of which could be described as "Total War" (Goebbels' term not mine), with little hope of victory and during which the civilian population was being subjected to incessant Allied bombing from 1942 onwards. The desperate nature of the situation in those dark days is probably unimaginable for anybody not directly involved. However, one can imagine that the desire to survive in such situations becomes focused and unbreakable - what's the alternative? The situation, regardless of how grim it was, must have been half an inch more favourable than being at war. Anybody left standing was still alive and would stay alive provided they were able to find some sort of shelter and get something inside their stomachs from somewhere. The tide for a human being hell-bent on surviving would have to turn someday.

The desire to forget was great, keeping the population in its firm grip in the immediate post-war chaos, yet freeing the mind to deal with more pressing matters. Channelling all your energies into the everyday mammoth task of staying alive must also have had something therapeutic about it and could clearly take your mind off the horrors of the previous years. People learnt to become first-class negotiators on the thriving black market. Friends and relatives who lived in the country were suddenly people you desperately wanted to visit and keeping your eyes open for anything edible when visiting rural areas became a skill that was constantly being fine-tuned to perfection in the years just after the war. Was it a real crime to procure potatoes from a farmer's field or coal from a railway siding if it meant your family was kept warm and reasonably well-fed for a week? Was an illegal contact with Allied personnel who provided vital goods and uplifting treats really a crime? These are questions I have heard from older Germans down the years. They are very hard to answer with "Yes". The Germans had their hands full surviving in those years and the survival game was a key element in developing a strategy for forgetting.

The key date representing a breakthrough for those Germans living in the Western Allied Zones was the Currency Reform of June 21, 1948 when the West German Mark (Deutschmark) was introduced. It was the beginning of the social market economy and it meant that people could buy sufficient food at reasonable prices. Life was still tough, the cities still lay in heaps of rubble, but the feeling of the worst being over was in the air. It was also the beginning of the division of Germany into East (the Soviet Sector) and West (the American, British and French Sectors). Just over a year later the two German states came into being: The Federal Republic of Germany, with the proclamation of the *"Grundgesetz"* (Basic Law) on May 23, 1949, and the founding of the German Democratic Republic on October 7, 1949. Bonn was proclaimed provisional capital of the Federal Republic while the East Germans understandably plumped for (East) Berlin. Germany had been divided and was going to remain that way for another 41 years. There could hardly have been many Germans overly bothered by this new development; the job of surviving was taking up all their time and efforts.

How can a people emerge from 12 years of brutal Nazi dictatorship, six years of war with the rest of Europe ending in total defeat (and anything between 50 and 70 million dead), three or four years of near starvation in the midst of economic and political meltdown and recover to be Europe's top economic power with a democratic system of government admired (and sometimes envied) throughout the world? Before attempting to answer this question I would like to remind the reader of the price Germany has had to pay for the consequences of the years from 1933 to 1945.

THE GERMANS IN 1949 - WHAT WERE THEY AND WHAT DID THEY BECOME?

When the worst was actually over and the two Germanys emerged in 1949, the division of Europe had been cemented. West-Berlin remained in the centre of the new German Democratic Republic, its open border offering a fairly simple escape route for dissatisfied East Germans. And as the fifties progressed, increasing numbers made use of it. The prospect of a united Germany in the foreseeable future remained a distant one. A divided Germany was the price for a war of aggression waged in search of "living space" by Hitler, the man ultimately responsible for the Second World War and the endless human suffering caused by it.

So how did the Germans cope with the fact that their people had followed, supported, fought and died for a cause so evil and destructive that Germans today still shake their head in disbelief, asking the eternal question: how was all this possible? It would seem that this problem in those post-war days was solved by not asking the question at all. When you have your hands full desperately keeping body and soul together, you develop a strict set of priorities and concerning yourself with unanswerable questions will clearly not be top of your list. Survive, eke out some sort of existence, work hard and hope for better days would seem to have been the German formula for life after the war. The Germans, after all, had already paid a huge price: families decimated, homes destroyed, a nation ripped in two and the hatred of, for the time being at least, the rest of the world. They wanted at this point in their history to get on with their fight for survival in a world of grim silence and stoic industry. Time may one day heal most of the wounds.

The question of what happened to six million Jews, however, was not something that was ever going to go away. And, to this day it still hasn't. The liberation of the death camps and the realization of what had happened must have seeped deeply into every Germany psyche in those years. Jews were not the enemy in any military sense, their extermination had no strategic purpose. Again, the answer was not to talk about it. We should remember also that the Germans had had 12 years of practice at "not talking about things" under the Nazi dictatorship. Old habits die hard.

Heinrich Böll (1917-1985), one of the best-known, post-war German writers and Nobel prize winner, wrote in 1984 an essay, "*Brief an meine Söhne*" (Letter to my sons – my translation) in which the following, sweeping, yet important sentence attempts to define the immediate, post-war German : "*Ihr werdet die Deutschen immer wieder daran erkennen können, ob sie den 8. Mai als Niederlage oder Befreiung bezeichnen*". (You will always be able to recognise the Germans based on whether they describe the 8th May as defeat or liberation – my translation). Böll would appear to be reminding us of the bitter truth that a large number of Germans were saddened by the defeat in war and those people would be present for a long time to come in the New Germany.

As the initial waves of denazification ebbed and normality gradually returned, people were starting to talk. Unfortunately, what they were saying did little to lighten the mood of observers who thought Germany had changed for the better. In November 1946 a survey in the American Zone showed that 37% of those questioned took the view that "the extermination of Jews and non-Aryans was necessary for the security of Germans" (Judt 2005: 58). In another survey in 1952, 25% of West Germans admitted to having a "good opinion" (Judt 2005:58) of Hitler. It could just well be that one was expecting too much too soon, but it reveals a disturbing fact that what the rest of the world regarded as evil was regarded as acceptable by a not inconsiderable number of post-war Germans. The "old habits die hard" interpretation holds again.

The above observations refer to Germans living in the Western Zones of occupation (later the Federal Republic of Germany). Developments in the Eastern Zone of occupation (later the German Democratic Republic) were rather different. In the East, dealing with the past was a relatively simple matter. Soviet denazification was a rigorous process of putting any Fascist (their term for Nazis) to the sword as quickly and efficiently as possible; after that the task was to build Socialism according to Stalinist doctrine. Any Germans who had been Communists before or during the war were welcome to stay in the Soviet zone and re-build a country to defend Socialism against the new Fascist state emerging in the form of the Federal Republic of Germany. And many did. The simple message was that all the ex-Nazis had already fled to the West and now it was time to defend Socialism under the caring hand of the Soviet Union. In other words, the Second World War could continue in the form of the Cold War. The Goodies were in the East and the Baddies were quite clearly in the West. The other important conclusion to be drawn from these facts, therefore, was that nobody in the new German Democratic Republic had anything to do with the terrible crimes perpetrated in the name of Adolf Hitler as they had spent all their time between 1933 and 1945 fighting against him and his band of criminals and therefore had no reason to lose any sleep over it. A history lesson bulging with simplicity and logic.

The GDR, therefore, was allowed to live the rest of its life as the Germany that fought against Hitler in the war. Its citizens were all anti-fascist heroes, fighting side by side with the Soviet Union until that glorious day in May 1945 came and a true anti-fascist state could be built. Anybody living in that country actually grew up believing this. It made things a lot simpler of course, but was also rather untrue. It was certainly true that the dyed-in-the wool Communists did tend to stay there after the war, just as true Catholics stay in the Catholic Church because they have nowhere else to go and their faith does not permit them to go anywhere else. It is also a fact, however, that many ex-Nazis made good new Communists; following orders in a totalitarian state was second nature to them and democracy was the last thing on their mind. There is also plenty of evidence to suggest that the Communist authorities in the new East Germany were actually using blackmail as a way of convincing former Nazis to throw in their lot with their system (cf. Judt 2005: 60-6). Such ex-Nazis were, after all, extremely vulnerable to blackmail; they were also used to a totalitarian system and displaying unshakable faith in a system of that nature.

Both new German states also had a common problem in the years immediately following the war: an acute lack of skilled, trained manpower. The only class to be able to call itself "skilled and trained" in these years were obviously ex-Nazis or men and women at least sympathetic to the Nazi regime. Where else were the two new Germanys to get their teachers, lawyers, doctors, engineers and technicians for their new future? Let us not forget that the Americans had no qualms about recruiting Werner von Braun for their developing space programme. In the last years of the war he had been developing Hitler's "*Wunderwaffen*" (miracle weapons), the V1 and V2, to wreak terror and destruction on Britain's towns. Now he was the slick, clever, "good Nazi" helping the Americans win the Space Race. A similar title was given to Albert Speer at the Nuremberg trials in 1946 as he escaped the gallows and instead sat out 20 years in Spandau Prison in Berlin before re-appearing in 1966 to publish his memoirs, providing himself with a comfortable nest egg for his twilight years. He claimed not to have known about the Jewish extermination plan, a claim so ridiculous that he must have spent every day of his 20 years in Spandau not believing his own luck.

A look at the claim "I didn't know what was going on" is perhaps a good way to end this section because it is one made by virtually every adult German that survived the war; it manifested itself in mass, selective amnesia throughout the former Third Reich during those years. Further questions on the topic were avoided, ignored and in many cases never raised at all. Everybody was obsessed with the desire for a new start to assure economic prosperity in the West or the New Jerusalem via Socialism in the East. Everybody in Germany in those years had many stories to tell but hardly any were willing to relate them. The goals of East and West Germany could only be achieved by total dedication; forgetting the past, or in the case of the GDR, re-writing it, was the first requisite for starting on the path to achieving them - for better or worse.

As the fifties began, the growing economic prosperity in West Germany was helping everybody to forget. West Germany's first Chancellor of the Exchequer after the war was Ludwig Erhard, a man whose watchword was always "prosperity for all". As the fifties progressed, the watchword was starting to become reality. A feeling of unity was aided by the fact that Germany at least appeared to be starting out on a level playing field after the Currency Reform, with every citizen over the age of 21 receiving the exact amount of money in the form of 40 marks of the new currency. A couple of weeks later they received another 20 marks, thus creating the slightly misleading but romantic impression that much of the adult population was equal in their economic misery on that date and that from that date onwards people had the chance to make something of their lives with the same 60 marks. It is of course important to remember that, as George Orwell cynically reminded us in *Animal Farm* (1945), "all animals are equal, but some are more equal than others" and the propertied classes and industrialists whose houses and buildings had escaped destruction through Allied bombing were in a much better position to make something of their lives – their first 60 Deutschmarks were hardly going to make any difference to their opportunities and future development. But Marshall Aid was flowing in and investment was made in new industrial infrastructure and new ideas and people were more than willing to throw themselves into the ultimate distraction in these years: work. Older West Germans often wax lyrical about this period, praising the uplifting mood of people rolling up their sleeves, making do with little but seeing economic progress gradually being made all around them. If, as many business pundits have often pointed out, economics is 90% psychology, post-war German's relatively optimistic mood after the currency reform promised hope for its economic future.

Political dogma and fighting were a thing of the past, the social-market economy functioned perfectly as post-war external and internal demand steadily grew with elderly Konrad Adenauer as Chancellor, offering a steady hand and a clear vision that West Germany belonged in the Western European Alliance with France as its main partner. With no military expenditure (the West German Army didn't come into existence until 1955), few debts to pay back and no overseas commitments, West Germany was able to focus on developing its economic prowess. All these factors contributed to a more or less smooth ride to impressive prosperity by the end of the fifties.

All these favourable factors were missing in the post-war British narrative. Crippling war debts with the Americans, military commitments all over the world (including a dogged determination to remain a nuclear power) thanks to the escalating Cold War, disappearing Empire and a workforce still in the grip of class conflict formed the general scenario in the British post-war years. Plagued by outdated machinery and equally outdated working practices, rising productivity and real improvement in the standard of living was barely discernible. The Britons' psychology at the time was also a massive hindrance: the overwhelming feeling was that a long and calamitous war had been won and a nation only had to wait for the good times to roll. Britain's reluctance to join the Common Market along with the Six (West Germany, France, Italy and the Benelux countries) in 1957 was also to prove a grave error as she chose instead to show allegiance, in trading and political terms, to the newly-founded Commonwealth and the USA.

Hundreds of thousands of East Germans were leaving the German Democratic Republic for the West in the fifties. West Germany was greatly benefitting from this welcome influx of men and women (many highly-skilled) who were determined to make a new start, after turning their backs on the very modest fruits borne by the sort of Socialism practised behind the Iron Curtain. The fact that its citizens were still allowed to enter West-Berlin unhindered had meant that approximately 3 million of them had settled in West Germany since 1949. Despite the fact that many economists had marvelled at how East Germany's own economic miracle had taken off in the fifties despite vast Soviet reparations and large-scale dismantling of everything that could be moved eastwards, many East Germans had lost any hope of genuine improvement. This haemorrhaging of East Germany via West-Berlin was finally stopped on August 13, 1961 with the construction of the Berlin Wall.

Real prosperity and ever-increasing spending power were the watchwords of the sixties in West Germany. Having a car meant you had made the first important step on the road to prosperity. Foreign holidays were the next big thing. Foreign cuisine and fitted kitchens followed. Good clothes, modern, clean, re-built cities, an extended *Autobahn* system stretching the length and breadth of the country and people enjoying a standard of living by the end of the sixties which would have been unimaginable only 20 years earlier. German products were of high quality and exports to the recovering nations of the Second World War (and the constantly booming US market) were exceeding all expectations. Industrial relations were peaceful and pragmatic and the labour force was well-trained and educated. Inflation was low, wages and salaries were high enough to allow real money to be saved, backed up by index-linked pensions and social benefits which generously assisted anybody losing their job (unlikely by the end of the sixties as Germany experienced for the first time in its history almost full-employment). Rented accommodation conformed to the highest modern standards and was affordable. More and more people were building their own houses and for the first time in their lives inheriting generous amounts of money. By the mid-sixties, hundreds of thousands of "guest workers" from Turkey, Italy, Spain, Portugal, Greece and Yugoslavia were flooding into the country as employers were desperately trying to solve a chronic shortage of labour and by the sixties, Germans were getting very choosy about what sort of jobs they wanted to do. Manual labouring work, refuse disposal work and jobs down the mines were increasingly being done by the newly-arrived guest workers. Even British construction workers got in on the act as they escaped the recession-gripped seventies and Thatcher-dominated eighties to help with Germany's construction boom.

In many respects, Britain was the exact opposite to everything I have described above. Although jobs were also fairly plentiful in the late fifties and early sixties in Britain, prosperity could only be described as modest, although the then Prime Minister, Harold Macmillan, pleaded otherwise with his famous, "You've never had it so good" quote (A claim that would, however, have been spot-on for the Germany of that time). And Britain's skyline had hardly changed at all. With the exception of ugly, born-to-fail housing estates of the sixties and seventies, Britain looked pretty much the same as it had pre-war. Towns looked old, dilapidated, out-of-date and generally scruffy. The first time I was able to make the comparison was in 1970 as I peeked out of the railway carriage of a train that had parked for what seemed like an age in Cologne railway station. I was on a school trip to Germany: one week in Königssee, a small, picturesque holiday resort town on the edge of a lake in the southern reaches of Bavaria. Presumably the Germans I saw walking along the platforms of Cologne main station in the early hours of a July Monday morning were on their way to work. I had never seen people in Liverpool going to work so early, nor did any of them look anywhere near as smart as these people. Their high-quality clothes actually fitted them and the people in them oozed a healthy confidence. Although the bewildered 13-year old didn't know it at the time, he was catching a superficial glimpse of Germany at the peak of its economic power. Unemployment figures and economic performance were never going to get any better than this, although wealth generation and general prosperity within that new Germany was to continue throughout the rest of that boy's adult life. More of that later.

The shadow of the past and the undoubted fears of its European neighbours meant that Germany kept itself in the background in the global, political sense after the war. It has, by and large, remained this way to date. Its refusal to participate in the 2011 quasi-military campaign to overthrow Gaddafi's regime in Libya is part of a long list of "not interested" signals German foreign policy has consistently given out over the past 60 years. It has been a loyal supporter of most Western alliance decisions but has baulked at military participation. Notable exceptions have been their recent involvement in the Balkan wars in the nineties and the support for US military measures in post-9/11 Afghanistan. If non-participation appears to be supporting inhumane, dictatorial activities, even Germany is occasionally willing to join in.

THE 60S AND 70S CLEAR-OUT

For most observers, the sixties were seen as the decade of revolutions; for some it was a more liberal view of sexual matters, for others it was pop culture, including fashion, hippiedom and quite simply "doing your own thing". All these things affected (West) German attitudes, which tended to be conservative, traditional and for want of a better word, stuffy. By the end of the sixties those had been changed forever (as they had, of course, in most west European countries). The Adenauer years had been remarkable for political and social stability and breathtaking economic growth based on sensible, almost patriarchal nurturing. As youth culture grew from its rock "n" roll roots of the late fifties into the Beatles' and Stones' generation, its culmination was the beautiful yet idealistic battle cry "All you need is love".

The German sixties therefore embraced all of the ideas, ideals and hopes of the younger, better-educated generation and there was a dogged determination to create a more open society. Openness in the German context, however, was going to lead Germans down some very disturbing paths. If it meant having the freedom to discuss anything and everything, then Germany was in a quandary; the younger generation suddenly wanted to be able to ask those all-important questions such as "What exactly did you do in the war, Dad?" Any reticence to respond could almost be seen as an admission of guilt or as a trick to cover something up. Further unpleasant questions such as "Did you know what was happening to the Jews?" were going to produce further turmoil. A generation gap developed in these years as younger people received fewer and fewer satisfactory answers to more and more uncomfortable questions.

A further swing to the left in the sixties exacerbated the situation as the younger generation became diametrically opposed to an establishment they believed their parents had become an encrusted part of. Even minimal probing was starting to uncover that some of the leading lights of industry and commerce were ex-Nazis. For many young left-wingers, the Grand Coalition of 1966-1969 was marred forever by the Social Democrats' acceptance of Kurt Kiesinger, a paid-up Nazi Party member during and before the war, as CDU (Christian Democratic Union) Chancellor of that particular coalition. When questioned about his membership of the NSDAP, he averred that opportunism rather than conviction had been his main motivational factor in the Nazi-dominated thirties. Those on the left were understandably unconvinced and many political activists chose extra-parliamentary paths to political fulfillment in these years, which lead to a hard, vicious core of terrorism by the mid-seventies.

When the SPD came to power in 1969 as the senior coalition partner with the Liberal FDP, the SPD Chancellor, Willy Brandt, stated in his acceptance speech that they wanted to "dare more democracy". The statement can be interpreted in a number of ways and the common consensus now is that it was to herald the end of the subtly authoritarian and patriarchal rule of Adenauer and to encourage everyday people to involve themselves in matters that concerned them. Brandt appeared more as an easy-going, older brother rather than an overbearing father. On the domestic front he upgraded much social policy in a period of economic stability and increased the number of higher and further education institutions: the university I now work at, the University of Duisburg-Essen, founded in 1972, is an example of such expansion. This and other such universities in this area have offered hitherto impossible opportunities to young men and women over the past 40 years.

Brandt's major legacy, however, remains in the field of foreign policy: major steps were taken to normalize relations with Germany's East European neighbours, notably Poland and the Soviet Union. Brandt's new approach also included the virtual recognition of the GDR as a sovereign state. For some, Brandt had given away large tracts of Germany's eastern lands; for others it was a reasonable price to pay in the pursuit of good relations with neighbours Germany had once treated so abominably 30 years before. When he spontaneously knelt down in front of the Warsaw Ghetto memorial in 1970 the world watched and believed it was seeing a new Germany, a Germany showing remorse and desire for reconciliation. It proved to be the beginning of what he himself called the "politics of small steps" which was a parallel development to détente in the seventies and ultimately led to the end of the Cold War and the fall of the Berlin Wall.

What Willy Brandt was doing in public was indeed capturing the imagination of the younger generation. The desire to open up, discuss and get out into the open what had happened in their fathers' generation was strong. Yet their fathers did not appear to have the same enthusiasm for honest and open discussion. The result was that the generation gap in those years became bigger rather than smaller. The idealism of the late sixties had also taught those wrapped up in it that the meaning of life was not just about the next fitted kitchen or new car. Virtually anything could be questioned, discussed, analysed and, consequently, changed.

Willy Brandt's successor, Helmut Schmidt, continued a fairly successful period of SPD-FDP government up to the start of the eighties, but inherited a terrorist problem that had its roots in those disaffected circles of young, extreme left-wing individuals who saw no "progress" possible through parliamentary democracy. Their aims remain to this day a mystery, aside from terrorizing high-profile businessmen and politicians (some with admittedly dodgy records from Germany's 1933-1945 history) and carrying out atrocity after atrocity throughout the mid-seventies. Terrorism was not the only problem Schmidt had to face in his period of office between 1973 and 1982. The quadrupling of oil prices at the beginning of the seventies hit all economies; unemployment rose ever steadily and Germany was no longer having its own way on the world export market as Japan muscled in on the electronics and automobile market. And the old-style heavy industries were starting to be run down, with particularly harrowing economic consequences for regions such as the Ruhr area and the Saarland.

Yet Germany still looked in fine shape to me. When I first started working here in 1979, it was like a different world from the place I left. The massive surpluses produced in the sixties and seventies had been invested wisely in infrastructure, well-designed towns and "dwelling and green" spaces which offered respite to city dwellers throughout the republic. And the people themselves always looked as spick and span as their sparkling towns. One must bear in mind that I had just emerged from strike-dominated, recession-hit, decaying Liverpool, a city which had been on a downward spiral for as long as anybody could remember. Britain (or certainly my bit of it) had been the sick man of Europe for a long time; Germany looked a picture of health.

The seventies were also a time when people in West Germany were starting to reap the rewards of their parents' and grandparents' grinding hard work and ability to keep and accumulate money. The generous pensions had made life rather comfortable and when the grandmas and grandpas were falling off their perches in the seventies there were not insubstantial amounts being dished out to grateful offspring. Sensible and solid investments in property, high life insurance payouts and general low inflation that had been typical of post-war Germany meant that people were now in possession of serious amounts of money. The seventies were the starting point for people in Germany to start buying big and to flaunt what they had. Their readiness to do so made an impoverished, young Scouser like myself feel that bit poorer as the seventies became the eighties in Germany.

Unemployment still kept rising, however, and by the beginning of the eighties there were the first signs that even Germany was starting to live beyond its means. An added problem was that the Germans were not producing enough children. Sooner or later they would run out of people to pay for the generous pensions they were now dishing out to older people who were exacerbating the problem by living ever longer. This contributed to the demise of Schmidt's coalition government in 1982, when their junior coalition partner, the FDP, threw their lot in with the CDU who claimed - as conservative parties often tend to claim - that they would balance the books more effectively. So Helmut Kohl became Chancellor in 1982, proclaiming the "Moral turning point". Nobody has ever satisfactorily explained to me since then what this was supposed to mean but it was redolent of Margaret Thatcher's promise, on coming to power, to "run a good household".

By the end of the seventies a new political party had emerged in Germany in the form of the Green Party (re-titled "*Bündnis 90/Die Grünen*" after re-unification, but still generally referred to simply as "The Greens"). This new party emerged for two main reasons: firstly, concern over environmental problems had been growing dramatically in the seventies, which meant that a party devoting itself primarily to such problems would find ready support. And support it did find, particularly amongst young voters who believed the established parties were not taking these problems seriously enough. Secondly, the SPD, the traditional left-of-centre German party, was beginning to lose its appeal among younger, left-wing voters; the technocratic, sober style of Helmut Schmidt paled in comparison to his more charismatic, idealistic predecessor, Willy Brandt. The extreme, revolutionary left-wingers in Germany either drifted into terrorism (and here we are talking about a minute minority) or set up camp with the Greens. That party to this day still accommodates a wide spectrum of left wing/ecologically-minded people who feel more at home in an alternative-style party than in the SPD which traditionally aims at representing the working man and woman. One further reason for this is

23

the fact that most Green voters probably do not come from those traditional working class homes that the SPD has always claimed to represent.

The Greens have now become an established party in Germany, entering the German parliament for the first time in 1983. They were a junior coalition partner with the SPD-led government between 1998 and 2005. At the time of writing there is a Green Minister for the Federal State of Baden-Wurttemberg, the first time this has happened since the founding of the party (the Fukushima incident in Japan made a big contribution to this success in the spring of 2011). It is also a fact that the Greens have been responsible for moving on progressive, ecologically-friendly policies in Germany for many years now, resulting in the country becoming a sort of standard bearer in such policies worldwide.

The most long-lasting consequence of the emergence of the Greens and its relative success on the political scene in the seventies and eighties, however, was that the Left in Germany had been permanently split. Helmut Schmidt's coalition government was to be the last SPD-led administration for 16 years when he lost a vote of no-confidence in October, 1982. The rather cosy dominance of the CDU and SPD in German political life was over for good, and the SPD was going to have to win back Green voters or form coalitions with the Greens themselves to win back power. This was not to happen until Gerhard Schroeder formed such a coalition in 1998. In the meantime the Kohl era was about to begin.

THE KOHL ERA

For me (although not alone with this opinion), Helmut Kohl represented an era of lethargy during which nothing much actually seemed to happen. If there was ever a problem, he would wait until it solved itself. It always seemed to me that he took the view that everything had progressed smoothly in his post-war lifetime, so why shouldn't it continue that way? All he needed to do was keep a closer eye on costs, tweak a few policies here and there and normal service could be resumed in next to no time.

In many ways, of course, he was right. The prosperity of the seventies continued into the eighties, people were still inheriting money like never before and Germans looked as well off as ever. There were, however, some disturbing cracks under the surface. The demographic imbalance was still there, i.e. ever fewer younger people were financing the pensions of an ever-increasing number of older folk. The situation was made more difficult by a consistent increase in the number of people out of work. I first heard the German expression "*Die fetten Jahre sind vorbei*" (The fat years are over - my translation) emanating from the mouth of my then German boss, Frau Karin G., the charming owner of a small language school in the town of Minden, Westphalia. I have heard the expression many times since then, used by Germans who sensed that the steady upward rise in growth was unsustainable. All growth, as we know, has to stop sometime and the eighties were certainly a turning point; by the end of that decade, things, to put it very generally, were getting tighter.

Kohl quickly realised that cuts had to be made. The usual targets were rolled into the firing line: unemployment benefit, social benefits and a whole range of tax perks. But ultimately, his government was only tweaking the welfare system, which was still generous. The major reforms that were needed in view of the ageing population were still being put off for another day. The word "*Reformstau*" (reform backlog – my translation) was the word used most frequently in connection with Kohl's government and any reforms made in those years tended to be half-hearted affairs. Kohl, it seemed, was a man ferociously intent on not rocking the boat.

In foreign affairs, Kohl often seemed out of his depth. Inept at foreign languages (unlike his predecessors, Brandt and Schmidt), he tended to muddle through as best he could. Thoroughly in agreement with the Americans' stance on deploying ever more missiles in Western Europe to counter what Reagan called the Soviet "Evil Empire", he displayed no new approaches to solving the problems of the East-West conflict. His deep mistrust of the East raised its head on a number of occasions; his comparison of the new Soviet leader, Gorbachev, with Josef Goebbels in 1986 caused dismay amongst anybody hoping for a positive change in the Cold War climate. His Foreign Minister, Hans-Dietrich Genscher, was actually much quicker grasping the fact that you could do business with Gorbachev.

Kohl also estranged large sections of his own people by clumsily re-inventing a phrase coined in a different context by the SPD politician and journalist Günter Gaus, by using his "*Die Gnade der späten Geburt*" (Grace of a late birth – my translation). Kohl was inferring that being born late absolved you from any guilt for the atrocities committed during the Third Reich; Gaus was actually referring to his own personal relief of not being old enough to have had to take decisions about life and death in a German uniform in the more atrocious acts of Nazi barbarism. Whilst there is plenty of general truth in the statement (and Boris Becker, Germany's Wimbledon tennis hero made similar noises in those years), people were expecting a more diplomatic approach from a German Chancellor.

Kohl was never quite able to shake off his image as the ponderous, provincial plodder; but this actually rendered him many political advantages. One advantage was that he was very easy to underestimate. He won general elections, was astute at outfoxing opponents, appealed to voters with honesty and straight talk and generally gave a favourable impression of the genial, relaxed, understanding uncle. Curmudgeonly, easy-going Kohl, standing at six foot four inches tall in his socks and weighing in at 19 stone, transmitted a feeling of well-being and general well-roundedness - an image aptly reflecting 40 years of German prosperity. The nasty medicine that Kohl refused to administer in the eighties at a sufficiently necessary dosage would actually be forced on his people at the end of that decade when events led to German reunification, earning Kohl the title of "The Chancellor of Unity". The events of 1989 have been well documented and the heart-wrenching pictures of people streaming through the breached Berlin Wall on November 9 will remain with everybody forever. A look back at what had been happening in the eastern half of Germany in the years leading up to that dramatic night might answer the question of whether Kohl deserved his title.

The building of the Berlin Wall in 1961 put an end to the stream of people who had been heading west out of East Germany since the end of the war. It also started a period of modest economic prosperity for the GDR. The escape hatch had been sealed and people were knuckling under, making the best of the situation. By Eastern bloc standards, of course, life in the GDR wasn't bad at all and as leadership changed hands in 1971 from the old Stalinist, Walter Ulbricht, to the younger Stalinist, Erich Honecker, certain restrictions were lifted, allowing travel in both directions from one German state to the other, albeit mostly in a West-East direction. A huge housing programme gave young marrieds reasonable living conditions and pensions and wages rose steadily. Your job was secure, nobody was homeless, medical care was free and everybody had enough to eat and drink. Women were all in employment and enjoyed a considerable degree of autonomy and independence (the memory of which had additional harmful psychological side effects on unemployed East German women in post-1990 Germany). The former GDR, therefore, didn't sound too bad at all. Until you experienced the reality behind the bald facts - which I did on frequent occasions in the seventies and eighties. There was a chronic shortage of almost everything; the only things in abundance seemed to be bread, booze, sausages and endless Eastern bloc literature.

Things generally ticked over, however, and people got on with their lives, unaware (or perhaps they weren't) that approximately every fifth person in their republic was working for the secret police (the "*Stasi*"), either on an informal or formal basis. The general appearance of the place could be described as ranging from drab to close-to-destruction. You could only travel to the seven countries of the Warsaw Pact and the only chance you had of treating yourself to anything you could vaguely call luxury (like a decent bar of chocolate) was having contacts able to supply you with Western Deutschmarks. People were generally coping with life in their half of Germany because they had no other choice.

And then came Gorbachev. It sounds simplistic, and there was clearly more to it than that, but you have to ask yourself whether anything would have changed if he had not appeared on the scene with his revolutionary ideas of *Glasnost* and *Perestroika* in the eighties. His willingness to allow Soviet satellites to do it their way - the so-called "Sinatra doctrine" - was the beginning of the end of the Soviet Empire itself. It took a few years, but once the dominoes started tumbling, the GDR's domino was bound to tumble with them. The opening of the Berlin Wall might have been the result of a misunderstanding on that November night, but once it was open everybody knew that the East German totalitarian party was over.

I am therefore asserting that neither Helmut Kohl nor the East Germans themselves were solely responsible for the fall of the Berlin Wall. The regular demonstrations vented long-held East German dissatisfaction with their regime and the steady trickle of East Germans heading West through new holes in the Iron Curtain in Hungary displayed their determination to vote with their feet. But without the dramatic turnaround in Soviet policy sparked by Gorbachev *and* the reluctance of Erich Honecker's successors in those autumn days of 1989 to dare a bloody re-run of the Chinese Tiananmen square massacre, the reunification might not have happened at all. It cannot be denied that Helmut Kohl wasted no time in grasping the chance of cementing German unity and praise is due for his decisiveness and sense of urgency in that crucial time. The "Chancellor of Unity" title, however, has been awarded, in my opinion, for simply being in the right place at the right time. "Cometh the hour, cometh the man", as the saying goes. Kohl was about to place the final pieces in the final part of this post-war survey of German history.

BEYOND NOVEMBER 9, 1989 AND THE UNITED GERMANY

Kohl's chancellorship up until November 9, 1989 can best be described as uneventful, uninspiring with few grandiose policy reforms, no sweeping changes, no visionary ideas. One of Kohl's favourite sayings is one coined by his predecessor, Helmut Schmidt, on the subject of visions. The latter was once said to have uttered: "If a person has visions, he should go to a doctor". Kohl was a Chancellor who dealt with real facts, not abstract concepts. When the Berlin Wall fell, we were suddenly faced with the reality of 17 million East Germans having the freedom, due to a sea change in Soviet foreign policy, to live where they wanted. The whiff of re-unification was in the air and Kohl's nostrils caught the scent before anyone else's; he focused on starting (and, of course, finishing) the job before more deeper-thinking and less hands-on politicians in East and West (and in his own country) had time to discuss whether it was a good idea or not. His Foreign Minister, Genscher, had been attempting to convince him for a considerable period of time that Gorbachev meant business. Now Kohl knew it was actually true and intuited that this was not the time to hesitate. He had a lot of people to convince, but once he realized that the long-awaited chance to achieve re-unification was there, he was determined to make it happen. Within three weeks of the Wall falling, Kohl had a ten-point plan for German reunification worked out.

Once Kohl had a concrete goal to go for, his skills as a diplomat (up to this time not one of his stronger points) improved immeasurably. Margaret Thatcher and George Bush were reassured that this was a new Germany, determined to encourage peace and harmony within the "European House" (one of Gorbachev's favourite expressions). Kohl also put in an admirable extra shift to convince his old friend Mitterrand that the French had nothing to fear from a unified Germany and any final resistance from the third of the old western power triumvirate had now been broken. The common sense politician Kohl also knew that the prospect of receiving billions of crispy Deutschmark notes would also soothe most Soviet fears about a re-emerging "Fourth Reich". He was right. 12 billion Deutschmarks and a 5 billion interest-free loan over 4 years did the trick. By the summer of 1990, Gorbachev conceded that a united Germany would have NATO membership and 350,000 Soviet troops would be withdrawn by 1994. The treaty to re-unify Germany was virtually in place.

The next step was monetary union. Kohl was aware that if the West German Deutschmark didn't come to the East Germans, they would come to the Deutschmark. They were already coming in their hundreds of thousands in the first half of 1990, placing severe pressure on the West German economy. Despite the euphoric events of this period, unemployment was moving ever upwards. On July 6, the currency union was created. Six days before that a West German "*Treuhandanstalt*" (privatization agency) had taken over all East German state-owned companies (which was virtually 90% of the East German economy and 40% of its employees). On October 3, 1990, Germany was officially reunified with five newly-formed federal states joining from the former German Democratic Republic. On December 2 of that same year, Kohl became Chancellor of this new Germany after his party (CDU) obtained 43.8% of the overall vote and formed a coalition with the FDP which obtained a very respectable 11% of the overall vote.

So much for the facts and figures of that whirlwind year in German history - a year in which the word most used was "*Wahnsinn*" (madness). As luck would have it, I was in Britain during these mad times. I had moved back in September 1989 and followed developments in the press and on TV (no Internet in those days). I captured a glimpse of what was happening when I made a visit to Germany at the beginning of November that year to pick up my car. I was lounging around the living room of a good friend watching a massive demonstration on TV on

Alexanderplatz in the centre of East Berlin, watching various prominent East Germans from the world of literature and opposition politics giving speech after speech in support of democracy, freedom of speech, free elections and free travel. I'll never forget the soft tones of Christa Wolf and the rougher murmurings of Stefan Heym, two iconic East German writers whose works I had been reading for over twenty years. I looked sideways at my friend and said: "Is this really happening?" It was all so hard to believe. It was even harder to believe that on the following Thursday, East Germans were marching through the Berlin Wall with that magic word *"Wahnsinn"* on their lips. By that time I was back in Liverpool, cursing my luck that I was missing history being made.

The euphoria was of limited duration. Large and detailed tomes could be (and probably have been) written on the difficulties emerging after reunification in 1990. On December 2 of that eventful year, in the first, joint, free elections since the end of the Weimar Republic in 1933, East Germans voted in large numbers for those parties which had least in common with their previous system and which supported free enterprise with as little state intervention as possible. Mass unemployment followed with all the social problems that accompany it, made worse by East Germans' inherent fear of this new and disempowering phenomenon. Add to that the psychological problems of loss of identity through loss of state; creeping paranoia as a feeling of inferiority enmeshed many who had drawn the short economic straws after the change (*"Wende"*) and the spooky revelations as to just how many hundreds of thousands of people had been spying on their fellow citizens during the GDR regime combined to produce a disheveled and confused people. The final factor which prevented the two Germanys becoming the best of pals was the vast amount of money the whole project was costing: West Germans were starting to feel it in their pockets as taxes increased and all manner of benefits disappeared. The crassest example was that of West-Berlin whose inhabitants lost virtually all of the generous subsidies they had been receiving for years. The cost of paying millions of East Germans generous West German pensions when they obviously hadn't paid one cent in contributions for over 40 years was of course economic madness. Not to mention unemployment benefit and costly re-training programmes. And a complete overhaul of the former GDR's stone-age and rotting telecommunications system and infrastructure was to place a staggering burden on public finances.

To be fair, some of this was paid for from taxes on some of the mouth-watering profits which West German companies were making in the first few years after re-unification. I can remember a juicy bonus plus salary increase in the summer of 1992 when the West German educational publishing house I was working for shared part of the bonanza provided by East German schools placing their first mass order of books. In the accompanying letter my employers wrote: "1992 has been an extraordinary year". These were equally extraordinary years for West German insurance companies, car producers, furniture stores, travel companies, building firms and anybody providing goods and services to solvent East Germans eager to make up for lost time on the consumerist front. Those who kept their jobs, found new ones and found their feet in the new world of the market economy fitted in well in the world that most West Germans had been happy in for the last thirty-odd years of more or less uninterrupted prosperity. Those who didn't make it tended to have an odd longing for the nanny state they had said goodbye to after the tumultuous changes of 1990.

The nineties tended to throw up three kinds of East Germans: those who wholeheartedly welcomed the change and who were doing very well out of it; those who had found their feet quite well, and had obviously improved their lot, but who still had some desire for an alternative to full-blown capitalism; and those still believed in socialism and wanted a new-improved, democratic GDR with the state still looking after you every step of the way from the cradle to the grave. Herein lay the roots of the "East-West conflict" which has stayed with us in Germany since the re-unification. Almost two-thirds of the former East German population still had something positive to say about their former state, whilst the vast majority of West Germans could not grasp for one minute how any East German with half a performing brain cell could miss anything about their former state. The East German cause wasn't helped in the nineties by a series of anti-foreigner atrocities carried out primarily in the new Eastern states. I will go into these issues in more detail in Chapter 6.

The reunification reminded us once again of how healthy the German economy actually was. How many countries would have had the financial means to take on the task of transforming and re-building a ramshackle, dilapidated, ailing country like the GDR without blinking? Well, West Germany obviously had and although there have been problems along the way, the former GDR is hardly recognizable to the one in existence at the start of the nineties and, in my opinion at least, the vast majority of its citizens would have to admit that their lives have improved beyond recognition since reunification. Further theories, details and analysis in Chapter 6.

Helmut Kohl scraped through the next elections on 16 October 1994 with a reduced majority. Kohl was slowly losing credibility with East Germans. Probably the most famous phrase associated with him at this time was, "In East Germany we will soon be witnessing blossoming landscapes". Words which rang very hollow in certain parts of East Germany as unemployment was still moving constantly upwards with a number of regions experiencing mass exoduses as people sought work in more prosperous parts of the country (or even other countries). Kohl himself became enmeshed in various corruption scandals towards the end of the nineties and ultimately lost the next election on 27 September, 1998 and Gerhard Schroeder became SPD Chancellor at the head of a SPD/Green coalition. Kohl resigned on the same night and left as the longest serving Chancellor of the Federal Republic of Germany (16 years), beating his idol, Konrad Adenauer by two years .

The new SPD/Green coalition had a lot of plans: they decided to close all nuclear power stations in an acceptable period of time and make renewable sources of energy a priority; in foreign affairs, Germany was to take a more independent stance (no involvement, for example, in Iraq); gay civil marriages were to be recognized; laws were passed to grant foreign citizens dual citizenship. The most far-reaching reaching reforms were laws to streamline and simplify the social benefits system. Many saw this as a dangerous development that would subject more and more people to poverty as their unemployment benefit entitlements based on their last salary were to be reduced to one year (previously two). After that period all benefits were to be means-calculated. The measures estranged many SPD voters. I will go into more detail on these major reforms in Chapter 7.

"The fat years" (to revive the phrase I employed earlier) really were over in Germany by the end of the nineties. The final eight years of Kohl's time in government had been occupied with the monumental task of financing and directing the re-construction of East Germany. Reunification had cost a fortune and something had to be done to balance the books and prevent the country falling into unprecedented levels of debt; something which would endanger the whole future. Unfortunately, it was left to a left-of-centre government to start the dirty work. Much progress was made in these years, aided and abetted by one of the sharpest Finance Ministers the SPD ever produced, Hans Eichel. Before the credit crunch put paid to everybody's plans in 2008, he was doing a very good job towards steering Germany towards a debt-free scenario.

Mention should be made of the symbolic importance of Germany's Green Foreign Minister during those coalition years, Joschka Fischer. While doing a fairly good job of keeping Germany on an independent yet co-operative footing on the international scene in those years, he also represented a sort of closure in post-war West German politics. He had been on the outer fringes of those left circles in the early seventies that had been involved in violent means to overthrow the state, or at least make futile, bloody statements in senseless acts of violence. He had even been captured on film causing a policeman actual bodily harm, for which he made a formal public apology during his time in government. In some small way he appeared to be the incarnation of the young radical who had grown up, showed repentance for the errors of his youth and was now serving society in a constructive way, yet still driven by firmly held leftist convictions.

Gerhard Schroeder asked the German electorate to judge him on whether unemployment fell or not. And they did. He won one more election in 2002, but with a considerably reduced majority and battled on for three more years before his party was forced to enter a Grand Coalition with the CDU as a slightly junior partner in 2005 after achieving the worst SPD election result since 1953. He resigned as leader and let the battle-weary Franz Müntefering muddle through under Germany's first female Chancellor, Angela Merkel, in a Grand Coalition with the CDU. His successor as candidate for the Chancellorship, Frank-Walter Steinmeier, fared even worse than Schroeder had four years previously, obtaining a frighteningly low 23% in 2009, the SPD's worst share of the vote since the founding of the Federal Republic in 1949.

So Schroeder's lack of success in making any significant dent in unemployment was to prove his downfall. But it is important to point out that he had carried out many overdue reforms which Kohl had omitted to introduce in his 16 years in office. In the final years of his time in office Schroeder had also passed legislation to take the pressure off the state pension system by offering subsidies to citizens investing in government-backed private pension schemes - a clear message to people that they were no longer able to fully depend on the overburdened state system. People were quite simply living longer and having fewer children, an imbalance which was in danger of destroying the pension system altogether. Credit should be given to Schroeder for finally doing something about it rather than just talking about it.

This policy of encouraging people to take responsibility for their own fate and rewarding them for showing initiative made the transition from a Red-Green coalition (1998 till 2005) to a Grand CDU-SPD coalition (2005 till 2009) and then to the present CDU-FDP coalition (since 2009) a relatively easy one. What Schroeder was eschewing were basic conservative policies. Merkel reverted to a small tweaking of those policies, hoping, presumably, like her former mentor, Helmut Kohl, that things would simply somehow look after themselves. As luck would have it, she hasn't been far wrong. The apparent smooth switching from centre-left governments to centre governments to centre-right governments in Germany since the demise of Helmut Kohl has questioned people's interest in and passion for politics. Some pundits have questioned altogether whether the usual traditional voters actually exist anymore. A repeatedly emerging expression, "*Politikverdrossenheit*", (disinterest in politics) has been on many people's lips over the last twenty years or so. As political scandals and minor (and major) tales of corruption have done the rounds in that same period, people have tended to tar politicians with the same brush and classic lines such as "They're only in it to promote their own interests" is a common criticism of politicians and their parties. More and more people are coming to the sad conclusion that nothing changes anyway, regardless of who you vote for.

This survey so far has concentrated primarily on the economic and political development of the former West Germany with special reference to its attempt to forge a new and positive role in Europe and the world. This attempt has been, by and large, a successful one in which all the political groupings and economic organizations consisting of industry, commerce, trade unions and church bodies have played important roles. The fact that the people themselves, supported by the millions of foreign citizens, quite simply got on with life, rolled their sleeves up and worked extremely hard, resulted in the creation of the economic success story which Germany has undoubtedly become.

But what have Germany's writers made of these developments since "Zero hour" in 1945? How have these critical voices made themselves heard in these years? What have been their main focuses of criticism, analysis and description in a period dominated by the aftermath of the Third Reich and its war, the division of Germany, the Cold War, economic recovery and staggering prosperity, terrorism, re-unification and Germany's development towards a multi-cultural society where the question of identity is clearly not as simple as it used to be? This section is an attempt to give a credible answer to these questions and to offer a brief overview of the historical survey of some of the major authors of the last 60 years.

The year 1945 also represented a deep cut in the field of literature. After the war a generation of authors just returned from the front were making themselves known. Writers such as Heinrich Böll and Wolfgang Borchert had been called up early in the war and in their early works they illustrated an impressive record of war and post-war reality. They characterize *"Heimkehrerliteratur"* (Literature of the returnees) which appeared at the end of the forties and beginning of the fifties. The literature of the immediate post-war period not only describes the problems of the men returning from the war but also provides an accurate picture of Germany's destruction. In this context, however, there was the tendency to remove the memory of National Socialism and its consequences as quickly as possible. This could only happen if the rubble and ruins could also be removed as quickly as possible.

A new form of German literature gradually emerged after the catastrophic collapse of Germany in 1945. A literature which concerned itself with the war, Fascism and the Holocaust, even if it was speaking almost exclusively of the presence of rubble (1945-1955) and the years of the Economic Miracle (1955-1965). In the West, literature was competing with consumerism and entertainment, yet was carving out opportunities for writers to develop individual, critical positions on that very society. The most important post-war West German writers of the day, who formed *"Gruppe 47"*, were particularly concerned with questions of political and societal morals and were a sort of replacement opposition. To a certain extent, they represented the official conscience of state and society. Writers in the West, such as Heinrich Böll and Martin Walser, critically reflected on the materialistic society that the economic miracle years had produced. Böll went on later to question the hysterical reaction of the powers-that-be to the terrorist outrages of the seventies and eighties.

Generally speaking, writers in the GDR were concerned more in describing the development of socialism in their part of post-1945 in as positive a light as possible. Most 1945 writers in East Germany had been in exile since 1933 and were more than happy to devote their writing to the task of helping the re-construction of a socialist homeland. This resulted in a genre of literature known as "socialist realism", creating works based on the belief that the socialist system was the superior one. Criticism was allowed only in as far as the work in question offered viable solutions to the problems raised. Most writers remained largely loyal to this principle throughout the fifties and even into the sixties; serious doubts emerged after the Hungarian uprising of 1956 and the Prague Spring of 1968, by which time many East German writers were publishing much of their work in West Germany only. Some even left the GDR, exasperated by censorship and restrictions, or generally disillusioned by the system. Those who wrote good literature about general human problems in East Germany found a ready audience in East and West and were normally able to avoid the wrath of the censors (and make a good living). Writers such as Stefan Heym, Christa Wolf, Günter de Bruyn, Hermann Kant and Franz Fühmann, to name but a few, lay testimony to this.

Other East German writers left, unable to tolerate the repressive nature of the Party's censorship. Others were forced to leave, even though their belief in the aims of Socialism remained as strong as ever. Wolf Biermann, famed "*Liedermacher*" and satirical poet of no little talent had his GDR citizenship revoked whilst on a concert tour in West Germany in 1976. For many in the GDR, this was the sign that reforms from within their state were not going to happen and further disillusionment in the form of inner-emigration ensued, particularly in the artistic and literary community.

Günter Grass produced in 1959 *Die Blechtrommel* (The tin drum), one of the major works of post-war German literature: an attempt to come to terms with the daily horror of the Third Reich through a child's traumatic processing of events in Danzig, Grass' hometown. Grass' subsequent works and frequent commentaries on international and domestic developments have never met with universal recognition and have frequently provoked anger and disdain from many sections of society. His look at post 1989 reunification finds its voice in his 1995 novel *Ein weites Feld*, (An extensive field), a lengthy, rambling work depicting reunification through numerous references to German social and literary history. The novel generally received poor reviews, the most devastating one from the pen of Marcel Reich-Ranicki, perhaps Germany's best known literary critic. A Polish-German Jew, who survived the Warsaw Ghetto (and consequently the Nazi extermination camps), Reich-Ranicki was an eccentric character, bringing German literature to the masses, primarily by hosting a TV programme called "*Literarisches Quartett*" in which he would discuss the latest literary works with other top critics. Whether his attack on Grass' major post-reunification work is justified or not, it is true that attempts to produce **the** post-reunification work didn't quite work. They tended to be serious, lengthy tomes which did little to impress the opinion makers Reich-Ranicki frequently invited to his cult series.

One well-written, comprehensive book *Der Turm* (2008) by Uwe Tellkamp, offered a look at life behind the wall from the perspective of a doctor's family in Dresden and generally received positive feedback. I ploughed through it and agreed that it went a long way to helping Westerners understand the intricacies and struggles of living in a totalitarian system. Further books by East

German writers giving insights into how East Germans were coping with post-1989 Germany tended to be of a more light-hearted nature. Hapless but likeable "*Ossies*", muddling through a new Germany with varying degrees of success seems to be the general formula used here and books such as *Helden wie wir* (1995) by Thomas Brussig use a satirical form which has moments of laugh-out-loud humour (not something I have often found in German novels). In a similar vein, although showing more subtlety and literary talent, Ingo Schulze brought out an impressive selection of short stories, titled *Simple Storys* (1998) and produced some of the most delightful lines depicting the East German, post-reunification dilemma, for example: "*Sie müssen mal versuchen, sich das vorzustellen. Plötzlich ist man in Italien und hat einen Westdeutschen Paß. Man findet sich auf der anderen Seite der Welt und wundert sich, dass man trinkt und isst und atmet und einen Fuß vor den andren setzt, als wäre das alles selbstverständlich.*" (You really have to imagine the following: suddenly you are in Italy, you have a West German passport. You are on the other side of the world, you are eating and drinking and breathing and placing one foot after each other and it's all totally normal - my translation). Refreshingly true, beautifully put, and to the point. The background of both Tellkamp and Schulze (sons of doctors and physicists), however, throws up the question of where all the East German working class writers are. Don't they have an interesting tale or two to tell about pre and post-unification histories?

The humorous side of coping with life in a reunified Germany also brought box office success in the cinema with films such as: *Go Trabi, Go!* (1991), *Sonnenallee* (1999) and *Goodbye Lenin* (2003). The first two trashy and trivial, the third one worthy of the international recognition it received. *Das Leben der Anderen* (2006) and *Barbara* (2012), two films depicting life in the Big Brother society known as the GDR, got well under the skin of anybody watching them and proved that East German writers and film producers could come up with quality cinema on the subject of Germany's recent history.

In recent years another section of Germany society has been making their voice heard on the literary and cinematic scene: the children and grandchildren of the guest workers from the sixties and seventies. Society now calls them citizens with a "migration background". They are people who have achieved varying degrees of success in integrating and finding their feet in a society in which they are clearly the minority and often from a totally different cultural background (i.e. Turks). Some already possess German citizenship; some are economic success stories, fully integrated and happy to be here. Others less so. Some are married to Germans, some wouldn't dream of doing so. Many have very ambivalent feelings about identity. Many are bilingual, others have poor German language skills. Some speak only German. All the emotions, doubts and fears of the vast array of different foreigners in Germany are being expressed through literature, theatre and film. Two examples spring immediately to mind: Lale Akgün's book, *Tante Semra in Leberkäseland* (2009) depicts the humorous autobiographical story of growing up in Germany within the bounds of two cultures (i.e. the German one and the Turkish one). A film which begins by addressing other problems of such a world, *Gegen die Wand* (2007) begins in a similarly humorous way, but ends with a chilling wake-up call. In the film a young Turkish woman living in Germany attempts to win her freedom from her overbearing Turkish family by entering a marriage of convenience with a young Turkish man who, after spending years in Germany and becoming totally socialized into a liberal and alternative German way of life, can offer her the freedom to lead a similar life of easy-going hedonism. The plan goes badly wrong.

The different attempts of various cultures to make their way in post-economic miracle Germany are presented in a plethora of fascinating literature emerging since the seventies. These writers are also describing the newest sociological developments in Germany in which some of the key questions seem to be: How well integrated are such citizens? Which problems of identity do they have? Do we have a multi-cultural society? Is such a society desirable? Such questions and more will be discussed in more detail in Chapter 7 of this book. In the meantime, literature will offer some fascinating insights into modern society, just as it has been doing continually in Germany since 1945.

SOME BASIC TRUTHS EMERGING SINCE 1945

Some basic truths have emerged since the last shots of World War Two were fired before midnight on May 8 1945: Germany has been on a steady course to real prosperity since the start of the fifties. It has fostered an enviable social market economy, a booming export industry with large, highly-esteemed, profitable companies in all branches of manufacturing and services and its people enjoy possibly the highest standard of living in the world. People know that things now are a lot tighter than they used to be, but the majority of the population still has a more than comfortable bolster to fall back on. The latest debt crises have created further doubt and uncertainty, but even at the time of writing and while such crises rage, Germany's unemployment rate is falling and the country is boasting the highest number of people in employment for 20 years.

Germany's democratic system has caused no concern to its neighbours since the end of the Second World War; never has there been a moment's fear of it falling back on old and sinister ways. It helped bring about the unification of its country at the end of the Cold War and offered all its citizens a chance to eat a piece of the delicious prosperity cake it has been baking since the start of the fifties. Latest figures on poverty and homelessness have been disturbing and the failure of the present government (2013) to introduce a minimum wage has no doubt contributed to this, along with the *Hartz* IV reforms introduced by their predecessors. But to quote a British acquaintance of mine who also lived a number of years in this country, "In Britain we have the haves and the have-nots; in Germany you have the haves and the have-mores". The comparison sums up rather accurately the different development of the two countries in the years since 1945. Unlike Britain, Germany also knows exactly where it belongs - in the centre of Europe, hand in hand with France, steering a non-interventionist and sensible course in foreign affairs.

The dark shadows of the past are always there, of course. The past, as we amateur philosophers know so well, never goes away. The generations since 1945 have tackled this dilemma in various ways and the German bottom line seems to look like this: "What happened was terrible and we will do everything in our powers to ensure nothing like that ever happens again. In the meantime give us a chance to show what decent human beings we actually are." Numerous attempts have been made to step out of the shadows and as time goes by more and more Germans can claim to have had nothing to do with the whole horrific chapter. By displaying tolerance, openness and compassion in their dealings with foreigners (abroad and at home), they are doing the only thing they can do. The Football World Cup in Germany in 2006 was a good example of this. "Feeling at home with friends" (the official motto of the tournament) set the scene for four weeks of sunshine, happy football fans and Germans seemingly having a good time in a relaxed and spontaneous fashion (including massive swinging of the German flag, hitherto unheard of since 1945). The improvement in Germany's image in the world during this time cannot be overstated. Many a stereotypical cliché about German stiffness and general earnest demeanor was put to bed for good during and after those four weeks.

The general success story that Germany undoubtedly is has also rubbed off on its citizens - no lack of self-confidence in this country. People generally look healthier, better-dressed and seem more prosperous than, for example, their British counterparts. The openness brought about by the explosion of youth culture and the expansion of political consciousness in the sixties has also left its mark on the people. The grey, conservative stuffiness of the Adenauer fifties was swept away by that glorious decade, helped along by more progressive, open-minded governments led by Brandt and Schmidt. The rights of women, minorities and the increasing awareness of ecological factors were direct consequences of the developments in those years. The terrorist attacks of the seventies and eighties, with no real coherent political plan behind them, intermittently put public life on red alert but was never a serious threat to democracy.

What became of the "guest workers" (*Gastarbeiter*) that streamed into the country at the beginning of the sixties? Most of them are still there. Most of them had not intended to stay longer than it took to get enough money together to go home, build a house and start up their life again back home. Yet Germany's continued and impressive economic rise in the sixties and seventies offered permanent, long-term employment for most of them. Wives, children and in some cases, parents, followed. More children were born, growing up bilingually, going through the Germany school system, thereby creating more reasons for their parents to stay longer. In 1950 there were 500,000 foreigners living in Germany, approximately 1% of the total population; today that number has risen to 6.7

million, accounting for 8.2% of the population. Most of the unskilled or semi-skilled jobs held by the fathers of today's young foreigners are no longer there and it is the big challenge to see whether this new generation is flexible enough to make a living in modern Germany. The signs are good, although there are intermittent warnings that integration is not taking place as smoothly and quickly as it should be. How this is to be tackled is the topic of endless debates in the media; even the briefest analysis of the complexity of the problem would overstep the scope of this overview. Suffice to say that the demographic time bomb ticking in Germany will require more people to be born and as things stand at the moment it is the 8.2% foreign proportion of the population which are, for want of a better term, producing the extra children necessary to pay the pensions of an ever-increasing older generation. There will follow a more detailed analysis of the situation in Chapter 7.

Germany since 1945 has been characterized by a staggering economic development which no Germans dragging themselves round their half-destroyed cities in that year could possibly have envisaged. The political and social stability Germany now enjoys has its foundation in the economic powerhouse that Germany is and has been for almost 60 years. Everything that has been achieved has been down to this unbelievable economic development. Resistance to the all-conquering might of the economy has been a rare occurrence, leading to, some might say, an obsession with money and everything that it can buy you. In other words, a materialist, consumerist society, the like of which has never been seen before, has emerged. Of course, it has been seen before, in the form of the USA. One reproach, therefore, has been that Germany has been Americanized, losing any sense of German identity and making money and material possessions a sort of replacement religion. Losing your German identity in those years after the war, however, was actually not a bad thing for most Germans, of course, and a conspicuous feature of German post-war development has been the Germans' rejection of any form of nationalism. Chasing economic prosperity was therefore seen as an acceptable occupation compared to the aggressive military adventures of the past. Consumerism is of course not restricted to Germany and is rampant all over the world, yet the impression remains that the therapeutic benefits of consumerism is covering up other German hang-ups.

Germany today is a prosperous, modern, progressive, liberal-minded, country, committed to the European Union (and recently to helping to solve the gigantic problems certain countries in that Union are facing) and to a NATO alliance with other like-minded, democratic nations. Its de-centralized, federal system enables fair treatment and allocation of resources to the 16 federal states Germany consists of. It is the fourth largest economic power in the world after USA, China and Japan, a remarkable achievement considering the size of the population of USA and China. It is a fact that Germany has come a long way since the dark days of 1945. In the next chapter I will attempt to describe what it is like to live there on a daily basis.

2   Everyday life in Germany

"If the world has come to an end and there are only two Germans left on the planet, you can safely assume that one will be selling a sausage and the other one will be consuming it."

Isn't it the same everywhere?

The expression "Everyday life" smacks of routine. The things that everybody on the planet does every day, wherever they live: sleep (a third of one's life, apparently), get up, go to work (if you have work), chastise the kids (if you have any), go shopping, have something to eat or drink, and watch TV. And unless you live in particularly strange places such as on the side of a mountain, up a tree or in a cave, to name three possibilities, the aforementioned activities will probably not be much different all over the world. One might assume that eating, drinking and TV viewing habits might throw up some differences, but globalization and Americanization have also taken their toll: fast food, hamburgers, soaps and reality TV have found their way to Germany and are steadfastly refusing to go away. Not even much to report on there, then.

I thought it would make sense, therefore, to concentrate in this chapter on what is actually really different about German everyday life. But even this plan is fraught with danger: a couple of years ago I was looking forward to fascinating all my friends and relatives back in England by revealing to them that everybody in Germany was obsessed by mobile phones and seemed to spend half their waking hours having endless conversations on them. Once back in England, I noticed that everybody was obsessed by mobile phones and seemed to spend half their waking hours having endless conversations on them. I was also going to wow them with the news about how popular satellite navigation systems are in Germany until I noticed that one in virtually every third car on Liverpool roads had one. IPods, iPhones, tattoos, piercings, Barcelona football jerseys, artificial nails and suntans seem to be so ubiquitous in the world today that it hardly seems worth pointing them out at all. Globalization, apparently, is succeeding in making us all look the same, or at least very similar. So, in an attempt to offer the reader something new and thought-provoking, I have observed long and hard and believe to have spotted enough interesting differences to prevent the thinking man and woman from skipping this chapter. Let us begin with the early morning alarm call.

The early bird catches the worm seems to be the Germans' watchword; it's not only at the swimming pool that Germans beat us to it. Before most Brits are even out of their pyjamas, the average German is at his desk, lathe, blackboard or any other place he is required to be to earn his daily crust. Whereas 9 a.m. is the average time for working life to begin in GB, by that time Germans have already been beavering away for at least an hour. By way of compensation for the early start, most companies allow a semi-official breakfast break round about ten o'clock when employees produce a tasty-looking sandwich with sturdy-looking German wholemeal bread from their briefcases. In the Adenauer days, this was lovingly produced by the loyal housewife who placed it in her hard-working husband's briefcase before he raced off to keep the economic miracle going.

EATING, DRINKING AND SOCIALISING

While we're on the subject of eating habits, it is true to say that when I first reached German shores, the midday meal was a hot one, and in the evening the German family reverted to bread, with various cold meats and cheese. This evening ritual was called "*Abendbrot*" (literally translated: evening bread). Sometimes a few gherkins, tomatoes and salads were thrown in to take away the stark frugality represented by that tasty, healthy, yet sometimes slightly dry German bread. The glass of beer that accompanied it made it something that hard-working German husbands and fathers could look forward to. I was fascinated and thrilled at the idea of drinking beer every night of my life and became an avid supporter of the "Evening bread faction" when I first arrived here. If I was ever invited to families with more pronounced boozy proclivities, the evening bread ceremony could, without too much effort, be derailed into a serious drinking session with put-hairs-on-your-chest short drinks being offered to ensure you had no trouble finding your sleep (finding your bed could sometimes be a more difficult project, of course). Back home in Liverpool, the evening meal was pie and chips and a cup of tea; I wasn't complaining, but the added alcoholic component offered at the German meal captured my imagination - and played havoc with my waistline.

Things are changing, of course. I observe that German eating habits are gradually becoming rather Anglo-Saxon: people tend to grab a sandwich or something cheap and cheerful at lunchtime and rustle up something hot in the evenings. In these busy, high-speed days the no-frills, age-old German *Abendbrot* is probably no longer in. It could also be that the evening beer so revered by Germans down the years is also being phased out as the Germans become ever more health conscious and less bound by tradition. Thomas Mann, one of the great German writers of the 20th century, once said about his evening quart of beer: "It creates in me peace, relaxation and desire for my armchair, an atmosphere of "It is over!" (Dorn/Wagner 2012: 9). The "it", one presumes, is referring to the passing day. This was Mann writing in the Germany of 1906 - a different world, a better world?

Drinking in Germany still remains an activity enjoyed largely within the confines of the home. The idea of going out for a drink to your local pub is an alien one and the spontaneity of "Do you fancy a quick pint?" is almost unknown. The tradition of the pint after work is an equally uncommon occurrence. Pubs, as we British know them, don't exist anyway. It's possible to imbibe an alcoholic beverage in virtually any establishment in Germany which sells food and drink, whereas in Britain the pub has been traditionally the place to drink alcohol. Germany do drink out, of course, but the drinking can take place in a whole host of different environments, be it a café, wine bar, restaurant, spit and sawdust bar, beer hall or, if you're feeling in a really casual mood, loitering outside your local kiosk.

If Germans do go out for a drink, they tend to frequent places appropriate for their class, age group, status, taste, and even sexual or political orientation. In a British pub, you might well find an old-age pensioner rubbing shoulders with a bubbly teenager or well-dressed businessman, but this would be unusual in Germany. Of course there are working class pubs in Britain where only working class blokes tend to go (whoever the working class are these days), but the liberal sprinkling of different types of people in most pubs in Britain has, for me certainly, lasting appeal. Germans tend not to go out just to drink; some sort of food is normally consumed with the drink. And no queuing at the bar for your drinks in Germany; you find a seat and drinks are brought to you and you get your own individual bill after you have decided you've had enough. This means the "rounds system", which remains popular in Britain, is virtually unheard of in Germany.

Having a drink in Germany is, as in most countries of the world, the most popular way of celebrating something or just generally loosening up the atmosphere. Germans find any number of excuses for opening a bottle of something intoxicating: starting a new job, getting a pay rise, being promoted, carnival, birthdays, wedding anniversaries, getting a divorce, christenings, building a house, buying a house, retiring, passing your driving test, passing exams or being made president of your local tree-cutting club. Any German with a modicum of self-respect will have a bottle of something in their fridge to celebrate anything they believe needs celebrating.

It has to be said that Germans take more out of drink than drink takes out of them. They drink a lot, yes, but are generally able to behave themselves when they have drunk a lot: the centre of German towns on Friday and Saturday night are not war zones witnessing drunken men and women descending upon the accident and emergency wards after gigantic drinking bouts have sparked off equally gigantic fights and caused horrific accidents and injuries. In fact most Germans regard a couple of fine wines with a good meal and coffee to follow as a good evening out. With many Brits the war cry seems to be: "Drunken oblivion, here we come" - otherwise it has been a boring evening. The fact that you can drink as much beer at any German football stadium in the land, insult the referee, scream at the top of your voice in support of your football team and go home without anybody coming to any physical harm says a lot about the generally positive way Germans handle booze. In Britain, the sale of alcohol in football stadiums has been banned for as long as I can remember. And we all know why: we don't appear to be able to handle it. That is not to say that alcohol-fuelled violence is unknown in Germany; or that there is no concern about the alarming increase in alcohol consumption, particularly among young people. But the consumption of alcohol does not seem to spark off the fighting spirit so well known in British towns every weekend. I have attended wine and beer festivals in Germany where staggering amounts of booze have been shifted and I have never seen a fight, something very hard to imagine where I come from. Lyric writer Bernie Taupin was surely displaying his British roots in 1973 when he had Elton John sing: "Saturday night's alright for fighting".

Eating out is generally more common in Germany than in Britain. There are two reasons for this: firstly, there are more restaurants to eat out in (particularly Italian, Greek, Mexican, ex-Yugoslavian, Turkish and Chinese), and secondly, restaurants are more reasonably priced here. A husband and wife with two kids don't need to take out a mortgage to eat out and what you eat amply fills you up and is positively tasty. Fast-food restaurant chains (apart from the usual suspects such as McDonalds, Burger King etc.) prevalent in Britain have not (yet) caught on in Germany and foreign restaurants here (particularly Greek and Italian ones) pride themselves on providing the personal touch and foster customer retention and build relationships a million miles away from the automated American style "Hi guys, I'm Jordan, what can I get you?" uttered by a robotic waiter, followed by the equally automated invitation to cast a glance at the plastic menu offering 7 different styles of French fries with a corresponding number of dips. Eating in a restaurant is something which Germans see as a treat they have deserved; perhaps it is a throwback to the days when people were starting to treat themselves in the economic miracle years. The habit has stuck and a reasonably-priced, restaurant in Germany with family-style customer service will always find a regular clientele.

Snacking has always been a popular German pastime and this revolves around what might appear to be the Germans' apparent obsession with the sausage. The Brits grab a pasty or pie, the Americans go for the hamburger, the Italians munch on a slice of pizza, but if the world has come to an end after a nuclear war and there are only two Germans left on the planet, you can safely assume that one will be selling a sausage and the other one will be consuming it. It fills the niggling hunger gap, takes less than 5 minutes to consume, can be eaten in a standing position and is very reasonably priced. Everyone eats them regardless of age, status or religion - even Jews and Muslims can choose the pork-free versions. Kids love them, pensioners at least know what they are eating and they can be consumed with the minimum of fuss and bother.

They are facing tough competition, however. Turkish and Arab vendors offer *döner kebabs* on every street corner now and the younger generation sees them as a slightly funkier alternative to the rather old-fashioned *Bratwurst* or

Currywurst (a specially spiced sausage with hot, curried tomato ketchup). But even these foreign vendors will normally offer a couple of the aforementioned German sausage variations for more traditionally-minded Germans. Not even the irrepressible march of the all-American hamburger has suppressed the German sausage and it is unlikely ever to disappear completely.

However, the preponderance of non-German businesses in the fast-food sector is slowly putting paid to the marvellous old German snack bars where all manner of German heart-attack food used to be offered to anybody brave enough to take the risk of considerably shortening their life by eating there. They were the culinary equivalent of today's non-safe sex. Oh what joy it was to enter them and sample *Bratwurst*, *Schnitzel*, pork cutlets, *Schaschlik* (skewered slices of meat, onions, peppers and tomato sauce), roasted half chickens, French fries, fried potatoes, potato salads and pea soups. If you couldn't find something there to still your more base desires for cholesterol-drenched goodies, you really did need to go and see a doctor (which you'd have to do anyway if you visited such establishments regularly). Nowadays, you're lucky to come across the occasional mobile snack bar with a fraction of the dishes I have just described. There are some exceptions, however; some elderly, normally overweight German souls slave away in such traditional places to prove that lean cuisine is something no real German worth his salt really wants any truck with. Motorway service stations also offer such culinary delicacies to make sure that truck drivers rarely reach pensionable age without at least a triple by-pass.

Doing your daily business and getting about

Daily routine also means shopping, going to the bank or post office, driving your car, using public transport and going for a walk through streets and parks. Do Germans do these things differently? Answer: well, yes, and as a Brit you notice differences. The main difference is that people tend to do things with fewer smiles on their faces and far less small talk, or in many cases no small talk at all. Germans want to focus on the job in hand and small talk tends to get in the way. The woman working behind the counter at the bank deals with your enquiry without engaging you in niceties about the weather. Walking on the street sometimes requires strong nerves and you need to stand your ground; if you are on collision course with somebody on the street, Germans seem to take a certain amount of pleasure in "psyching you out" to see who changes direction at the last minute. Still being accustomed to British norms, it's normally me doing the chickening out. They are not good at queuing (although, after years of practice, they still do this rather well in East Germany), rather reluctantly let you get off the bus before they get on, can be impatient at supermarket check-outs and look positively uneasy if you smile at them. And the less we say about driving a car in Germany the better. This all sounds rather negative, but walking around the average German town is rarely an uplifting experience, and if you are waiting for a stranger to cheer up your life, you may have to be patient. The famous exception proves the rule, of course, but my general take on this is: "If a stranger talks to me in Germany, he is normally a nutcase, drunk or wants money."

By pointing out these examples I am not being anti-German; or claiming that Germans are unfriendly. They just find it hard to talk to strangers. Once they are convinced a stranger means them no harm, he's as friendly as the next man. But initial wariness seems to be an inbuilt mechanism. Stop a stranger on a street in Germany and the person in question will require a few seconds to establish whether you're friend or foe. Once they have decided you're the former, amicable and co-operative inter-human relations can commence. Germans just need a bit more time than other nationalities; it's just the way things are. Stop somebody on the street in Britain and they generally smile; in Germany they are more likely to start off the exchange with a brief, but deep, questioning look of suspicion. But once you surmount the initial barrier, things work efficiently and well.

Nobody (and least of all the Germans) can claim that Germans are good at small talk. I usually turn to my "Baker's test" to illustrate this. For the duration of my 35-year residence in Germany, I have been making at least twice-weekly visits to my nearest bakery and I have never got past an exchange of information extending beyond the reason for my entering the bakery, i.e., to buy a loaf, rolls or cake. I have patronised local bakeries for periods lasting from six months to six years and nobody has ever expressed the slightest desire to know where I came from, what I thought of the day's weather or Germany's latest results at the World

Cup (and there have been eight of them and the same number of European Championships since 1979). The women concerned have all been pleasantly efficient, sometimes good to look at and even proffer the odd non-committal smile or two. But the bottom line remains that all they are really concerned about is giving me what I want from the formidable selection of delicious German bread available (in exchange for money, of course). Their message seems to be: "If you want to buy bread, you will get it here. If you want social intercourse, talk to somebody you know. I don't know you, so why should I talk to you?" I am exaggerating now in order to make my message clear, but I believe it clarifies the general rules of combat at the bakery. (These "rules" generally also apply in similar retail outlets such as supermarkets, butchers, dry cleaners, etc.).

WORKING LIFE AND THE GERMAN ART OF COMPARTMENTALIZATION

Let's get back to the topic of something that Germans are supposed to be so taken with: work. Yes, I suppose they do take it seriously, in the sense that they follow their basic instinct summed up in the phrase, "if you're going to do something, do it properly". After all, they couldn't have created the economic miracle without some intrinsic desire to work hard and well. They also tend to believe that where you work, for example, is a place where you work, not where you play or make friends. Even if they form a friendship of sorts with colleagues, Germans are clear in their minds that the people they work with are colleagues and not friends. The step from chatting amiably with a colleague and actually inviting them to their home is often a step many Germans are cautious about taking. This is not to say that it doesn't happen at all, in fact, in recent years, as Germans themselves have become less formal, it happens more frequently. But many still fall back on the old watchword "*Dienst ist Dienst und Schnaps ist Schnaps*" (literally, work is work and schnapps is schnapps). You separate one from the other because your colleagues are not your friends. This is particularly the case with your superiors or colleagues considerably older than you. The working atmosphere in Germany is an example of what we might call compartmentalisation. Put simply, you go to work to work, not to socialise or discuss your nephew's forthcoming wedding. It's perhaps worth mentioning that the above points do not quite correspond to East German company culture where people are used to sharing more personal information. A throwback, I presume, to the old socialist days of "let's all be pals together", where happy comrades sat on happy tractors, happily fulfilling their productivity norms.

The office gay wit and banter often witnessed in British companies is harder to find in Germany; British companies doing business in Germany are sometimes rather taken aback by the relative stiffness and coolness of their German counterparts, in, for example, meetings. Cracking a joke to relieve tension can go badly wrong. The German attitude tends to be: "If you're trying to be funny, I can't take you seriously. And if I can't take you seriously, I can't do business with you." It takes time for some British business people to realise this and by the time they have, it's often too late.

Germans are constantly confronted with the tricky question of whether to call their colleagues by their first or second name. Again, major changes can be witnessed as people have generally loosened up in the workplace and more and more people are just casually introducing themselves as "Helmut", "Melanie" or whatever they happen to be called. This is particularly the case in newer branches of industry such as advertising, information technology or marketing. People working together in manual labour or tradesmen's jobs have automatically been using first names since the start of the Industrial Revolution. It is also common in academic circles. In other more traditional and let's say, staid branches of endeavour such as local government, administration and banking, there may well be more resistance to this casual way of addressing each other. The trend towards a less formal approach, however, is clearly evident and will doubtless continue.

Germany, however, is still a long way from the first name culture rampant in Britain these days where everybody seems to call everybody by their first name. Doctors, dentists, bank managers, binmen, they're all at it. You have the feeling in Britain that you may as well call the Queen and the Duke of Edinburgh "Liz" and "Phil" the next time they're opening a community centre in your neighbourhood. It probably will never get to that stage in Germany as using your first name in German normally demands that you use the more intimate sounding "*du*"("you" in English) as part of the deal. If anybody "offers" you the "*du*", you can't really say "no", unless you really want to insult them, of course. I've never really wanted to insult anybody so much that I have refused it. What sometimes happens is that one drink too many has lulled you into offering or accepting a "*du*" which you rather regret in the sober light of the breaking dawn. The English language, thankfully, does not have these awkward, burdensome alternatives.

HOME SWEET HOME

Only 43.2% of Germans own their own home (Source: www.facts-about-germany.de/2010). I use the word "only" because it is a considerably lower percentage than in Britain. Why is this? I believe there are two major reasons. Firstly, there is, quite simply, an ample supply of good quality, affordable rented accommodation to be had in this country. There is little evidence of overpriced, low-quality flats that tend to be the only alternative on offer in Britain. Secondly, the cost of renting in Germany has risen little in the thirty or so years I have been here; it is seldom necessary to spend much more than 20% of your net income on rent. Germans therefore see little reason to commit themselves to mortgages when they can live at a reasonable cost in quality, rented accommodation. As the German housing market is also very stable - with the exception of "cool" and prosperous towns such as Cologne, Hamburg, Düsseldorf, Frankfurt and Munich - there is little need to rush into property before prices become either prohibitive or too good to miss.

Psychologically, there doesn't seem to be the British obsession with "getting on the property ladder" anyway. When the Germans eventually do get round to investing in property, they tend to have a house built according to their own specific requirements. Generally, they are far bigger than British houses with large gardens front and back, a cellar, an attic, a utility room, guest room and plenty of space. A "two-up, two-down" favoured by many couples starting on the property ladder in Britain is uncommon here and Germans are often mildly shocked at the relatively small amount of space their Anglo-Saxon neighbours have to live in.

The topic of space is an important one for Germans. Being the second most populated country in Europe (after Belgium, I believe), it is perhaps understandable that they appreciate a bit of space. If a couple move in together, they tend to take 80 or 90 square metres as a minimum size required for two grown people. If a child appears on the scene, we are then talking about 120 plus. There are of course exceptions to this, but space seems to be a commodity Germans particularly crave.

Germans furnish their apartments and houses tastefully and well; their fitted kitchens are often a sight to behold and no expense is spared on good furniture and the latest electronic gadgetry. Cleanliness and tidiness is the norm, particularly if the household is run by older, more conservative German women with a leaning towards sparkling, spotless rooms with everything in its rightful place. For the modern German woman more interested in pursuing careers than maintaining perfect dwellings, cleaning ladies from various central and eastern European countries can be had at affordable prices.

As most people live in flats, there is an increased sense of anonymity in the way people live their lives in Germany, particularly in the bigger cities. A brief encounter in the corridor or lift often creates little more than a grudging acknowledgment of a fellow flat dweller in the form of a curt, grunting *"Guten Tag"* (Good day). The curter the *Guten Tag*, the less likelihood there is of the person indulging in anything we could describe as conversation. It's a generalisation of course, but Germans like to keep themselves at a certain distance from their neighbours and, as we have already seen, from strangers in general. Often you don't hear from them until you're doing something that bothers them: music/kids/wife/husband too loud, steps not cleaned, snow not cleared from in front of the building, etc, etc. A friend of mine was once reprimanded by a neighbour because her vacuum cleaner was making too much noise! Quite what she was supposed to do about that, I do not know. An older custom, which I believe is dying out, is to outlaw any noise between the hours of 1 and 3 p.m. This, apparently, was the time allotted for the post-lunch snooze.

A HEALTHY MIND AND BODY - OTHER DISTRACTIONS

Other leisure activities enjoyed by the Germans are the same ones any of us enjoy anywhere in today's world, particularly the digital world, which entails spending hours on the internet maintaining links via social networking, playing computer games, surfing the Web and wasting hours on YouTube. It is rare to find a German without a hobby or sporting interest, some of them rather expensive, like skiing, sailing or horse riding; some are more down-to-earth like hiking, jogging and swimming. One thing that struck me when I first came to Germany was how seriously Germans took their health. This manifests itself in the vast number of sports clubs that exist here; 70% of Germans older than 14 are members of groups, clubs or organisations (Source: www.facts-about-Germany.de/2010). They are not all sports clubs, but it would appear that this is the Germans' favoured way of keeping in trim. It also gets them out of the house and gives them a chance to meet people.

A healthy body also deserves a healthy mind and Germans are no slouches on the education front. The "*Volkshochschule*" is an adult education centre which can be found in every town nationwide. Heavily subsidised by state funding, the trusty *Volkshochschule* has been in existence for over a hundred years now. Virtually anything can be learnt there from pottery to nuclear power station construction (I am joking about the nuclear power stations, but there is an impressive list of courses available). It's another way for Germans to make sensible use of their time. Many other adult education centres of a more commercial complexion offer further possibilities to improve skills in, for example, foreign languages, business and technology.

No report of everyday life can miss out the ubiquitous role that TV plays. Germans don't seem to watch as much of it as the British do. Neither do they have that irritating habit of leaving it switched on when nobody is actually watching it. Nor do they reach the pits of bad manners by eating while they watch it or when you visit them. Pats on the back all round there. But is German TV actually any good? Generally speaking, "No" (a bit like British TV has become, actually). There are the usual portions of dubbed American TV series and films, reasonably well-made documentaries and German feature films (most of them no better than average). Then we move into the really poor stuff: reality TV (just as bad as in Britain), quiz shows (ditto), and German TV series (ranging from predictable rubbish to vaguely entertaining - but rarely anything better than that). The Germans have also discovered stand-up comedy and despite the never-ending quips about the German sense of humour, such shows presenting up-and-coming comedians are actually sometimes quite funny.

Chat shows are something you can watch virtually every evening; there are three currently running simultaneously on three different channels on Friday evening. On German chat shows there are never less than four or five guests and the producers of such shows have hit on the brilliant idea of inviting guests bound to have geometrically opposing views, thus ensuring a lively and, better still, noisy debate. All sounds fine in theory, but unfortunately the same producers fail to communicate to their guests that there is one fundamental rule that must not be broken, i.e. only one person is allowed to speak at any one time. Consequently, after a fairly civilized start, guests all begin talking, or in some cases shouting, at the same time. This is the moment when I invariably reach for the remote control, either for another channel where you can understand what is going on (provided you want to understand what is going on, of course) or decide on another form of entertainment altogether, which is normally the best option.

German TV at least manages to transmit the news well: in the same formal style, with the same greetings and goodbyes, no emotion shown and no fuss created. And followed by the weather. I can never remember the format or presentation being any other way and quite frankly, I wouldn't want it any other way. The privately funded channels jazz it up slightly, but most people feel a certain affinity to the public channels and their sober transmitting of news, good or bad. The same applies to TV reporting of football: straight, to the point, minimalistic. In Britain we now have a second commentator who constantly feels the need to comment on what the main commentator has just commented on. Do we need this? German TV producers, thankfully, don't think so, and for once I wholeheartedly agree with them.

WORLD CHAMPION TRAVELLERS

And then we have holidays; no nation travels more than the Germans. Go anywhere in the world and you'll find them: the young adventurer trudging across the Himalayas, the party animal in Spain, the prosperous pensioner sipping cocktails on cruise ships and culture vultures studiously viewing the sites of the ancient Incas in Mexico: Germans seeking, sun, sea, sand, salvation, relaxation, enlightenment and anything they can't get at home. A genuine desire to see and experience foreign cultures, generous holiday entitlement and top-of-the-range prosperity has combined to make travelling the Germans' favourite waste of time. In my experience, Germans tolerate no economizing on the following three items: their car, the furniture in their home and their holidays.

Germans prepare for their holidays with an attention to detail sometimes bordering on the obsessive. They are so determined to find out as much about the place they are visiting beforehand that you sometimes wonder why they bother going there at all. Based on what they have gleaned from various up-to-date, quality guides, they often plan their schedule like a military campaign, with little left to chance and every opportunity taken to explore everything they think their chosen destination has to offer. On the one hand, it is a laudable approach to travelling as it makes sense to work out in advance what you want to see. But on the other hand, it also takes away the certain tingle of excitement about arriving in a place without any prior knowledge, opening your eyes, speaking to the locals and just experiencing whatever comes your way.

It remains a fact that Germans do love to travel. People in their fifties are constantly talking about the monumental travel plans they have once they reach retirement age. At the other end of the age scale, students plan similarly ambitious trips to distant and exotic climes before they finish their studies and settle down to build that house I was talking about earlier. Or, if they don't build that house in their thirties and put off starting a family till as late as possible, you can guarantee they will be investing most of their double-income-no-kids earnings into as many spectacular trips round the world as possible. So where does this lust for exploring the world actually come from?

We have already established that Germans have the necessary dosh to finance such globe-trotting projects. They go on expensive trips around the world because they can afford to. I feel, however, that the ghosts of the past are a further motivating force. They desire to go abroad, not inside a tank or aircraft carrying bombs, but with a message of peace and a desire to show the world that Germans come with a need to learn about other cultures. They wish to prove that they can behave well on their travels and appreciate mentalities different from their own (a quality which is, by and large, sadly lacking in some of my compatriots). The pent-up desire that East Germans had to see the world after they obtained their freedom hardly needs any explanation: they are, quite simply, making up for lost time. It could well be that Germans (particularly from the younger generation) are escaping from the more rigid confines of their own culture. Letting your hair down abroad is much easier when the neighbours are not watching and perhaps tut-tutting. If you do what the natives do, you are accepted, perhaps even liked. And you are contributing towards improving the image of Germans - something most Germans, deep down, want to do. All these factors contribute to the fact that it's hard to escape from them, wherever you are in the world.

Ever-recurring rituals

A couple of culinary rituals which Germans still hang on to need to be mentioned: the weekend breakfast and coffee and cakes. After a busy week, during which there is little or no time for a "proper" breakfast, Germans take great delight in slowing down on Saturday and Sunday mornings and indulging in what they call the "Family breakfast". There is probably something similar in Britain, particularly on Sundays, when the Brits gorge on the "Full Monty" heart attack breakfast *and* the Sunday newspapers. But the German weekend breakfast simply requires a little visit to the local bakery and back. The Germans, you understand, need to munch on fresh rolls at the weekend and these can only be had at your local bakery, of which there are many hundreds of thousands. I have caught the disease and every weekend join the lugubrious queue of bread roll purchasers just dying to start their weekend off with an extended breakfast during which the whole family can rediscover themselves, set new records for bread roll-eating and perhaps even talk to each other. They must consume a record-breaking amount of these things because people walk away from bakeries on Saturday mornings overloaded with bagfuls of those crispy, circular creations, soon to be covered with butter, various types of cheese, sausage meat, jams and the like. Bearing in mind that the average German family only consists of 3.3 people (husband, wife and 1.3 of a child), the orders barked out in bakeries, "*12 Brötchen, bitte!*" (12 rolls, please!), always seem slightly incongruous. Where on earth do they put them all?

Coffee and cakes is archetypical German tradition. Often scorned by younger people, generally loved by the older ones, it stubbornly refuses to go away. Younger folk scoff at the stiff rituals it requires: served anytime between three and four (Sunday is the main day); immaculate tablecloths; plates armed with sparkling and pristine cake forks and neatly folded serviettes, carefully placed for every invited guest; cakes strategically and tastefully arranged across the central section of the table and the coffee lovingly poured by the senior female member of the household. I have myself become a bit of a sucker for these civilized coffee slurping rituals and can now understand why many households on Sundays still, with a certain zealous alacrity, uphold this cake-gorging ceremony. I am not a huge fan of German cake and the aforementioned female coffee pourers have a nasty habit of forcing you to eat far more of the dreadful stuff than you actually want to, but, like the family breakfast, it provides a pleasant hour when people make an effort to sit together and talk. And if it is followed by something a little stronger, even a die-hard cake hater like me can survive it.

This brings us to a German tradition witnessed in everyday life right through the year - the German birthday. Coffee and cakes also play a major role here, often being the fulcrum of the whole celebration. Having a birthday without coffee and cakes would be quite unthinkable in most German families: a bit like a British Christmas without mince pies. Another unusual thing (for Brits at least) is that you don't buy the birthday boy or girl a drink in Germany - they buy you one. It is also true to say that phone calls are more important on this special day than cards. If you are there on the day of the person's birthday (or on a day assigned for the celebration of it), you shake the person's hand or kiss them and give them their present. I have often had questioning looks from Germans as I hand over the obligatory card; it would seem that they find it strange to be receiving a card wishing them in writing what I am also saying to their face. Cards generally do not play the massive role they play in Britain. If you do give them or send them one, they tend to read it, thank you and put it back in the envelope where it will never be seen again. We, on the other hand, see it as a fairly good value for money investment as they are then displayed for a good few days at Christmas, Easter,

New Year or on birthdays (and for a few days after).

Generally speaking, birthdays in Germany are important. Forget one and you might be in trouble (a bit like us forgetting to send somebody a Christmas card). Miss a "big" one, i.e. 30, 40, 50, etc and you definitely are in trouble. Birthdays really are the chance for families to get together and bury the hatchet and they therefore play a part in ensuring that relatives and friends don't just simply drift apart. In that sense, if you haven't contacted somebody on their birthday for many years, you really are saying you don't want to have anything more to do with them (a bit like our threat to cross somebody off our Christmas card list). Often younger folk have two different types of birthday parties: one where their older relatives can come, have coffee, a gulp of sparkling wine and leave generous amounts of cash and expensive presents - a boring but profitable PR exercise. The other one is for their similarly aged and like-minded friends, where they can drink a lot, behave badly and finally get to know that girl (or bloke, of course) they have been ogling for a goodly while. The party can go on as long as they want as the meddlesome, elder relatives aren't there to interfere and embarrass. A further example, I suppose, of the compartmentalization I mentioned before.

Christmas comes but once a year and many Germans utter a heartfelt "Thank God". For those not interested in consumerism, religion, Christmas carols, family tension and unhealthy diet, and I count myself as one of them, it can be a huge damp squib to be endured rather than enjoyed. In that respect, then, it's not much different than Britain and the reservations most Brits hold about the festival of peace and love; but there are some additional aspects of a German Christmas which make it very different to the British one.

As a rule, the German Christmas does not require you to drink until you drop. Alcohol is involved, as it always is in Germany, but it is not consumed in seriously dangerous quantities as it is during the British yuletide revelries. A couple of mulled wines too many at your local Christmas market is about as far as it goes on the alcohol abuse front. Christmas office parties as I know them in Britain, with everybody off their heads and people doing embarrassing things with people they shouldn't, don't really exist. If there is an office do, a table at a local eating place is reserved, people enjoy a meal appropriate to the time of year, perhaps roast duck, have only one drink containing alcohol (because they are all driving, of course) and drive home alone.

The build-up to Christmas in Germany is dominated by the Christmas market, an interesting and quaint collection of stands and stalls selling Christmas decorations and gifts, mouth-watering Christmas delicacies and the infamous mulled wine (*Glühwein*) which is now, I have been told, available in most British supermarkets during the Christmas period. On the four Sundays before Christmas, Advent is celebrated and the Advent crown is displayed along with all manner of Christmas foliage and on each Sunday one more candle is lit as Christmas approaches. The concept of the candle is an important one when talking about the German Christmas, as it is the pre-dominant mood-maker, creating an atmosphere of inner reflection, stillness and contemplation. No jovial, cracker-pulling, raucous ribaldry of a British nature here: Christmas for the Germans is a serious matter and serious behaviour is expected.

Christmas Eve (December 24) is when the German Christmas reaches its zenith - anytime between 5 and 8 p.m. German families peacefully and harmoniously gather round the (real) Christmas tree (and sometimes with real candles) with soft yuletide melodies in the background as the *Christkind* (a figure resembling somebody who is not quite Baby Jesus, but not quite Father Christmas either) descends (only symbolically, of course) and the presents are opened. A meal is prepared; Germans cook something fancy on this special evening, but definitely not turkey with stuffing as we know it. The mood is sombre and reserved, the lights are low and by the time the family has gone to bed, Christmas is, to all intents and purposes, over for another year. December 25 and 26 are official bank holidays and more food is served up, either at home or in a restaurant, but the jolly festivities that we pursue in Britain are generally not in evidence.

I have myself "done" the German Christmas and find it hard to come to terms with. After my first experience of it with a German family, I went to bed on Christmas Eve suffering from deep and serious depression. The mood of inner reflection and soul searching was so at odds with what Christmas had meant for me in my previous British life that I actually wondered whether it had been Christmas at all. The next day (December 25) was for the German family I was staying with more or less "just another day"; I spent most of that day wondering where the presents were, the Christmas crackers, the Christmas pudding, the Queen's speech, the endless supply of mince pies and generous doses of Scotch. Not to mention Slade screaming out "So here it is Merry Christmas, everybody's having fun" on the Christmas Day edition of "Top of the Pops". Some cultural bridges are just too tough to cross and the "German Christmas Eve versus British Christmas Day" bridge is one of them. Other British expatriates tend to agree with me on this one: the peaceful nature of Christmas markets, mulled wine and civilized, subdued and well-behaved, atmospheric revelry in the build-up to Christmas in Germany is an improvement on Britain's hedonistic madness, but the German Christmas Eve is verily one step too far.

An annual festival in Germany which consistently provokes mystification and bafflement in me is Carnival. Taking place in the week before Lent in predominantly Catholic areas of the country, i.e. the South and Rhineland, it is historically the period when Roman Catholics have one last, pleasure-seeking bash before starting their period of fasting in the weeks before Easter. They are allowed to eat, drink, fornicate, dance, be merry and generally behave as badly as they want before it all comes to an end on Ash Wednesday when they renounce all pleasures of the flesh for a few weeks. In other words, everybody goes mad in those five or six days. Having no feeling of tradition for such things means that I only ever have one question racing through my head during these "mad days" (*die tollen Tage*): "What on earth are all these people doing dressed up like complete idiots, drinking, dancing and cavorting about the streets, singing songs which have no rhyme nor reason?" My question seems even more justified when many of the very same people foolishly gyrating before my eyes during Carnival are, in normal life, as stiff as the proverbial broom and possess as much spontaneity as a North Korean robot. Germans press the spontaneity button during those days, let themselves go and come back again on Ash Wednesday with a thumping headache, ready to continue with whatever their daily lives demand as if nothing had happened.

My main gripe with Carnival is that point about spontaneity. It really does seem false to suddenly appear ludicrously happy, behave in a way which is normally alien to you and dress up in clothes which could be described as the German version of Bollywood. Anybody harbouring liberal values about how we should lead our life would have nothing against people doing such things if that actually floats their boat. But why should they want to do it just because it's that week in February when people decide that they should want to do it? I suppose the same argument could be made about celebrating New Year or having a good time on your holidays, i.e. "I'm supposed to be having a good time now, so I better be having a good time, or at least appear to be having a good time". Everybody tends to do it, regardless of their cultural background. Anyway, if culture means: "The way we do things around here", then they will be celebrating Carnival this way long after I have shuffled off this mortal coil. So I'll let them, lock myself away on the days in question and leave it at that.

GERMAN EVERYDAY LIFE: BETTER OR WORSE?

The answer to the above question could be: "neither better, nor worse – just different." When comparing cultures, this is often the compromise answer. Everyday life anywhere in the world normally means you are attempting to achieve one or more of the following things: get to and return from your place of work, buy products which will feed you or improve the quality of your life (i.e. shopping) and complete rather mundane tasks like going to the doctor's or the bank. None of these things is particularly exciting but hopefully this chapter has pointed out some interesting differences which have now become second nature to me but might have surprised readers not familiar with Germany. The question of better or worse is perhaps of secondary importance: a shop is a shop, a job is a job, and a tram is a tram wherever you are. However, these activities always involve people and the generally relaxed way British people go about everyday life would put Britain into a 1-0 lead.

The variety and depth of what's on offer outside what I have called "everyday life" provides a crucial equalizing goal for Germany. There is no denying the quality of most things around you, from restaurants, cafés and bars to the variety of leisure activities available. German towns tend to look clean and modern with a public transport system and infrastructure to match. If you have anything like a reasonably-paid job in Germany (despite the breathtaking amount of stoppages at source), you will be able to afford a nice flat, decent food and a weekly night out and still have enough left over to save for that all-important holiday in a country you haven't been to before. Inflation has never been a huge problem (with the exception of the catastrophic post - 1st world war twenties) and the vagaries of the housing market and the price of mortgages don't play havoc with your spending plans - as they regularly do in Britain.

The fact that I have now spent over half my life here would seem to suggest that Germany is a better place to live. I can't really argue with that. A human being is happy or unhappy for a variety of reasons; the quality of the 18 or so waking hours I spend on a daily basis in Germany is certainly one major reason why I am still here. Despite the fact that many Germans themselves are prone to complain about their own country, the number of natives who actually leave it and settle in another country forever is comparatively small. A German economic refugee is a rare bird.

When people, both German and British, ask me why I (still) live here, I flippantly reply: "Because of the bread and the beer". I could have mentioned any number of other things which make everyday life in Germany a pleasant experience: clean toilets, punctual trains and trams, heating and plumbing systems that work. This sober listing of creature comforts and amenities says nothing about any emotional attachment I have to the place; perhaps I don't have any. I once thought I had a deep attachment to Berlin, a place I lived in for ten years at the turn of the century. I made a nostalgic trip there a few years after I left and visited all my old hunting grounds, thinking it would stir emotional intensity and deep feelings. It didn't – it rather created a damp squib of reflective confusion. I quickly realized that places without the people you spent them with are inanimate objects: bricks, stones, pieces of wood and iron. In the same way, my love of clean toilets and chemical-free beer are certainly not an expression of any deep passion I have developed for my chosen country of residence. What I do have from my time in Germany are emotional attachments to German people. When a certain Herr Mack (one of the first Germans I ever met in Germany) offered me a beer in his garden all those years ago and was patient with my faltering German, he was displaying two aspects of the German character often not associated with them: spontaneity and patience. Germans have symbolically been offering me bottles of beer regularly since that spring day in 1978; the purity of their beer and toilets have contributed to the quality of the experience but it is important to remember that at the end of the day it's our relationships with people that matter. During the many years I have spent here I have learnt that it is wise to persevere with Germans as they reveal, in the course of time, further qualities worthy of high praise. Their bark in the coolness of everyday life doesn't win them many points; but we need, of course, to dig deeper to figure out what makes them tick. Let us get digging in the next chapter.

3   The Germans

TYPICALLY GERMAN OR TRANSCULTURAL?

Writing this chapter is a difficult call. The danger of generalising, and stereotyping, is ever present and, of course, "the German", as such, does not exist. Every human being is different and individual, regardless of the influence of the culture he or she is surrounded by; their behaviour patterns are influenced by a large number of different factors such as gender, their genes, class, age, education, regional origin, upbringing and the immediate situation people find themselves in. I therefore agree that the "typical German" doesn't exist, but I have lost count of the number of times that I have heard Germans themselves say: "That's typically German". They must be saying it for a reason. This chapter, therefore, focuses on why the phrase actually exists.

This chapter also focuses on the things that Germans generally do which British people, for example, generally don't. Germans (generally) wait for the green man at the pedestrian crossing; Brits (generally) don't. If it is typically German to do that, then I think any German can happily live with that statement and condone this sort of behaviour: waiting for the green man to appear is a positive "typically German" characteristic as it reduces the risk of road accidents and sets a good example to children. I expect the German reader, by the same token, to accept negative statements, such as "Germans aren't good at forming a queue". Any rational human being would agree that queuing is a very fair method to employ if a number of people want a similar thing or things at the same time and place (e.g. rolls at the bakers, tickets at the box office, inoculations during an epidemic). The Germans' reluctance to do so, therefore, would then have to be registered as a negative "typically German" characteristic.

There is also a need for caution when describing the habits of a "nation" because things, quite simply, change. When I first came to Germany in 1979 there was indeed a lack of queuing going on here. Things have, I am happy to say, improved in this respect. Whilst not yet being world-class queuers like us Brits, life in the bakeries of Germany have over the years become far less of the brutal free-for-all than it used to be. Society, particularly in the modern, fast-moving, global world is in constant flux and it could well be that the well-travelled Germans are picking up some good habits including, for example, the queue-forming one. Take also the example of baked beans in tomato sauce, a delicacy unheard of when I first moved here; now they're available in every supermarket. Many tourist resorts offer beans with their cooked breakfasts and they seem to have made their way into some German households at breakfast time. Next thing you know, they'll be tucking into beans on toast for lunch. Well, perhaps not...

As ridiculous as it sounds, the baked bean story brings us nicely to a relatively new concept in the field of Cultural Studies and that is transculturality (Welsch 1999). Transculturality suggests that Herder's concept of the nation, characterized by "internal uniformity and clear separation from what is outside" is dead in the water. Transculturality implies "internal diversity, permeable borders, cultural blending and manifold cross-cultural connections" (Welsch 1999:194-213). In other words, global communications, mass migration and economic interdependence (and, of course, your average German holidaymaker tucking into his full English breakfast in Greece), are moving us towards a world of hybrid culture. The downside to this could well be that it will become a world where we all eat hamburgers, use a computer, have an iPhone and like Take That and the Eurovision Song Contest. Forgive the brief lapse into infantile polemic, but I believe that such examples make clear that things in Germany are not as German as they used to be; the march of transculturality plods on, but does not necessarily always improve the quality of our lives.

Despite the fact that the Global Village is thriving and likely to do so for a very long time, there are still plenty of differences to get our teeth into and I presume that anybody reading this book will want to find out what is different about the Germans. What does make them tick? What makes them so successful? What makes them different to us (by "us", I mean the British)? Why are they so obsessed with sun loungers? (Only kidding). So good at taking penalties? (Kidding again). Putting it really simply, if I buy a book on Italian cooking, I'm going to be mighty disappointed if there is no section on pasta. A book on modern Germany, for the same reasons, I believe, should tell us something about the way the Germans behave.

Of course, the cries of "You can't /shouldn't/mustn't generalize" will not go away; however, I have checked with a lawyer and I have been informed that it is not a punishable offence by law to generalize. And as I have also been careful not to make any of the generalizations appear insulting to any Germans reading the book, I don't envisage any libel actions against me, either. The Oxford Advanced Learner's Dictionary defines the word generalize thus: "to make a general statement about something and not look at the details"; the first part is self explanatory but I will attempt also in this chapter to look at the details of why Germans behave the way they do. This requires me, therefore, to look at the details. Sometimes there is no immediate answer to the question of why a certain culture behaves the way it does, of course, and we are back with the age-old definition of culture as "the way we do things around here".

As far as possible in this chapter, comments and observations about Germans will be based on my experiences. I mention this because I am often accused of prejudice even when I make a statement about Germans which has evolved from something I have experienced on a number of occasions. How can it still be a prejudice when I frequently experience a behaviour pattern in Germany which I have never experienced anywhere else? Two more final points before we move on. Firstly, the Germans I refer to in this chapter are primarily, unless I am referring to national characteristics moulded pre-1945, West German. Secondly, for the reasons already mentioned, any statements made about the "Germans" are almost always made in the general sense. Many German readers will want, from time to time, to screech at the top of their voice: "I don't do that!" I understand your concern, but generalisation means that at least 51% of Germans do. It is generalisation based on observations made over the course of 35 years. But it's definitely not prejudice.

In 2011, a book came out in Germany entitled *Die deutsche Seele* (The German Soul) by Thea Dorn and Richard Wagner. Both well-known as writers and media personalities, Mrs Dorn is in her early forties and Mr Wagner touching sixty; consequently, the book covers topics which might be considered more traditional cornerstones of the German mindset. In an attempt to come to grips with the complicated concept of the German soul, they choose 63 catchwords (in alphabetical order) and devote anything between three and twenty pages on each of their chosen topics. Younger Germans may well be dumbfounded by some of their choices: *Abgrund* (abyss); *Kleinstaaterei* (scattered regionalism); *Männerchor* (male voice choir); *Ordnungsliebe* (orderliness); *Schadenfreude* (malicious joy); *Wurst* (sausage) and fifty-eight other words which Dorn and Wagner believe are lurking deep within the German soul, defining the way Germans are. Younger Germans might even find it hard to take many of the items on the list seriously, and many would claim that such old-fashioned notions have nothing to do with modern Germany and, more importantly, modern Germans.

However, the book has had an important part in reminding us, and Germans themselves, that Germany did not only come into existence after 1945. The trauma of the Third Reich has lead many Germans to present themselves as a liberal, modern, tolerant forward-thinking nation which is determined to distance itself from events pre-May 8, 1945. Their book is a successful attempt to reacquaint Germans with concepts often mocked these days but which have a lingering influence on what and how they actually are today. Scattered regionalism (*Kleinstaaterei*) may seem like a crashingly boring and non-descript notion, but modern Germany has a federal state system today which has its roots in that very concept. Having a chapter on the sausage (*Wurst*) seems like a mildly ridiculous idea, but have you ever found a German town which does not have a sausage stand? And do you know how many different types of sausage there are in Germany? Orderliness (*Ordnungsliebe*) is another topic which younger Germans baulk at because it smacks of rigidity and lack of spontaneity, but I cannot deny that I myself have become addicted to tidy German towns, spick and span cafés and impeccably clean bathrooms over the last 30-odd years. It might be cool to be untidy, but the German attachment to tidiness is without doubt a positive trait and Dorn and Wagner rightly point out that the German desire to lead an orderly life is a deep-rooted one. It comes as second nature for a German to get things organised and these organisational powers have been another building brick in the German success story.

Where Dorn and Wagner start going too far is in their treatment of the more sinister elements of the German character as discussed, for example, in their 18-page treatise on the concept of the abyss (*Abgrund*). Quoting from the great German philosophers, poets and composers – the usual suspects, Nietzsche, Goethe and Wagner (the other Wagner, of course) - they develop the idea suggesting that deep down, every German is somehow fated to push himself over the cliff, falling ever deeper into the abyss, gripped by some Teutonic death wish and all to the profound tones of Wagner's *Götterdämmerung* (twilight of civilization). It reminds me of Woody Allen's premise that it's hard to listen to Wagner without imagining German tanks rolling eastward into Poland and this chapter seems to be suggesting that at the end of the day the Germans are just itching to make that final descent into the deep, whilst dragging us all down with them. If that's not reminding us of the self-destructive, apocalyptic journey Herr Hitler took his fellow countrymen on, then I don't know what is. It seems to me to be rather a cop-out, suggesting that the Third Reich happened because, "well, the Germans are prone to that sort of mischief from time to time. It's in their Romantic temperament, you know". Alternatively, the authors might just be showing off how well read and clever they are.

Whilst reminding us in a detailed way that the culture we have today is the product of at least a thousand years of history, the book is strangely archaic and in stark contrast to the image of Germany a younger generation of Germans would like us to know. A much more modest compendium, *Die Tagesschau, das Große Deutschlandbuch* (2012) gathers together a number of TV news reports concerning Germany and German history and looks at modern developments since 1945. Interestingly, there is even some overlapping with the topics covered in the Dorn/Wagner book. The importance of football, for example, is stressed. The question of whether Germany still sees itself as a "*Kulturnation*" (no real English translation for this expression, apart from the rather lightweight "nation of culture") is also under scrutiny. Generally speaking, the book concerns itself more with the achievements of Germany since 1945 and its role in the world since the end of the Cold War.

The book also reflects the general trend for modern Germans to blow their own trumpet more than has been the norm since 1945. Many believe that the World Cup in 2006, hosted by Germany, represented a turning point in the way the country presented itself: spontaneous, open, friendly and able to party. Nobody doubted the Germans' ability to organise such an event; the fact, however, that they could also have fun at the same time surprised many. The book also mentions the Germans' desire to find a new role in Europe, this time helping to integrate rather than dominate. The path which Adenauer chose for Germany in the fifties, firmly anchored into a Franco-German alliance and with a view to stabilizing Europe in peace, has continued since the end of the Cold War. Chancellor Merkel, whilst not being the Greeks' and southern Europeans' particular darling at the moment, would fervently claim that she is endeavouring to keep the European Union together by suggesting that countries like Greece, Spain and Portugal get their house in order. The general argument is that modern Germany's role is now to help and support: a helpful, well-meaning neighbour rather than a bossy, nasty threat.

THE GERMAN IDENTITY PROBLEM

Being European suits the modern German image. Few Germans are happy with the sentence: "I am proud to be German", while "I am happy to be European" comes naturally and is a legitimate solution to the problem of having to show any sort of nationalist feeling. In many ways, then, Germany provides an excellent example of the transculturality we briefly discussed at the beginning of this chapter. One almost has the impression that a neutral nationality would be the most favoured option for most younger Germans. It is an interesting fact, however, that German patriotism is as fervent and strong at a German international football match as in any country and the idea of being neutral on such occasions would never enter the average German's head. The football field – the one place where

Germans can show their national pride with a clear conscience? A notion worth considering.

So what is German identity? Who are they? Regional identity is another way around the "problem" of answering this question and we now realise why Dorn and Wagner included *Kleinstaaterei* in their index. Loyalty to one's own region or town is important in defining the German's picture of himself/herself and for this reason they are usually anxious to find work in their own area; the lament about having to leave friends and family is a heartfelt and genuine one that I have often heard if suitable employment cannot be found within a thirty mile radius of their home town. Dorn and Wagner also back me on this one, devoting five pages to the concept of *"Heimat"* (home); the final sentence of the chapter proffers the romantic assertion: *"Heimat* is one of the most beautiful words in the German language" (Dorn/Wagner 2011: 237 – my translation). In this sense, identity is restricted from the bigger picture (i.e. the country) to the local (the region, the town or even the house). We (Brits) are lumbered with the old saying "An Englishman's home is his castle" and in a similar way Germans seem content to carry the cumbersome burden of *Heimat* around with them. Patriotism is out, but local patriotism never has been and is unlikely ever to go away.

This would also explain the Germans' attitude to home ownership. When they buy (or more than likely build) a house, the chances are it will be in the area of their birth, be spacious enough to house a largish family (or perhaps two generations) and will stay in the family's possession until the end of time. There is little or no evidence of buying and selling, moving around the country and up (and sometimes down) the property ladder as the British do. It is also a no-risk approach which has reaped dividends over the years and also reflects the more cautious approach to personal finances that Germans possess. Generally speaking, Germans loathe having debts and are traditionally big savers. It is an approach to finances which the German Chancellor is currently recommending to debt-ridden south European states.

Most of the characteristics I have described here point towards a people less inclined to leave their comfort zone than other nationalities; a step-by-step, sensible approach to life where risk-exclusion plays a vital part, backed up by a sober analysis of the overall picture. I have observed these behaviour patterns throughout my years in Germany and there are numerous examples of them in other parts of this book. I have also expressed cautious criticism of such behaviour both in this book and in real life, hinting, perhaps, that Germans tend to be predictable, over-cautious and, well, sometimes plain boring. For a number of reasons, however, I have started to change my mind. Maybe it's advancing years, maybe all this time in Germany is starting to Germanize me; or maybe I have quite simply seen the error of my ways. You can't argue with results and the typical characteristics I have just attributed to Germans have certainly in no small way contributed to the overall success story of post-war Germany, at least in the economic sense.

A culture is defined to a large degree by its language. Few people argue that German is a beautiful language. French is purported to be the "language of love", English the language of Shakespeare, Italian the sunny sing-song melody of all things gay and light-hearted. To the foreign ear, German is guttural, harsh-sounding and can sound rather fierce, especially when they insist on placing the all-important word "I" at the beginning of a sentence which is supposed to be a request. A German will rarely say: "Can I have?", but rather "I want", which can sound positively threatening and bossy to the British ear and tends to ruffle feathers rather than soothe. More sinister observers take delight in reminding us that it was the language used by the evil Nazis - the British are forever re-cycling the wearisome jokes about "Ve haff vays off making you talk!" It's all about British prejudice, a traditional stick to hit the Germans with when jingoistic, ill-informed factions in other countries (like Britain) decide to have a go at them; it is certainly not something we should be particularly proud of but is something we still do on a regular basis.

In their seemingly never-ending efforts to gain a better reputation with their foreign neighbours, Germans in fact tend to abandon their own language at every possible opportunity. Modern German is littered with Anglicisms, using English words when there are perfectly good German words to perform the same speech acts. In doing this, they are diluting their own language and culture. It would seem that they would rather be identified with a foreign language than their own and to be part of an international community where English is the preferred language of communication. This leads to the rather surreal situation whereby a German develops an international identity by avoiding his or her own German identity.

This unusual development is logical and understandable when seen in the light of modern German history, however. The extreme nationalism of the Third Reich and the tragic and gruesome consequences of that regime have induced in Germans a deep and real aversion to any sort of nationalism; any sign of preference for one's own language over a foreign language could be interpreted as being nationalistic, something your average German is most anxious to avoid.

The examples I have mentioned here point to a people determined not to follow any path which has even a slight nationalistic flavour to it. It is very difficult for any German to utter the words: "I am proud to be German". The closest they get to such a statement is: "I am proud of what Germany has achieved since 1945". By this they mean the obvious things like the economic re-construction of the country, the development of a functioning democracy, the country's non-interference in military conflict or perhaps even their consistently impressive performances in European and world football championships. Emotional statements of national pride are out – a cautious listing of post-war achievements is as far as most Germans will go.

In the light of these facts, Germans feel it is therefore imperative that they present themselves well in the eyes of the world. When a right-wing act of violence takes place or when a luminary from the public domain allows him or herself a faux-pas when referring to a particularly delicate matter (Third Reich, race, the 2nd World War, foreigners, immigrants), the first reaction is always: "What will our international neighbours think of us?" It will indeed be a long time before Germans don't care what the neighbours think.

German virtues?

There is an expression in German called "*Die deutschen Tugenden*" (The German virtues). It is disliked by many Germans as it refers to characteristics which have almost become stereotypical of the German character: strong will, discipline, hard work, order. The problem lies, I believe, in the military connotations associated with these terms and the disturbing possibility that Germans still hanker after the sort of military successes these virtues helped to deliver in the dark but victorious days of the Third Reich. The fact is that the four "virtues" mentioned are actually positive when used in other non-military contexts. What's wrong, for example, with being hard working? This shows quite clearly that the spectre of the Third Reich hangs like a dark cloud and refuses to go away - people are perturbed when certain words and expressions are used. You will never hear a German politician use the word *Volk* (people) due to its unpleasant association with Nazi terminology. *Euthanasie* (euthanasia) and *Rasse* (race) are other no-nos. The worst possible insult is to call somebody a Nazi or anything inferring that the person being insulted may be a Nazi. Legal proceedings may ensue. All this makes for a tense atmosphere at times and normality still seems far away, even today, almost seventy years after the Second World War.

Ben Donald offers an excellent example of this problem with words and expressions in his moderately funny, sometimes insightful and consistently polemic *Springtime in Germany* (2007). He describes how the German government and businesses, wishing to "instil a feel-good factor in the German people" during the World Cup in Germany (Donald 2007:135), funded a fairly extensive media campaign which included billboard posters, TV clips and newspaper with the ubiquitous motto "*Du bist Deutschland*" (You are Germany). Great idea until it transpired that an identical slogan had been used at a Nazi convention in 1935, complete with a picture of Hitler, aimed at spurring young people on even more. Ooops.

There are other German characteristics which also become a problem when taken too far. Being a perfectionist is all well and good, and Germany wouldn't be the splendid place it is today without generous amounts of it, but overdo it and you can be entering a world of constant dissatisfaction, mood swings, insomnia and lasting depression. Striving for the best is a good idea, but sometimes second best is worth mentioning in despatches, too. I am always amazed at the deep vat of misery that Germans fall into when their national football team "only" comes second in a World Cup or European Championship. Only second! The Queen would be knighting the entire England squad if they came "only second" in anything!

Donald approaches the task of defining what being "German" is by using a list of catchwords à la Dorn/Wagner. (In fact his book came out five years before theirs, so perhaps they adapted the idea from him). He reduces the list to fourteen, four of them appearing in the Dorn/Wagner book. He takes a more humorous approach and doesn't hold back with outrageous mickey-taking when he deems that the Germans deserve it and you have the general impression that he feels happiest when he is having a go at them. His grasp of German philosophy and history is certainly a match for Dorn and Wagner; he just hams it up for comic effect whenever he gets the chance. (You would never catch the Dorn or Wagner team making such cracks as: "Who were *Sturm und Drang*? Didn't they make hi-fis?"). This illustrates excellently the fact that highly intelligent Brits find it hard not to tease. The closest Dorn and Wagner get to this is a whimsical and subtle use of irony when covering some of their fairly heavyweight concepts. Donald briefly enters various aspects of German life, mercilessly makes fun of it after a brief, pithy, entertaining analysis and moves on to the next subject at breakneck speed, hardly pausing for breath.

One particularly good chapter is the one on *"Angst"* (fear, anxiety, anguish), a topic also covered by Dorn and Wagner. In this chapter, we find Donald's thesis that the German soul is influenced to a large degree by Romanticism. Donald touches upon a number of concepts also covered in Dorn /Wagner's book. All three authors agree that the following concepts are vitally important in understanding what makes a German tick: *Heimat* (home), *Selbstwahrnehmung* (self-perception), *Vergangenheitsbewältigung* (coming to terms with the past), *Sehnsucht* (longing), and *Wanderlust* (travel for travel's sake – quoted in Donald 2007: 65). I would agree that they might, to some extent, explain those aspects of German character and behaviour still alien to me, even after spending 35 years of my life with them.

Let's take them from the top: *Heimat* - something we have already covered, but certainly a solid refuge which Germans cling to in troubled times. *Selbstwahrnehmung* - the search for identity, a particularly difficult undertaking in the light of the recent past, which is also linked to the task of *Vergangenheitsbewältigung*, an ongoing problem which will probably be around for many generations to come. *Sehnsucht* - described by Donald's German "tutor", Manny, in the book as "a longing, for something better, for completion and for some absolute state of rest and perfection that is destined not to be achieved"(Donald 2007: 64). Remember what I said about Germans being perfectionists? *Wanderlust* – been anywhere on this planet without meeting a German?

Donald also neatly summarizes the influence of the Lutheran reformation of the 16th century and the German philosophers at the end of the in his chapter on *Angst* (cf. 2007: 68-73). He describes Protestantism as encouraging hard-work as a way to heaven and Kant encouraging the German mind "to reduce the world into neat systems so that it can be better understood and, if necessary, improved". Donald also directly notes how Kant himself realised that "Germans are praised in that, when consistency and sustained diligence are demanded, they can go further than other people". Unfortunately we are back with one of those controversial German virtues again: the strong will. In other words, the Germans, as Donald neatly sums up, "don't do things by halves".

According to Donald, the Germans' way of dealing with *Angst* is the creation of order, summed up perfectly in the classic phrase *"Ordnung muss sein"*. (We must have order – my translation). As in most things in life, the maxim "Everything in moderation" is a reasonable guiding light and as long as the creation of order is not stifling and nonsensical, most rational human beings can happily live with it. And, generally speaking, this is the case in Germany. The German mind does have a tendency to want a plan and a structure and the average, less organised Brits can adapt to it without too much trouble at all. It must be said, however, that the days are long gone when only Germans slavishly kept to rules and regulations; in fact, the modern British obsession with Health and Safety regulations means that we are becoming, in this respect, the "New Germans": a nation where schools have to provide goggles for pupils if they wish to play conkers outside in the playground, creating an over-cautious world in which faceless bureaucrats make up ridiculous rules in order to remove any element of risk from our lives.

Despite a general feeling that life is loosening up in Germany it is still a fact that anybody reading this chapter might paint themselves a slightly disturbing picture of the way Germans are, and with no knowledge or experience of Germans you might race to some unpleasant conclusions: a country of work-obsessed, serious, deep-thinking, self-analytical perfectionists who are forever racing around the world, avoiding risks and searching for their true identity and being constantly anguished about their past and what the rest of the world thinks of them. Well, even most Germans themselves would agree there is some truth in all those things, but all human beings are experts at fighting their own neuroses on a day-to-day basis and the same rule probably applies to other cultures. Where would the Brits be without their obsessive pre-occupation with the weather? Or the Americans' desire to protect the rights of all their citizens to carry arms? Or the Ukrainians' fear of homosexuals? The Germans, however, do seem to have an above-average share of hang-ups. Perhaps it is precisely this fact that spurns them on to work very hard at being "good "(and their desire for self-improvement is a truly laudable one). They have endeavoured since 1945 to be peaceful neighbours, first-class democrats and to create a stable, prosperous, tolerant country in the centre of Europe. Oh yes, and they managed to bring about unification for their own country in a peaceful manner, bringing freedom and prosperity to 17 million East Germans and is the leading light in East-West reconciliation and co-operation. So why don't we love them?

The question is a complex one. We normally like the Germans, respect them, envy them and praise them and their impressive country. However, I have never heard anybody in Britain profess their love for Germans (excluding, of course, for individual Germans, like their wife, husband or children). I think the reason why we cannot speak of love is explained in everything that has been discussed in this chapter so far. The long list of factors we have discussed has not created a carefree, easy-going, relaxed sort of folk. When you meet Germans for the first time, they invariably look glum. Statistically, they cannot be very high up in the table of nations that smile the most. If you have a suggestion, they are sceptical, not to say downright hostile. They often point out what can go wrong before admitting there is potential in an idea you might have. As they are not superficial people, they don't do small talk, which makes them appear standoffish and distant. They are to-the-point, direct, don't want to waste time and are keen to get on with the tasks of the day. In short, they are efficient, focussed, hard-working, take life rather seriously and can therefore appear rather tense. In a nutshell, relaxing sometimes doesn't come easy. All these things can make people think that they are rather inhuman and cold.

My experience shows that when you get to know a German, they are invariably the exact opposite of inhuman and cold. They need time, their *Angst* has to dissipate and when the Romantic restlessness has settled itself and an *Ordnung* with which a German can feel at home has been established, he or she could well turn out to be the best friend you've ever had, displaying an admirable gamut of positive characteristics. The following spring immediately to mind: generous, intelligent, reliable, loyal, decent, genuine, thoughtful and good.

The British are more easy-going, willing to engage in small talk and smile at strangers, have a joke and be generally relaxed. But English history tells a story more likely to create more congeniality: united a thousand years before Germany, the English only suffered one foreign invasion and two civil wars during that time and were even described as "this happy breed" by a certain William Shakespeare. Germany, by comparison, was a disunited landscape consisting of a myriad of warring factions, principalities, fiefdoms, counties and dodgy alliances, supporting equally dodgy landlords, dukes, barons, princes and emperors. Any stranger you met could be an invader, nasty foreigner or antagonized vigilantes from some nearby village or else an imperial spy. The more recent history of Gestapo snoopers in the Third Reich or State Security agents in the former GDR is hardly going to allay your distrust of strangers, either. It is no coincidence that the German for "a total stranger" is *ein Wildfremder* (literally "a wild stranger"). The implication is that a stranger is wild, so make sure he isn't before you relax. Some instincts linger on down the generations and it is one of my theories why Germans look tense and uneasy during the first few seconds of any encounter with a stranger.

Germans reading this may well think this is a huge load of twaddle. But I have thought long and hard about why Germans need more time than virtually any other nationality in new situations with new people. Adroitness in the first few seconds of such encounters does not give people the impression of friendliness or warmth; but the fact remains that it would have been very surprising if Germany's history had created a happy-go-lucky, cheerful bunch of trusting folk. The more aware we are of the past which helped to create the Germans we meet today, the more we can understand the way they behave. This is true, of course, of any culture. But the fact remains that Germans invariably need time to weigh up any stranger coming their way; being on the receiving end of this crucial "weighing-up phase", however, can contribute to creating negative first impressions about Germans which can be described as "standoffish", "distant", "cool" or, in extreme cases, "hostile". Despite the fact that judging people on first impressions is generally accepted as being unfair, it is also true to say that many (or perhaps even most) people still do so. And those people who do set great store by first impressions and who are not willing to persevere when experiencing initial German reserve might not get past first base in their attempt to get to know a German.

The problem is also exacerbated by that seemingly deep-seated German aversion to small-talk. On the one hand, we could (and perhaps should) praise the German desire to avoid superficiality; on the other hand, reality teaches us that without some ritualistic and phatic communication at the beginning of any social intercourse with a stranger, it would be virtually impossible to meet anybody new. The classic "Do you come here often?" can actually lead to beautiful, fulfilled, happy marriages. Less ambitious souls can even talk of equally beautiful one-night stands a few hours after this classic chat-up line. Either way, without those five crass words the two people involved would not have met each other. "Cold today, isn't it?" is another classic one-liner which many Germans would find hard to bring themselves to say, although equally meaningful relationships - or further exciting one-night stands - can emerge from such uninventive, conversational openers.

IDENTITY THROUGH PROSPERITY?

What defines the Germans today? Has there been a continuous link since 1945, holding together a nation through post-war, Cold War and post-Cold War years to the present day? (I will leave East Germans out of the equation at this stage and refer you instead to Chapter 6). I would proffer the suggestion that the

80

uninterrupted period of prosperity that began in the late fifties and which has resulted in impressive purchasing power and economic stability has created a nation used to having money and thoroughly enjoying the security and opportunities this has created. Generally speaking, the average German today is a well-off German. The vagaries of the modern economy and the challenges thrown up by the post-industrial revolution and globalization have cast shadows over the unprecedented boom years of 1953-1973 and the gap between rich and poor has also noticeably widened, with all the unpleasant consequences this creates. Yet the material gains amassed in those years and beyond are nestling happily in German bank accounts to the tune of 4,715 trillion Euros (source: German Federal Bank statistics 2011). Interestingly, this money is in the form of cash and short to medium-term investment bonds. In other words, Germany is also a nation with impressive amounts of liquid cash at its disposal. This is further helped by substantial amounts of money being inherited in Germany today - in its June 15, 2011 issue, the newspaper, *Das Handelsblatt* reported that 2.6 trillion Euros will be inherited by the end of the second decade of this century.

Such economic comfort is bound to have an effect on individual personalities; to quote a German saying: "Money isn't everything, but it calms the nerves". Self-confidence grows when you have money in the bank. Driving a comfortable, modern car is better than the daily terror of having to hope that your old banger is going to start on a freezing cold January morning. Good quality food tastes better than cheap variations and you generally look better in better-quality clothes. The list could go on forever and nobody would question the Germans' decision to enjoy all these things and more. The immediate post-war generation of the fifties and sixties, who had kept their money together by keeping a prudent household and saving at every opportunity, has been replaced by a more consumer-related one, more relaxed about casting caution to the wind. The danger residing in this way of life is that you become less and less satiated as you consume more and more and there are undoubtedly numerous cases of such frustration all over modern Germany. I am not suggesting for one moment that only Germans suffer from the age-old frustration of not finding happiness through money. I am not even suggesting that most Germans believe that happiness can be achieved through spending it. It is, however, an undeniable fact that Germans are in a better financial position than any other nation to find out whether money can do the trick. And, as I look around me, I see many trying.

Modern Germans are used to being able to do what they want to do; quite simply because, generally speaking, they have the money to do it. A large and ever increasing middle class, which includes families who would previously have been part of the comfortable working class, has impressive purchasing power. Doing without plays a minor role in the modern German psyche; expectations are continually high and rarely thwarted. Psychologically, there might be a price to pay and sociologists, educationalists and (some) parents fear that younger generations are losing a sense of proportion, expecting too much, too soon and regarding work as something that gets in the way of having good times in exotic places, driving top-end-of-the-market cars and wearing equally impressive clothes. Put simply, the underlying fear is that the modern generation is spoilt, soft and getting softer.

So should we see the modern German this way? Obviously it is a generalised picture and it would be unnatural if younger generations did not want to reap the benefits of previous generations' economic successes. The march of consumerism continues unabated across the world and we are all encouraged to grab a piece of the action and keep the party going; it just so happens that Germans have more cash and have, consequently, fewer excuses to be party-poopers. Unfortunately a new insidious materialism has been created in which many people are defining themselves by the brands they wear, the places they visit and the lifestyle they aspire to. And the Germans, thanks to the economic legacy they have inherited, will be indulging as long as supplies last. And judging by the statistics quoted above, the supplies will not be used up in the conceivable future.

Chapter 1 reminded us that Germany was long considered an economic giant but a political dwarf and it is true to say that many Germans since the war have therefore seen their own country first and foremost as a successful economic concern. The business of international politics and world affairs took backstage while the people were happy to keep their noses to the grindstone and out of other nations' affairs. Some have argued that a nation obsessed by economics and creating prosperity has been created; consequently, the Germans themselves have become obsessed by the economy and the nation itself had degenerated into one huge prosperity-creating apparatus, lacking a soul and moral purpose.

This might all sound rather far-fetched and extreme. Yet I myself have experienced many situations here in which the topic of money has been the only thing people actually talk about. I have met a number of Germans, whose sole topic of conversation has been what things cost, what one's pension will be later (and many angst-ridden Germans are convinced there won't be any pensions later), the price of car insurance and the best way of screwing the Inland Revenue. One should also bear in mind that such conversations have often take place at parties, where presumably people are supposed to be relaxing and having a good time. Perhaps it's no worse than the Brits' obsession with house prices and the endlessly boring conversations revolving round that particular topic.

Some readers will wonder why I am even mentioning how prosperous modern Germany is and what exactly my problem is. Why shouldn't they enjoy the life of plenty? Asking why today's Germans are bouncing around on puffy white clouds of comforting prosperity is rather like asking the question: "Why does a dog lick its own balls?" Answer: "Because it can". Modern Germans are enjoying the good life because they can. Any clear-thinking human being would behave in the same way. My problem is that generations are being created who do not know what it means to do without, are not actually sure how wealth is created and, more dangerously, are increasingly unable to put themselves in the position of people less fortunate than themselves. I am not claiming that Germans are insensitive to the less better off; they have been raised in an environment in which social justice is (and always has been) an economic principle of all the leading political parties, stretching back to the Adenauer/Erhard era when "Prosperity for all" was their watchword and striven for by all Chancellors and Finance Ministers since. Germany has never had a radical leader like Margaret Thatcher making statements such as, "There is no such thing as society" and thus encouraging members of that society to be selfish. The population as a whole seems very aware of the fact that social tension and political instability will ensue if equality is not maintained. More importantly, the lessons of history have made Germans acutely aware of the consequences of such tension and instability. But as the modern cult of individuality also prospers it cannot be denied that the further away you are from poverty, the less likely you are to understand the situation of people afflicted by it. And that danger is undoubtedly growing.

Another problem lies with the people actually enjoying the benefits of this widespread prosperity: the ever-increasing rise of the middle classes and their seemingly endless supply of cash provided by breathtaking amounts of (mostly parental or grandparental) savings and inherited wealth is producing a people seemingly unable to enjoy the simple things in life, to be happy about being alive, to be happy with less or little. Quite frankly, it is in danger of producing a generation of listless bores; there is a tendency for such people to be impressed by nothing, often assuming that the next, bigger, more expensive experience is going to be the better one and it sometimes resembles the picture of the man looking for the black cat in the darkened room or the kitten playing with the ball of wool. The days are over when the weary Germany miner downed his first beer in one in the pub after his shift, laughed and joked with his mates and greedily slurped down his wife's homemade soup later before collapsing into bed an exhausted, yet contented man. A decent day's pay for a decent day's work and peace of mind.

Many readers will say that these are the ramblings of an out-of-touch socio-romantic, hopelessly nostalgic and clearly trapped in an over-idealised time warp. Yet many Germans have admitted to me in more lucid and honest moments that all the trappings of prosperity, or in some case of luxury, have not brought them peace of mind and that satiation has kicked in with a vengeance. The problem has been exacerbated by how easily such trappings are obtained. Bob Dylan mentions in his autobiographical book, *Chronicles* (2004), something he had heard from a former American Poet Laureate, Archibald MacLeish: "He (Macleish) said the worth of things can't be measured by what they cost but by what they cost you to get it (sic)" (Dylan 2004: 112). At this stage of Germany's economic development, much is being given free of charge and some people's characters are suffering badly as a consequence.

The German *Sehnsucht* for the perfect fitted kitchen or motor car or for the ultimate holiday experience has led them down some unfulfilling paths. The Economic Miracle has soothed the nerves but not the souls. It has encouraged many

Germans to take up Eastern religions and philosophies, question the whole quest for ever greater material wealth and, in more extreme cases, the whole purpose of their existence. Their trips to foreign climes where the indigenous population had a fraction of their wealth, yet seemed to exude a lot more happiness than they could ever muster have also got them thinking about whether the prosperity trip is the right one. The fascination with the simpler life, however, is often a short one and before long more expensive projects are being planned, be it another exotic trip to an even more exotic place or the long-term renovation of a rambling, mediaeval cottage in the south of France to enable alternative-style holidays with equally prosperous friends.

Some will accuse me of envy; others of being a killjoy, simply rehashing the typical complaints always expressed by the older generations about their younger successors. There may be truth in that: my mother often angrily stated that I didn't know the meaning of hunger. I sincerely believe now that she did and I didn't, just as millions of post-war Germans did and their children and grandchildren didn't. My German partner's father once stated that he never takes a warm room for granted. Another 40s + German businessman I knew at the end of the seventies said that the difference between him and his daughter was that she opened the window when it was too warm in their apartment while he turned the heating down. Presumably, these people from the old school have more peace of mind than people used to being warm, well-fed and financially comfortable. The examples could go on forever, along with that well-known generational conflict.

On the positive side, there are many Germans who are very aware of the limited satisfaction money and possessions can bring and who use the wealth they have to invest wisely in their children's and grandchildren's education: those Germans who buy healthy and natural food, book holidays and trips with an educational purpose or with a view to improving the health and cultural capital of themselves and their families. Or who give generously to charity and organisations which improve the lives of people much worse-off than themselves. Millions of Germans do voluntary work all the year round in churches, privately and state-run charities and sports clubs.

The fairer and more equal distribution of wealth across all classes, which ultimately makes life in Germany a better place to live in than Britain, is something I am genuinely envious of. My grouse is that despite the fact that Germany is arguably the most affluent country in the world, it also seems to be the country with the glummest faces and the highest number of grumbling citizens. A number of reasons have been put forward in this chapter to explain why, but ultimately it remains the great Teutonic mystery, destined to remain unresolved.

In the meantime, I'll just go to the fridge and remind myself how good German beer is and raise my glass to all those miners who agreed with me all those years ago and who were seemingly happy with what they had.

FINAL THOUGHTS: WHAT IS THE MODERN GERMAN?

The modern German is the product of everything that has happened in German culture since German culture has been in existence. The particularly extreme period of German history culminating in the Zero Hour meltdown of May 8, 1945 and the resulting Cold War years of the forties and fifties have, of course, made a particularly big impact on the way Germans are today. The major developments of German history and culture dating pre-1933 culture have also left their mark and linger on through the generations; concepts such as the desire for an orderly approach to life, for example, will always be noticeably present, despite the march of transculturality and globalisation. Particular familiar characteristics of Germans can still be discerned. German economic development, however, and the Germans' push to forge a new identity since 1945, largely devoid of nationalist or patriotic fervour, have undisputedly made the biggest impact on mentality, personality, attitudes and way of life.

The fruits of economic success have made it a first-class country to live in but have not made every German in it happy - a healthy scepticism of virtually anything remains the lasting impression. The German search for something better has two consequences: the country keeps improving and its people remain restless and grumpy in their efforts to keep it improving. The Germans have still not figured out how to have one without the other; it is unlikely they ever will. The final message I have (and it's a happy one, you'll be pleased to know) is that I sincerely believe they are going to work on this most difficult of projects exclusively within the borders finally settled on October 3, 1990 when Germany eventually became united after 45 years of division and Cold War conflict. I can also recommend anybody outside those borders to come and observe the project and let the Germans, whoever they are, pleasantly surprise you. They might even give you a smile.

4   An Englishman in Germany – one man's journey

"SETTLING DOWN WITH A NICE GIRL FROM MINDEN AND STAYING THERE FOR THE REST OF MY LIFE WOULD HAVE BEEN MUCH SIMPLER; AND A LOT LESS PAINFUL, COMPLICATED, INTERESTING AND EXCITING."

WEST AND EAST GERMANY, APRIL 1978 - SEPTEMBER 1978

Neuss, April to June 1978

Although I always state that I have been living in Germany since 1979, the journey actually began in April, 1978 when I spent six months here as a student. Those months convinced me that Germany could offer me a future. The question I am most frequently asked by Germans is: "What brought you here?" I have had a glib answer ready for years now, and it is: "Annarosa Winkler". It's not a lie, but it's not wholly the truth either. More often than not romance is involved when people move to a foreign country and the final decision in my case to try life in Germany was influenced by a woman of that name.

Liverpool Polytechnic (now more grandly known as Liverpool John Moores University) required its foreign language undergraduates to spend six months in the countries of the languages they were studying. My first stop was the *Pädagogische Hochschule* in Neuss, i.e. Neuss teacher training college, just over the river from Düsseldorf in the North-West of Germany. Student life there couldn't have been more different to the way of life I had left in Liverpool: no student bar(s), every student seemed to own a car and drove off home every evening and/or weekend to either study hard, do sport or some part-time job. Being a student didn't mean (as it did and still does in Britain) partying, drinking, smoking pot and getting laid at every available opportunity, while desperately trying to keep to essay deadlines and pass exams when need be. My German colleagues seemed to be rational, sensible, prosperous, attractive people who saw the time they spent studying in a radically different way to their British counterparts. To put it in the proverbial nutshell, there didn't seem to be any social life; well, certainly nothing that we could discern as social life. The fact that the institution we were registered at didn't appear to have much notion about what to do with us didn't help matters;

I had fears that our time in Germany was going to end up the same way as our time during the previous year in France: a time of drifting through summer desperately trying to find some natives to talk to. Help was at hand, however, as a group of students suddenly appeared to have a remit to look after us. And just like Herr Mack, the kind gentleman who made such a lasting impression on me in the two weeks preceding this official stay (see Chapter 2), look after us they did. They offered company, advice, accommodation and constant help with our far-from-perfect German. They seemed to have an endless supply of patience and willingness to help. If the Germans were trying to make a good first impression on me, they were doing a damned fine job.

What also impressed me, though perhaps frightened is the better word, was the structured way they went about their lives. There seemed to be a purpose and plan to everything they did. Aimless lounging around, talking witty but gibberish nonsense was not on their agenda. In Liverpool we did little else, finding any excuse imaginable to retire to the student bar to crank up the madness a notch or two. Whenever I plucked up the courage and made the hesitant but sociable suggestion: "Let's have a drink sometime," the person I asked would normally come up with a definite place, time and a depressingly detailed plan as to how he or she thought the evening might then proceed. I found that "dropping in on somebody" was uncommon, and presumably not welcome. Questions such as "D'you fancy a drink?" were normally met with confused looks of miscomprehension. The lack of a student bar or friendly pub on the corner prevented the sort of spontaneity I was used to and enjoyed back home.

The early starts to the day in Germany also proved an almost insurmountable challenge. I was living with a fellow student, Petra, and her family for the first month of my stay and was astounded on the first morning to hear a knock on my bedroom door at six o'clock. Struggling to the kitchen and being presented with a daunting selection of cold meats, cheese and morning drinks at this time in the morning was a dumbfounding experience; being supervised by Petra's well-meaning but persistent mother hardly helped my mood: she was determined I wasn't going to leave the house without something substantial inside me. All I really wanted was my bed again. Petra's hectic shuffling in the background, anxious to "miss the rush hour traffic before seven", pushed me over the brink on most mornings. My English brain couldn't come to terms with the fact that there would be anybody on the roads at this unearthly hour; and how, pray tell, could you have a rush hour at 6.40 a.m? But this was Germany and everybody in this area was hurtling towards the main city, Düsseldorf, at that precise moment. On those mornings in the month of April 1978, bright, sparkling Petra, an extremely fit student of P.E and English had an unkempt, grumpy, confused Englishman by her side wishing he was back in Liverpool where life was civilized and lecturers didn't even dare suggest offering seminars before ten o'clock.

It was a difficult start and my travelling companion and mate Mike G., who had been given accommodation with a couple out in the sticks, was feeling the same way. His situation was even worse as he had a young wife and six-month old baby back in Liverpool. We were British: unstructured, without ambition and therefore feeling rather confused in get-up-and-go Germany. But I was also slowly realising why Germany was the economic motor of Europe, with the highest standard of living, and miles ahead of us in most matters. The fact was that they got themselves out of bed early, grabbed life by the scruff of the neck and gave it a deep meaning before the average Brit had scratched his balls and thought about getting the kettle on. I'm outrageously simplifying things, of course, but there's a solid grain of truth in it. I felt hopelessly inadequate in those early days.

Germans could also enjoy life; they just did it differently to us. I noticed that the home was the central hub of partying, not the pub. One incident (for want of a better word) brought this home to me. Returning to my lodgings one Sunday evening, I found Petra's parents seated round the dining table with two friends. Without any great ceremony (who says Germans can't be spontaneous?), I was invited to join them. They were about to tuck into what looked like a more exotic and enlarged version of the breakfast I had been trying to force down all these weeks in the very same household. There were extra salad dishes as well as cold meats, fish and a staggering variety of different bread types. The other important extra dimension were the liberal quantities of alcohol they were knocking back and pushing my way every time my glass was threatening even to get half empty: beer, schnapps, digestives, liqueurs, you name it and they seemed to have it. My German hosts seemed to be genuinely enjoying the company of their gregarious English guest as my German became better and better with every gulp of the local brew that came my way. I was adapting admirably to the German tradition of the "*festliches Abendessen*"- a special evening spread (my translation). The booze eventually caught up with me, of course, and I hastily thanked all and sundry for their great hospitality before concentrating on the few blurred paces to the bathroom to begin the customary search for "Hughie" (think about it). As I lay prostrate on my bed, watching the ceiling doing its customary magic tricks, I realized I was still a novice at this German drinking lark. At the same time, I congratulated myself on holding my own - at least I hadn't ruined the family's pristine tablecloth. I told myself that I would be back for more in the future as I slumbered off. The evening visit to the bathroom had at least spared me the gruesome pain of my first German hangover; the six o'clock hammering at my bedroom door was bad enough. It inevitably came and I was fairly shake-free as I carefully knocked back Frau L's killer coffee. Thankfully she didn't seem to notice the damage her generous hospitality had inflicted upon me the previous night.

A young woman I met at the teacher training college in Neuss kindly offered me the use of her flat for the rest of my stay there; she would move in with her boyfriend until the end of June, when I would be moving on elsewhere. Mike joined me and we were able to have the best of both worlds: slumming around in the true British student tradition whilst enjoying the friendship of some very pleasant, helpful young Germans. They showed generosity, too, not asking a pfennig for the use of their apartment. Any spare pfennigs we had were invariably spent in Düsseldorf's Old Town or on going to watch Borussia Mönchengladbach play (and normally win). This was the team Liverpool beat in Rome to win the European Cup the previous year. Mike and I had been there. Liverpool actually beat Mönchengladbach again in the semi-final that April and we were able to hold our heads high as we beat FC Bruges in the final; our German friends looked on as if we were nuts as we went wild when Kenny Dalglish chipped the winner over the Bruges' goalkeeper. They apparently hadn't seen British football supporters before; well, definitely not Liverpool ones.

Looking back, the in-built superiority we enjoyed, basking in the glory of

Liverpool's great team of the late seventies, helped me overcome the rather sad realisation that I came from an inferior country. An alarming statement, perhaps, but everything I witnessed and experienced during my stay in West Germany put Britain in the shade. Perhaps it isn't so surprising, considering the state Britain was in at the time: by the end of the seventies it had become an under-achieving country economically, with frightening, anarchistic elements and social divisions and poverty that hadn't been seen since the dire thirties. My home town, Liverpool, was leading a pack of post-industrial British towns going nowhere. Its citizens were leaving the place in tens of thousands, going anywhere that offered some sort of future. By mid-summer, I was starting to see Germany as a sort of escape route out of a country which seemed to be a grim black and white film called "Going-nowhere Britain". Germany seemed to be in high-definition colour (and definitely going somewhere).

That is not to say that I didn't miss the easy-going, relaxed way of life I had left behind in Liverpool; whilst I admired the no-nonsense efficiency of German life, I also noticed that many tended to take things just a little too seriously. It also struck me as early as 1978 that many didn't actually appear to be particularly happy despite all the trappings of wealth and prosperity. My first inkling that it takes a lot to make a German happy was starting to take within me. But even then Germany had, to use a modern football analogy, a place in the Champions League; Britain was, on the other hand, fighting relegation.

East Berlin, July 1978

My time in Neuss came to an end at the beginning of July and a promising intermezzo was about to begin in a very different part of Germany. It was, in fact, officially speaking, another Germany: the German Democratic Republic, the Germany surrounded by a wall running from the Baltic Sea in the North to Czechoslovakia in the South. For all intents and purposes the East Germans were 17 million prisoners living under the Marxist-Leninist system imposed upon them by the country liberating them from Nazism in 1945. The state was officially founded in 1949 and the building of the Berlin Wall in August 1961 cemented the division from the West for the next 28 years. And I was now going to get behind that wall for four weeks as a participant in the "*Hochschulferienkurs*" (University Summer School) at the Humboldt University in East Berlin. I was originally chosen to go to Greifswald, a town you may have heard of. However, Mike decided to get back to his wife and child and I was more than grateful to take his place in East Berlin. As corny and dramatic as it sounds, my stay in the GDR's capital turned out to be a veritable life-changing experience.

As I was travelling on my original visa issued for Greifswald, I was obliged to cross the border in the North West corner of the GDR to get to Berlin. I was able to have a look at Lübeck, birth place of Thomas Mann, before getting on an antiquated train belonging to a rail company with the spooky name, "*Deutsche Reichsbahn*" – a relic from the days when Germany spoke in the language of empires. The border guard gave a robotic, distant, vaguely threatening impression as he stamped the visa into my passport.

I had to change in Schwerin and decided to kill the half hour with a drink at the station restaurant. It was spacious, dark, sinister and looked positively unhealthy. I nuzzled on an unpleasantly tasting beer and surveyed the scene: scruffy with a definite end-of-the-world touch to it. Just time for a burst on my banjo, I thought, and I made my way to the toilets.

What awaited me there would remind anybody familiar with the film "*Trainspotting*" of the scene when our desperate protagonist, suffering from a bad case of diarrhoea, finally finds a toilet in a grim pub in Edinburgh. The film's subtitles read: "Scotland's worst toilet". In my film, the subtitles would have read: "The **world's** worst toilets". If I had come directly from Liverpool to Schwerin, I would have been shocked to the core; coming straight here from West Germany, where you could generally eat your dinners from most toilet floors, this picture of loathsome and disgusting depravity, consisting of a stomach-churning variety of green, brown and yellow poisons not challenged since the Red Army took the town in April 1945, was a shock even to a Scouser used to dodgy Liverpool toilets. If this was Socialism, I might have to reconsider my own political beliefs pretty quickly. As I had no exit visa and my train was leaving in 5 minutes, I had no option but to push on to Berlin. I was hoping the standards in the capital would be a little higher.

By about 10 p.m. we were pulling into Berlin-Lichtenberg. The student hall of residence was supposed to be close, in the area known as "*Schlachthof*" (slaughter house). I didn't like the sound of the name, but armed with my official letter and the address of the hall I marched into the night. Berlin was darker than any other city I had visited before as no street lamps seemed to be turned on. I cautiously pushed on and approached a man who was clearly a little unsteady on his feet. He shuffled off, seemingly unable to follow my gist. I had no more luck with the second fellow. The next man I literally stumbled into was actually lying on the ground. A few yards further on, another man fell to his knees. I slowly realised that I was probably the only sober human being within a one-mile radius. I assumed it was closing time at various taverns near to the station. I was starting to panic, trudging rather aimlessly through ever darker streets. After about 15 minutes or so a tall, dark, gangly young man wearing sandals and a check shirt entered my line of vision. He seemed to have his wits about him and, more importantly, didn't reek of the local brew. I tried my luck and my luck was in. He knew where the halls in question were and after whisking me onto two different trams and marching me down a couple of concrete avenues, he led me to the doorway of the very building that was to be my home for the next four weeks. I was met at the desk by a welcoming and efficient East German student called Thomas who turned out to be an FC Magdeburg fan - but we all have our problems. He took my particulars and I was in. The name of the fellow who got me there was Thomas Consmüller, a student of dentistry. The twenty minutes or so I spent with him shuffling through the dark night of Berlin-Lichtenberg had been enlightening: he had told me that there was no unemployment in the GDR; public transport cost 10 pfennigs a ride; to study you needed to have the equivalent of "A" levels and to have completed your three-year military service. He seemed reasonably happy. We exchanged addresses and I got a postcard from him in Prague when I got back to Britain. Thomas, the chap at the reception (for want of a better word), showed me to my room. I got undressed, made it to a bed and drifted off. I spent my first night next to Berlin's "*Zentralviehhof*" or central abattoir, described so vividly by Alfred Döblin in his 1930 masterpiece, *Berlin Alexanderplatz*.

I woke up next morning to find I had shared a room with seven African students from a variety of Eastern-bloc socialist states. They were amiable, spoke idiosyncratic German and were after my transistor radio from that first morning until the day I left four weeks later. They tried to barter but nothing they had tempted me in the slightest.

Sharing a room and its meagre facilities with seven other people was quite a shock to the system and at best the hall of residence could be described as adequate for sleeping in but not much else. In total contrast, we were swept off every morning to the Humboldt University where a sumptuous breakfast buffet awaited us. Anywhere we went to during our stay there seemed to go via "*Ostkreuz*" (East crossing). There was, of course also a "*Westkreuz*", deep into West-Berlin. Same town, different world.

The *Hochschulferienkurs* was superbly organised and very possibly the best four weeks of my life. Students of German from all over the world, high quality lectures on language and literature, visits to open-air classic concerts on the ramparts of old monasteries, Brecht plays, comedy shows and visits to all manner of cultural establishments and historical buildings. What made everything even more wonderful for the Western participants were the incredibly cheap prices, made even more ridiculously cheap by the endless supply of Eastern Marks, courtesy of a Yugoslavian fellow student who had interesting black markets contacts in town. When those contacts dried up, he would nip over to West-Berlin and buy some there. For the first (and last) time in my life, money was no object.

My time in East Berlin was further sweetened by meeting Boshana, a classically beautiful Bulgarian I came to know in the first week of my stay; we were inseparable for the remaining weeks in the GDR capital. I never quite worked out what she saw in me, but it was reciprocal love at first sight and I wasn't complaining. A cynic might say that her interest in the West was greater than her interest in me. But I still wasn't complaining. In fact, none of the Western students were complaining about our East European fellow students' fascination for the West: it generally made us more interesting than we actually were. Their interest in life in the West was insatiable.

It was equally fascinating to observe the different nationalities during those weeks. The Russians and Poles, locked in an endless bout of drinking competitions which the Russians usually won; the optimistic and elegant French and Italian Eurocommunists; the sceptical Americans (one of them would keep reminding me at every possible occasion of the danger lurking, with the never-ending mantra: "never forget, they're Commies, Neil, they're Commies"); the poorly dressed but alarmingly pretty Romanian and Polish girls and the smart, charming but Mafiosi-style Yugoslavians. And the Africans from Socialist "Brother states" wandering around affably, smiling all the time whilst trying to get their hands on somebody's transistor radio.

And then, of course, there were the East Germans themselves. The teaching staff were presumably all loyal party members; bright, thorough, eager to help with any questions you might have. They were obviously well-trained in tackling the uncomfortable questions some of us confronted them with. The East German students whose job it was to look after us coped admirably: always available, always cheerful and generally speaking, a joy to be with. Some openly discussed politics, but they generally toed the party line. Others were more cautious, withdrawing from conversations involving topics which were, in their opinion, off limits.

On the few occasions that we were left to our own devices we were able to explore parts of East Berlin which were not on the programme. Apart from low prices for the basics: bread, staple foods, accommodation and public transport, the GDR seemed to have little else to offer. The actual quality of the aforementioned products and services ranged from below average to appalling. The concept of service in the retail sector did not exist; the temptation to punch waiters in bars for sheer insolence was ever-present and strong. Generally speaking, however, we just laughed it off, left and continued drinking in some other dubious-looking socialist tavern.

The disturbing fact was that, as a GDR citizen, your country was your prison until you got to 60 or 65, depending on your sex. I came to know the reality of this situation when I regularly visited an East German couple I got to know at the university who lived in a street which ended at the Wall. To visit people in any of the houses further down the street required a special permit. To walk a few yards further on might get you prison (or worse). I have a photo of Boshana leaving Beate and Lutz's place and there is the Wall, 30 yards behind her. I still shiver every time I see it all these years later.

Even so, I had the time of my life in those July weeks of 1978. It was clear that the powers-that-be were pulling out all the stops to impress their visitors and have us go home feeling that life behind the Wall wasn't as bad as that mischievous Western propaganda made it out to be. *I* was certainly impressed. But when I tried to visualise the reality of life beyond the cosseted world of that superbly organised summer school I could easily imagine the difficulties you would encounter in that country as a normal GDR citizen if you wanted anything more than the regime believed you needed. And if you thought you needed to travel anywhere outside the Eastern bloc, you were entering dangerous waters.

When I left the GDR at the end of my stay, I was confronted with the glaringly obvious fact that I would never see any of those East Germans again unless I made the effort to visit them. If I didn't make that effort, our friendship would remain a purely postal one, with all the restrictions that entails. As my train crept over the Berlin Wall at *Friedrichstrasse*, anti-tank devices on my left, the Reichstag just over the border in West-Berlin on my right, I felt sad, relieved, exhausted and aware that I was lucky to have been born where I had been born. The tragic picture of the German division had come into view and it was going to stay with me till that fateful and unforgettable night on November 9, 1989.

Vlotho, August 1978

One of the remarkable things about my stay in East Berlin was that I didn't set foot on West-Berlin soil once. I got on the train at Berlin *Friedrichstrasse* and didn't leave it till I got to Hanover in West Germany. I was to spend three weeks at the *"Gesamteuropäisches Studentenwerk"* in Vlotho on the River Weser. This pan-European study institute carried out research and offered seminars on all aspects of divided Europe since 1945. I was also to be re-united with all the students of my year who had been scattered all over East and West Germany since April.

The institute provided a well-balanced, studious look at the problems caused by the consequences of the Second World War and had the most comprehensive selection of literature on the subject in Germany. The seminars we participated in made excellent use of the reference material at the institute's disposal. The programme was a welcome change to the one-sided approach to post-war history offered by the Humboldt University in East Berlin. I was also back in the world of ultra-clean toilets, slick towns and bristling prosperity. This environment was far removed from East Berlin's crumbling, urban Eastern bloc gristliness: we were accommodated in crisp, modern single room dormitories, surrounded by hilly, green landscapes weaving round the peaceful River Weser.

In the German tradition I was now becoming used to, the whole stay was organised and executed brilliantly. On a personal level, my knowledge of the German language and culture had come on leaps and bounds; I had been in three completely different German environments and felt that I had learnt more in six months than I had through ten years of schooling. The country and its people had received top marks right across the board. The fact that I met and fell in love with a young German woman in Vlotho added the final clincher. I returned to Britain with only two things on my mind: Annarosa and Germany.

FIRST BRITISH INTERMEZZO: LIVERPOOL, OCTOBER 1978 TO AUGUST 1979

Annarosa was the deciding factor when it came to taking the plunge and trying my luck in Germany, although there were other reasons, not least the lack of opportunities in Britain. The fact, however, is that it is not a "and they-lived-happily-ever-after" story. It turned out to be a "lived-sort-of-happily-ever-after-without-her-in-Germany" story, which is basically what this autobiographical chapter is about.

I visited Annarosa just after Christmas in 1978. From the Bielefeld area where she lived, I moved on to East Berlin and stayed with Beate and Lutz for a few days. If I thought East Berlin was dark in July, the scenes of deep-frozen, black despair on the streets of East Berlin in January were beyond the beyond. Boshana had got wind of my coming and had flown in from Bulgaria. This made things, well, a little complicated. The details of my stay under these circumstances can be kept for another book when I have found a suitable pseudonym. Suffice to say that I learnt a lot in those days about East European moral proclivities. It was also the continuation of the learning curve on the differences between East and West. In some ways East Germans were virtually the same as West Germans, in other ways totally different. I will go into this in more detail in Chapter 6 of this book.

I finished my degree in the summer of 1979 and managed to get a teaching job in Minden, Westphalia, a 45-minute train drive from where Annarosa lived. I threw my worldly possessions into an offensively-coloured orange rucksack (they were all the go in those days, you know), got into the car of a German exchange student I had got to know at the polytechnic, and she drove me there. I started my first real job at the Bénédict Languages School in Minden on August 1, 1979.

Minden, West Germany, August 1979 to August 1982

Minden is a small town of approximately 70,000 inhabitants in the most easterly corner of Westphalia, about 50 miles west of Hanover and 70 miles north-east of Dortmund. It is situated on the River Weser in an area known as the *Weserbergland*. It is not famous for anything in particular apart from being a reasonably quaint and attractive place with an atmospheric old town and a 1000 year-old stone cathedral. The *Mittellandkanal*, one of Germany's longest canals, straddles the Weser in Minden, linking east and west.

After a couple of short stays in temporary accommodation, I eventually settled down in a ground-floor apartment, offering no frills but a pleasant view out of my window of the old city wall and the river which flowed gently past in the summer months and regularly burst its banks in spring, the water reaching just below my windows at peak times.

I found my feet fairly quickly, working hard during the week and spending the weekends with Annarosa. Her parents were helpful, understanding people. Their household was run meticulously and the father's innate stiffness left him after the second beer and we had some worthwhile conversations. I was mildly surprised how often the war was mentioned and slightly troubled by the use of the word "Adolf" when referring to the man who had about 60 million deaths on his conscience. Hitler was made to sound more like a lovable, cranky uncle rather than the brutal, half-insane dictator he actually was. The Third Reich years were the "time under Adolf" rather than "those dreadful years". One evening the father reminded me that it was the British who invented the concentration camp during the Boer War. I obviously remained the diplomatic, young Englishman and listened politely (well, I was drinking his beer and Dimple whisky at the time). He regularly admonished the British for "milking the cow dry" when referring to the European Common Market. I wonder what he'd say about the Greeks today? Nevertheless, he admired our football teams and general sense of fair play and didn't push the concentration camp topics. And neither did I.

I actually found Annarosa's views on what a man of my age should be doing slightly more disturbing. She held certain views which were foreign to me. The fact, for example, that I had no driving licence disturbed her greatly. Having no car was the obvious consequence of this, something else which seemed to trouble her deeply. Neither did I seem to be making any concerted effort to get a driving licence, a further minus point in her mind. My British "habit" of frequenting a local drinking establishment with my Scottish colleague, Ian J, in Minden was also something she did not approve of. I was getting important lessons on one version of the German way of life.

Life in Minden I found generally pleasant; a friendly feel to the place, most things within walking distance and places to walk in pleasant green countryside. There were also approximately 10.000 British Army personnel and dependants stationed there and I quickly made contact with some, exacerbating my "problem" of going to pubs and drinking.

The only real contact I had with Germans was with my students, most of whom were too young (the day school young ladies, training to be foreign language secretaries) or too old (the evening school clientele who were catching up on the English they never had at school) for socialising with. Occasionally we met up for a drink or meal after class and I was treated well in a polite and hospitable way. My definition of politeness, however, changed when I was actually invited to a German (adult) student's home. The man in question, Ewald W, early forties, wife and two kids, took me to one side a week after I had had a tasty lunch with his family because he wanted to "have a word with me". I couldn't imagine what I had done wrong but I was about to find out. There were two problems: firstly, I omitted to

100

take a little gift for his wife. Secondly, and this was the more bizarre one for me, after asking for a second helping, I didn't actually *finish* that second helping.

My first real blunder in Germany was due to a lack of cultural knowledge; since that day other Germans have claimed that Ewald had been rather harsh, although they all agree that the conventions he was referring to do exist. It illustrated, too, that Germans are not reticent about stating their opinion, something I was to have repeated experiences of in the years to come. I was slightly taken aback by his frankness but was determined not to make the same mistake again; I never have and I have Ewald to thank for that. The cheeky bastard. The lesson for me, however, was that according to German cultural norms I had been, in fact, the cheeky bastard.

By the spring of 1980, Annarosa decided we didn't have a future. So any future in Germany was going to be without her. To say this was a blow is to state the obvious. I almost panicked and went back to Britain but I wasn't sure what I would be going back to. Thatcher seemed to be giving up on my home town, Liverpool. Britain generally seemed to be going nowhere. I still had more than a year on my contract and I was also making new contacts. The fellow living next door knocked on my door one day in early 1980 and introduced himself: Holger K, in the book trade, intelligent, lucid, lively - and after a few drinks, outrageously entertaining. He became a close friend during the Minden years. Somebody else I got to know was Rüdiger L, husband of one of my students. He was almost twenty years older than me, an eccentric maverick, a disaster zone and womanizer, a drinker, erudite and unpredictable. When I met him in 1980 he was married to a beautiful, sophisticated woman. When he died in 2002 at the age of 62, he was penniless, alone and an alcoholic. Watching the gradual decline over 22 years took a lot out of everybody he was close to. Despite everything, he remained my most loyal friend till his untimely end. Apart from their friendship, these men were instrumental in honing my German to near native speaker competence in those days. I can still hear the subtlety and beauty of their discourse from those days and copied vast chunks of elegantly sounding German. "That's the way to do it", I tell my students today: listen carefully, breathe the language in and imitate without a guilty conscience.

Owing to the presence of the British Army in those days, I was leading a strange double life. Breathing in German life and culture whenever possible, but enjoying the tried-and-tested British way of life through the Salvation Army Red Shield outlet which offered, tea, pies and British Sunday newspapers. There was even a bar next door on the first floor which offered booze at almost GDR-style prices. I got my bacon and sausages from the NAAFI courtesy of Sarah, wife of Chris, a gung-ho Army Air Corps helicopter pilot I met just as he was about to be punched by a German bouncer one night as he was leaving, and I was entering, some seedy drinking hole. Dave, a lovely Cockney chap (yes, they do exist) and colleague of Chris, also became a great mate. He was married to a French woman who was constantly unfaithful. They later divorced. Chris was also constantly unfaithful to Sarah, but they never divorced.

It is easy to forget in these post Cold War days that West Germany was right on the front line of East-West hostilities. The British Army was there for an important purpose: defending the West from the Soviet threat lurking less than a hundred miles further east. West Germans were very aware of this and many were grateful. Despite this the Brits didn't have an exactly untarnished reputation in Minden. Tales of bad behaviour going back as far as the sixties were rife. For example, a large number of British "Squaddies" went berserk in 1966 when England won the World Cup. Although "Squaddies" were banned from most German bars, there was regularly trouble of one sort or another. Strangely enough, conversations with Germans of the older generation revealed a more positive attitude to the British presence there; one of them enthused about Montgomery having his headquarters just down the road in neighbouring Porta Westfalica. Another was a big Churchill fan and praised the British Army's sense of tradition and discipline. The younger generation of Germans were not so enthusiastic, wondering why so many young men actually joined the British Army voluntarily, the military conscription system being very unpopular in Germany at the time. In a rather snobbish way, they looked down on the more traditional aspects of British Army life. Younger, more educated Germans were (and still are) decidedly anti-militaristic and the flak I got a year or two later when Maggie's task force was re-taking the Falklands from Argentina came as a further reminder of this. I let the criticism bounce off me by rather churlishly pointing out that British people took pride in standing up to dictators. My relations with the local populace cooled off for a few weeks.

I was an unusual species in Minden. I was British but could speak German, didn't have short back and sides and had nothing to do with the Army at all. But since Annarosa had jumped ship, I was living life on a number of different levels: diligent, rookie English teacher, sociable drinking partner to compatriots from the BAOR (British Army of the Rhine – or in this case *off* the Rhine), intelligent conversationalist with intelligent Germans and an oddball, slightly lonely observer of German life and culture.

Living in an area not a million miles away from the East German border meant I met many older Germans in the school who were from some interesting, far-flung places of the former German Reich. I was confused and forced to take a crash course in modern German history and Vlotho and the Institute there had given me a good grounding. In Minden, the school's administrator, Herr Z., told many a heart-rending tale of how he had to leave Silesia with his parents when the Poles moved in and the Germans moved out. "Which Germans? Which Poles?" I asked myself. The cleaning lady, Frau H, never referred to Minden as her home - that was in East Prussia, where the Russians were now in control. I wasn't even 100% sure if I knew where East Prussia was (or rather: used to be). Then I met young Germans who spoke German with a Polish accent. They explained that they grew up in Poland but were actually German. How was this possible? There were never ending stories of people leaving East Germany before it became the GDR, i.e. in the Soviet Occupied Zone or when it was the GDR before the Wall was built, i.e. 1949 till 1961, or after the Wall was built, i.e. post 1961. Some left legally, most illegally, some still had family over there, some not. Most hated their former home in the GDR, some still had a liking for it. The permutations were endless, the stories often thrilling, confusing and surreal but the bottom line was that they all came west in search of a decent living and, by all accounts, they had got what they were searching for. The fruits of the West German Economic Miracle were being sampled by an astounding variety of people. And that didn't include hundreds of thousands of "Guest workers" from Turkey, Yugoslavia, Spain, Portugal and Italy (most of them in the neighbouring "*Ruhr* area", 50 or so miles down the motorway heading westward). My story was the simplest: a lad from Liverpool eating at the low table of the Economic Miracle, but getting more than enough nutrition to keep a smile on his face.

My relationship with East Berlin was re-kindled in 1980/1981. It was a four-hour train trip from Minden (though I sometimes hitch-hiked) and I was always warmly welcomed on any weekend I decided to go. I used to get a day visa at Berlin-*Friedrichstrasse*, "leave" East Berlin just before midnight and "re-enter" just after. The East Berliners I visited were always pleased to see me, were over the moon about receiving a bar of Western chocolate or a pack of coffee and I spent relaxing hours wandering around the city or walking or rowing in the some of the green lake land areas on the outskirts of the city. Beate and Lutz were now divorced, which meant that I met their new partners and could actually increase the number of people I knew, whilst also increasing the numbers of places I could actually stay at. I was also getting to know West-Berlin, getting off at Zoo station and exploring. This was actually more of a challenge as I didn't know a soul there.

Returning to Minden after these East Berlin weekends was an edifying experience; after the frugal, difficult life over there, my life in Minden seemed like pure luxury. It wasn't, of course, but the journeying back and forth was always a "count-your-blessings" exercise which undoubtedly did me the world of good.

Then, on one of those East Berlin weekends, the hand of fate, Beethoven style, came a knocking. Sparing the reader the mundane details of exactly how, where and when it all happened, I met a woman. After meeting each other virtually every month for six months, with all the problems posed by distance, nasty border guards, endless queuing and the Berlin Wall, I decided to find out which options we had if we wanted to stay together, which, we had decided we did.

I obtained an appointment at the British Embassy in East Berlin and the Vice-Consul told me I had three options: 1) I could move to East Berlin. 2) My girlfriend could apply for an appointment at her local registry office to marry (i.e. me). If this appointment was granted, it was tantamount to her obtaining a visa to join me in the West after our marriage, or 3) we could forget the whole thing. We plumped for Option 2.

1: Getting our first socialist pep-talk at the Humboldt University in East Berlin. I'm top left on the back row (1978).

2: Boshana was a hard woman to take your eyes off – here's me failing miserably in East Berlin (1978).

3: In Beate's street - Korsörer Strasse, Berlin, Prenzlauer Berg. The street ended where the Berlin Wall started (1978).

4: Silvia contemplating a life on the western side of the Brandenburg Gate (1981).

5: How many times did I walk over this bridge to my riverside apartment by the river Weser in Minden? (1982).

After the GDR authorities took approximately nine months (was the number a coincidence or an example of precise East German cunning?) checking our application, we finally obtained our appointment: June 17, 1982. This was a public holiday in West Germany, quite a funny joke as it was the Day of German Unity, commemorating those who died in an uprising against the GDR regime on 17 June, 1953. Was it a rare display of humour on the part of the GDR? Or even compassion? Probably neither. At least my girlfriend's relatives in West-Berlin wouldn't need to take a day off work to come to the wedding.

After that eventful summer I was going back to Britain to do a Post-Graduate Teacher Training course at the University of Wales in Aberystwyth. I would be accompanied by my wife, boasting a GDR passport, no English and no professional qualifications of any use in Britain. Thatcher's policies of neo-liberal capitalism were pushing unemployment through the roof. I would be a student again, supporting two people on a student grant. I felt sure the savings I had accrued in Minden would save us from poverty in the first instance, but the Option 2 choice I had made wasn't going to be an easy one. Settling down with a nice girl from Minden and staying there for the rest of my life would have been much simpler; and a lot less painful, complicated, interesting and exciting.

Germany had become a sort of home and in my heart of hearts and as I crossed the bridge over the Weser for the last time and looked down on the Minden street I had lived on for the best part of three years, feelings of trepidation greatly outnumbered any feelings of optimism.

Second Intermezzo: Liverpool-Aberystwyth-Milton Keynes, GB, August 1982 to September 1984

Approximately two weeks after our wedding, my wife received a telegram from the authorities that she was to pick up her new GDR passport, pay off any debts she had, de-register from any authorities she had to de-register from, pick up and pay for her plane ticket to London Heathrow (via Prague) and leave the GDR at a pre-arranged border crossing where her exit visa would be waiting for her. She could then fly west to take up residence with her husband, British citizen, Neil Deane. And all within 72 hours. This was called "*Familienzusammenführung*" (reuniting of families), GDR style.

As the subject of this book is Germany, I will cover the following two years in Britain in the most perfunctory way possible. I completed my teacher training, Silvia took courses in English, we moved to Milton Keynes where I worked in a Comprehensive School for a spell, didn't like it and seriously doubted the wisdom of my decision to have left Germany and also of marrying somebody I had only known for a year or so in an East –West weekend relationship. I'm sure she felt the same way. In the middle of all this my mum was diagnosed with lung cancer. In the meantime I had got a job at the Inlingua School of Languages in Mannheim in the South West of Germany and started on September 10, 1984. On my second Monday in the job, September 17, I got a phone call at the school from my dad that my mum had passed away the previous evening. She was 55.

Mannheim, West Germany, September 1984 till April 1989

It was not the most auspicious of starts to my next slice of life in Germany. I was desperately short of funds, mum was gone, I was in a shaky marriage and in a part of Germany I knew very little about. After a few hours in Mannheim I started to wonder whether I even knew the German language; this was no longer clear, pristine "*Hochdeutsch*" (High German) as spoken in the area of Hanover. This was a difficult dialect with an almost incomprehensible accent. My first impressions of the city itself weren't particularly uplifting either: ugly, industrial and generally rather gloomy. There was a slight improvement when we were able to rent a reasonably-priced, pleasant, roomy flat, and only a stone's throw from the school I worked at. It was very central, close to Mannheim's most famous building, the "*Wasserturm*" (water tower). Also a stone's throw away from the "*Nationaltheater*" where Schiller's "*Die Raüber*" (The robbers) had its opening night on January 13, 1782. Further down the road, near the Rhine, was the magnificent castle where Mozart had composed and conducted at round about the same time. Mannheim even had a half-decent football team in the first division of the *Bundesliga*, Waldhof Mannheim, a team I occasionally watched on the other side of the Rhine in Ludwigshafen, home of the giant chemical company, BASF.

BASF was not the only important company in the area; Daimler Benz was present in Mannheim, as well as ASEA Brown Boveri, Lever Sunlight, Boehringer and John Deere. Freudenberg was in nearby Weinheim and Heidelberger Druckmaschinen in Heidelberg - all large companies of world-wide repute. There was a large university in Mannheim and nearby Heidelberg had the oldest in Germany. Heidelberg itself was worth a visit with its famous castle, and surrounding it in the East was the *Odenwald*. Beyond the Rhine in the West there were the vineyards of the Palatinate Forest (*Pfälzerwald*) which offered attractive wine-tasting and hiking possibilities. France was an hour away, as was Frankfurt to the North, and the Black Forest to the South. Another half hour in a southerly direction and you were in Baden-Baden and then Freiburg. Mannheim then, was surrounded by some real gems.

After I had escaped the gristly shackles of the Inlingua school and marketed myself as a language trainer, servicing some of the companies mentioned in the previous paragraph, I started to make some decent money. I had passed my driving test in Britain (Annarosa would have been proud) and bought my first car. I had followed millions of Germans and made that first car a VW "*Käfer*", or Volkswagen "beetle". I have never understood men's love and adoration of cars, and German men are particularly guilty of this affliction, but it is the only car I ever did actually (sort of) love. It represented the economic miracle years like nothing else, was a real piece of history and really did have a lovable, cuddly character.

Some of the students I was teaching were interesting characters: people in high-ranking positions, explaining to me their stories of business deals and encounters all over the globe. I realized again how tuned-in Germans were internationally; virtually every product and service they were selling was aimed at the export market. The message "Export or die" seemed to be throbbing through their veins and they all seemed so aware of what was going on in the business world around them. The German desire to do things to the best of their ability was always bubbling under the surface. Owing to the insights I gained into German in-company practice in these years, I began to realise why Germany was top of the class: only the best was good enough. Although my experience of comparable British companies was limited, I found it hard to believe that my compatriots would show the same level of commitment I was experiencing on a weekly basis in Germany. The British attitude to foreign language training was the most glaring example of this, but that was only the tip of the iceberg - the Germans were ahead in terms of training, attitude, inter-cultural awareness and the commitment to getting things right. The contrast with what I knew about the average British attitude to such concepts was a stark one. It was (and is) hardly surprising that we lag behind.

Obviously the bigger picture is a more complicated one. Some of the reasons why Germany was in the sound position it was in by the mid-eighties have been analysed in Chapter 1. German companies and industry have been generally organised in a different way since 1945, circumstances in Britain and Germany have been different, and the chance for a brand-new start was possible in Germany while Britain had other massive obstacles post-1945. I would merely conclude that the people I came into contact with in those German companies showed a desire to improve both themselves and the performance of their own companies; this attitude and commitment has kept the German success story going for many years and will probably do so for many years to come.

Perhaps some of this push for excellence had rubbed off on me too, as I started and successfully completed an advanced TEFL qualification in 1988. On the personal front, however, things were going downhill fast. My wife and I separated in 1987 and she moved to West-Berlin where her mother and siblings now lived – I suppose you could call it the final completion of the *Familienzusammenführung* which had started in 1982.

It was somehow, as Dickens might say, the best of times and the worst of times. Professionally and materially, I was making my way in the world. Personally things were falling apart. In a strange way, Mannheim was the least favourite German place I lived in. But looking back, it was clear that the personal circumstances caused most of the problems, not the place. Germany no longer represented the care-free life of a bright-eyed, bushy–tailed young Englishman living on the banks of the Weser and witnessing the fascinating freshness of German life and culture unfolding before him - and dipping into the extra spicy spark of life behind the Berlin Wall as a fascinating extra whenever he wanted. Life now consisted of working round the clock, running a business, paying speeding fines and coping with the consequences of a failed marriage. I met other interesting people in Mannheim but never made friends of the calibre of Holger K. and Rüdiger L. They now seemed far away, as did the world they were still living in.

The British Army was not present in Mannheim, of course. We were deep into the American Zone (as it used to be called) and I had virtually no contact with anybody connected to the military. Anyway, why should I be making new contacts? Meeting new people was something you did in your teens or early twenties. The fact of the matter was that I was now thirty and entering a phase in which people are supposed to be either settling down or be settled down. Instead, I was virtually out of a marriage, starting a new relationship and trying to find my feet again emotionally. And somehow, slowly starting to fall out of love with Germany itself. The people in Mannheim and surroundings had a roughness I hadn't experienced in Minden; neighbours were snappy and disagreeable; people hardly ever seemed to smile. Driving a car in Germany also forces you to confront some of the more disagreeable elements of the German character: impatience, unnecessary aggression, stubbornness and sometimes sheer bloody-mindedness.

I was also mixing in circles of people who were enjoying prosperity at full-tilt. Such people, however, are not always the most interesting people in the world to be with. Listening to a 20-minute discussion on whether the latest BMW has automatic side mirrors or not didn't personally provide me with much intellectual or emotional stimulus. Skiing holiday stories were also one of the topics which sent me heading for the door. Money just didn't make people any better; it simply gave them more boring topics to talk about. As there seemed to be more prosperous people in this part of the world than anywhere else, I was increasingly surrounded by more and more people boasting such tiresome topics in their conversational repertoire.

I almost reached breaking point once when a young man I was teaching from the University of Mannheim was genuinely depressed because he had just received an offer of a job in which the annual salary was slightly less than 100.000 DM. He was, of course, going to turn it down. That was big money in those days but this chap wanted more. I learnt the phrase: *"Die Ansprüche steigen"*, (Expectations get higher – my translation). About seven years before I had heard the owner of the language school I was working at in Minden that "*Die fetten Jahre sind vorbei*", (The fat years are over). I was confused, but it was a learning curve about the way Germans often see things: Doom and gloom (First statement). Desire for ever more (Second statement). Seems contradictory, but aren't all human beings contradictory? This would simply seem to be a unique German example of contradiction.

As I entered the second half of the eighties in Germany I could see the emergence of consumerism on a big scale. It was developing in Britain, too, but without the massive purchasing power the Germans had at their disposal. In Mannheim, the revolutionary ideas of the late sixties and early seventies seemed to be being replaced by men knitting in Green cafes or by an "I'm all right Jack" philosophy encouraged by the Kohl government of the time. Despite rising unemployment, there didn't seem to be any noticeable hardships and Kohl's glib comment: "*Weiter so*" (Carry on regardless – my translation) summed up the era rather well.

The desire to leave Mannheim had become almost an obsession. In the New Year of 1989 I saw an advert in a British newspaper seeking EFL trainers in Offenbach near Frankfurt on Main. I would be employed by a British training company working for Siemens. It would be initially a six-month contract. I feverishly packed up what I needed, sold or gave away the rest and moved to Offenbach on 1 April, 1989.

Offenbach, West Germany, April to August 1989

By moving to Offenbach and joining a team of expatriates teaching German engineers in week-long intensive courses out in the *Franconia* district of Northern Bavaria it actually meant that I was leaving Germany, if not physically, at least mentally. We were sent like task force combat units to a place called Bad Kissingen where we were cooped up together with groups of CPs (the jargon for Course Participants) for days on end. My new colleagues came from Britain and the Commonwealth and had been teaching wherever EFL teachers were needed in the

6: Mannheim's most interesting landmark – the water tower. Otherwise, there wasn't much else to write home about (1985).

7: The depressing reality of the Cold War: no-man's land at the Berlin Wall (1986).

8: Rüdiger took this one on a trip to Dresden. I had, as usual, a stack of Oxford University Press books in the boot (1995).

9: There aren't many photographs of Rüdiger without a glass in his hand – and this is not one of them. I was also adapting to the German "*Leitkultur*" by drinking as much Pils as possible (1997).

world. There was no need to speak German (many of my colleagues didn't). The only real contacts we had were with the students when we were virtually always in a teacher-student mode. Otherwise we were with each other, drinking, talking rubbish (or usually both).

The closest I got to German culture was visiting a charming old tavern on the south-east outskirts of Frankfurt where Goethe is supposed to have supped a few goblets of wine before inviting the odd fair maiden back to his place for a nightcap. I also visited his house in Frankfurt and spent many a pleasant hour wandering around the cathedral area or in the trashy *Sachsenhausen* district of the town where Japanese or American tourists did the usual embarrassing things.

My colleagues' general attitude to the Germans we were teaching disturbed me. More often than not, they despised them, calling them robots, humourless, predictable, dull and boring. OK, perhaps middle-aged German engineers, holed up in a hotel for two weeks, grappling with a language they might have had some contact with 30 years previously in school are not exactly a barrel of laughs. But the merciless persecution of the CPs went too far sometimes and smacked more of post-imperialist arrogance than anything else. I prided myself on being a "*Germanist*", a lover of German life and culture and fought hard not to become like some of my more vindictive colleagues.

Having said that, I did enjoy my compatriots' company when we had time off together. It was like being at university again: banter, communal piss-taking, heavy drinking, bad behaviour, arguments about football, philosophy and any other subjects that came into our heads. We had fantastic times in Frankfurt, Düsseldorf and Amsterdam and I realised it probably wouldn't have been as much fun with Germans. They were a great bunch of blokes: a dry, laid-back New Zealander; a highly intelligent and inventive bloke from Cambridge; a friendly, down-to-earth Mancunian; a lucid charming Cockney from the Jewish East End of London, and a sex-maniac from Leicester. There were many more I could mention, suffice to say that during the time in Offenbach I re-discovered how great it was to be back in a British environment again, albeit still in Germany. I had turned my back on German culture for six months and felt seriously better for it.

I am sure some smart psychologist could define my state of being during that time. I had spent the best part of ten years soaking in and experiencing German life and perhaps I had simply had an overdose. Rather like having a dreadful hangover due to a certain drink, and never being able to drink, or even smell, that drink again. We all went our separate ways in August of 1989 and I got a job, on a one-year contract, at the University of Liverpool, starting at the beginning of October. I genuinely believed it was the end of an era and I would be staying at home for good. Wrong again.

Third and final British Intermezzo, September 1989 to December 1990

I had hardly been back in Britain two months when the Berlin Wall came down. I cursed my luck and longed to be in Berlin. It was November 9, 1989. The damned thing had caused me so much grief all those years - and I wasn't in the country when it was finally dismantled. In fact I had just missed the monumental event by five days: I had travelled back to Minden to pick up my car from Holger K. Watching a mass demonstration on *Alexanderplatz* on his TV on November 4, we couldn't believe our eyes and ears as speech after speech by anybody who was anybody in the GDR demanded ridiculous things like free speech, free elections, the right to travel and democratic reforms. Little did we know just how quickly it was all going to become reality.

The period in Liverpool did me good; it was a chance to cut down on the food and booze I had been enjoying a little too much of in Germany. A period of consolidation, getting to know my home town again, re-assembling myself for whatever the next step was going to be. I had notions of settling down in Britain again, but the cool, clinical voice of British economic reality was going to throw its nasty spanner in the works again. My one-year contract at the university could not be made permanent or even extended and at the end of October 1990 I was unemployed. There were then two happy events: Mrs Thatcher's era came to an end on November 28, 1990, and just before that I had got a job as Sales Manager for Oxford University Press, working for their German distributor, *Cornelsen*, in Bielefeld. The "New" Germany had been in existence exactly three months when I packed my bags, threw them into the back of a hired van and made my way across the North Sea via Hull to Rotterdam and on to Bielefeld - the place where I used to

114

change trains after seeing Annarosa every weekend all those years previously.

I was divorced, had a steady job, steady, non-German girlfriend and everything was going to work out fine. Germany, once again, was the future.

Bielefeld/Rheda-Wiedenbrück,Germany, January 1991 to April 1993

My remit in the new job was to market the ELT (English Language Teaching) products of OUP in Germany at institutions of higher and adult education. "In Germany" was the frightening phrase. Germany is a big place (and had just become considerably bigger) and living out of a suitcase was going to be the order of the day, travelling the length and breadth of the country in a Volkswagen turbo-diesel estate car packed to the brim with OUP's latest goodies. I was about to get a crash course in German geography, but in a bizarre, masochistic way I was looking forward to the new challenge. Something different, I thought.

After the initial novelty of staying in hotels and visiting a different part of Germany every week had worn off, the job became a lonely grind. Most of my time was spent either behind the wheel or killing time between school visits in the most meaningful way possible. In the summer months this was less of a problem: sitting around Bavarian beer gardens or on the banks of the Rhine in some picturesque Rhineland town were challenges I could easily cope with - more a holiday break than real work. But in the depths of winter, sitting in some smoky bar or watching TV in yet another soulless hotel room, things looked decidedly different - not to mention snow-bound, nightmare traffic jams regularly raising their ugly heads and fouler tails.

I eagerly awaited my first trip to East Germany, now called "the new federal states". There were five of them. The larger cities there - Leipzig, Dresden, Magdeburg, Rostock and, of course, the Eastern part of Berlin, were getting their first makeovers. There was much uncertainty in the air and many East German teachers I spoke to seemed almost paralysed as the new state worked out how many teachers they could afford. In the rest of the economy, anything up to 75% of the companies which existed in the old regime were being put into administration or sometimes simply demolished. The spectre of unemployment was everywhere as most East Germans of employable age feared for their future. West German companies had done very well out of re-unification, of course, making record profits as East Germans lucky enough keep their jobs made up for lost time: the demand for cars, fitted kitchens, furniture, electrical goods, foreign holidays and clothes went through the roof and West German companies could hardly keep up with the demand. 1992 was not only a record profits year for my employer, Cornelsen.

The task of re-building East Germany was going to be an immense one and observing this transformation from behind my car window in those days was painful yet fascinating. Most pundits reckoned it would take a couple of generations - they were just about right; as I write this now in 2012, twenty years later, East Germany has little resemblance to the East Germany whose potholes I was cautiously navigating my way round in the early 90's.

The moment I was looking forward to most of all was my own personal reunion with the Brandenburg Gate, this time without the Wall. The moment came in mid-February 1991 when I took the underground from West to East Berlin, accompanied by a cousin of my ex-wife. It was early evening with freezing temperatures, a snowy wind swirling across the open spaces on *Unter den Linden*. We had left *Friedrichstrasse*, the first station in the East (or last, depending on which direction you were coming from). I was astounded that we were able to get out of the station without any of the usual hindrances I had grown used to for over a decade. No armed border guards. No electronic doors locking me in while nasty officials scrutinized my passport. No mirrors everywhere. No customs officials taking my bags apart after finally reaching the front of endless queues. No penetrating questions about the nature of my visit to the capital of the German Democratic Republic. Nobody taking my hard-earned cash from me for my visa and the daily compulsory exchange of 25 Deutschmarks. It was now a normal station; you got off the train and went to wherever you wanted to go to. But I still couldn't believe it.

Walking to the Brandenburg Gate from the East, I found my stomach was starting to fill with a mixture of trepidation, disbelief and total joy. As we got closer, the wind seemed to bite more than ever, as if it was asking me: "Do you really want to go through with this?" Snow swirled across *Pariser Platz*, the square directly surrounding the gate, no-man's land from August 13, 1961 till November 9, 1989. Over the years I had stood in front of that square with so many different people from East and West and I had often wondered what thoughts had been whirling round their heads. Now there was no Wall and I was walking towards the Gate itself, my legs shaking. I stood right underneath it and cried as I thought of all those years of frustration, sadness and, for some, death. I croaked out the pathetic sentence to Reiner, my companion: "I don't believe this". He replied: "I still don't myself".

We walked back to *Unter den Linden*; I was determined to find the traditional old Berlin pub I had spent a fantastic evening in with my student friends in the summer of 1978. After searching in the freezing cold for a quarter of an hour, we eventually found it: *"Zur letzten Instanz"*, right next to the central Berlin law courts, a few hundred yards from *Alexanderplatz*. We cheerfully gulped down large beers and got into conversation with an intelligent-looking East Berliner with whom we happily engaged in good-humoured but erudite conversation till midnight about domestic and international politics. The world really had changed.

THE GERMAN REGIONS

My job on the road gave me a unique opportunity to get to know virtually every region of Germany. As the months went by I visited them all. The Northern central area of the old West Germany, the *"Ruhrgebiet"* (the Ruhr area) is the former industrial heartland of the country, where mining, steel making and manufacturing had its heyday from the start of the 20th century up until the end of its 7th decade. The towns there sound grimy and rough: Dortmund, Gelsenkirchen, Essen, Duisburg and Bochum - unattractive, concrete conglomerations that continued growing through those seventy years, producing down-to-earth, hard-working folk, great football teams and admirable working class solidarity. As I live in one of those towns today (Essen), I can confirm that this is still true. As we progress further west and south, we travel through the more attractive, and occasionally, gentler towns on the Rhine such as Düsseldorf, Cologne, Bonn, Coblenz. Mainz is where the Rhineland starts to come to an end and the Palatinate begins. Here is where serious wine-growing starts, including Wiesbaden's famous sparkling wines. The general character of the people up the Rhine is of a more cheery and easy-going nature, where the favoured tipple is wine rather than beer.

Forty miles further south and you're in the Mannheim/Heidelberg region and beyond that Baden and Swabia. The towns surrounding Stuttgart boast hundreds of medium-sized businesses which form the backbone of modern Germany's economic power. Not that it's short of large employers: Mercedes Benz, Bosch and Hewlett-Packard are the three biggest. This is Silicon Valley German style, replete with prosperous folk and high employment everywhere. And it must be heaven to be a student in the nearby town of Tübingen, Germany's second oldest university after Heidelberg. The Black Forest dominates to the south west of Stuttgart and further to the West you're in towns with the most hours of sunshine in the country such as Karlsruhe, Baden-Baden and Freiburg. France is nearby and the cuisine starts to get seriously good. Lake Constance and the Swiss border are a few dozen miles south; you can eat your dinner off some of the sidewalks there.

Moving East, we're into Bavaria and viewing some equally impressive towns with glorious pasts: Ulm, Augsburg, Nuremberg (don't mention the war), Regensburg and, of course, Munich. 180 miles further north-east, heading towards the Czech Republic, you hit Coburg, a beautiful little town where Queen Victoria's husband, Albert, was born. And while you are at it, take in Bamberg, equally fascinating and offering the weirdest beer you're ever likely to taste: "Smoked beer" (*Rauchbier*). Like drinking a pint of British ale with three dozen packets of smoky bacon crisps mashed into it. Disgusting. But the locals get upset if you don't down at least one glass.

The three southern federal states, Bavaria, Baden-Wurttemberg and Hesse were always delightful places to travel to, particularly in summer. *Cornelsen* colleagues also directed and accompanied me to some exquisite culinary delights when I was in their area, which made the stays there even more enjoyable. If you ever decided to spend holidays in Germany, you couldn't go wrong winding your way through some of the regions and towns I have just described.

Moving further east and heading north through the new federal states (i.e. former East Germany) was an entirely different matter. Not that they didn't have their fair share of impressive historical architecture; the problem was that much of it looked like it was about to collapse. Terrible roads, cuisine which had not advanced much further than spuds and sausage and hotels which offered as much comfort as a Black Forest youth hostel (but with a little less charm).

The conversations with East German teachers, however, almost made up for the hardships I had to endure to actually get to visit them. They opened up on virtually any topic, they appeared human and more than willing to talk about the monumental events that had enveloped them and offered valuable insights into life in the GDR and how they saw the immediate future. And they actually seemed genuinely appreciative of the free books I was giving them.

The further north you got in East Germany, the grimmer it got. By the time you reached the north-eastern corner, you were beginning to wonder if there were any people left. The vicious circle of people leaving due to lack of jobs always means less tax revenue, less investment and less purchasing power and even fewer jobs. Fewer jobs mean more people leave and so the downward spiral creating permanent ghost towns, cranks depressingly into place.

Heading along the Baltic Sea coast to places like Rostock and Stralsund always offered a window of brightness, although economically things were not much better. I personally find people in coastal towns always seem in a better mood - I put it down to the sea air, or to the perennial thought that you just get on a ship to somewhere if life gets too difficult. This had been the way out for thousands of men in my home town for as long as people could remember. John Lennon's dad, Fred, was a prime example of this. I imagined, rather naively I suppose, that this was what kept many people on that Baltic Sea coast reasonably happy in the first years after re-unification. In their mind at least, they could get on a ship going anywhere and end up serving cocktails in Cuba. Or was it just large quantities of beer and schnapps which had kept them going since the wall came down?

Move further west along that coast and you're back in the "old federal states", this time leaving the Baltic sea in the East; Lübeck is historically fascinating, Kiel less so and before you know it you're heading towards the North Sea. Head inland and you're in a real city again: Hamburg. The town with the most millionaires in Germany, a gigantic port with a breath-taking history and a deliciously contrasting world of hanseatic orderliness and tawdry night life. Hamburg is a place you can never get enough of.

Head south on the motorway and two hours later you're in Hanover. The town itself is nothing to write home about but it has a couple of things going for it: it provided England with a few kings at crucial times. The inhabitants speak the purest and clearest German in the country and I knew a nice bloke there I could drink with – he was a good friend of Holger K's from my Minden days. There was a pub next to the entrance of his apartment building where Champion Jack Dupree, a legendary US bluesman, used to boogie-woogie deep into the night. Knowing people in towns where I could actually stay over often gave me a boost and reminded me that I didn't always have to play the archetypical travelling salesman and stay in an anonymous hotel. It often resulted in some vicious hangovers the next day and a shaky hand on the autobahn, but it was generally worth it.

Berlin, April 1993 to September 2003

So ends a brief and very subjective look at the Germany I was traversing like the proverbial headless chicken in the early nineties of the last century. It was basically a chance to see Germany for free. After a couple of years I realized, however, that nothing was free. My health and my relationship were suffering and I could not envisage doing the job in this form for the rest of my life. *Cornelsen* was merging its marketing department, up to now based in Bielefeld, with the editorial department, based in Berlin. I moved with them to Berlin at the beginning of 1993 with the promise that I would have an office in Berlin and would only be on the road for half of my working time: a step in the right direction. I jumped at the chance. My partner didn't, and at the beginning of September 1993 I found myself in Berlin, alone. The details of this calamitous time are probably best kept to myself.

Working in a German company on a day-to-day basis was an interesting revelation. People who work in publishing houses are well-educated, come from good homes, are liberal-minded, well-read, in some cases idealistic and, generally speaking, rather boring. Although I was happy not to have to be on the road day and night, I also realised that people working in offices start becoming rather cabbage-like and not the most fascinating people to spend your working hours with. The lighter moments were my contacts with English native speakers in the editorial department and down to earth "*Ossies*" (the general term by this time for East Germans. West Germans were known as, surprise, surprise, "*Wessies*").

East Berlin, where I lived, was still a fairly desolate place in those days. 90% of the residents on this side of town still had no phone, and that included me. There was one supermarket within a one-mile radius. Streets and housing were in a deplorable state. Unemployment remained high and feelings of optimism about the future were rare. The flat I had rented had been refurbished by *Cornelsen* but most of my fellow residents in the streets around me in former East Berlin were not so lucky.

Just a year or two before I moved there in 1993, the adjacent streets had been witness to violent and long-lasting street battles between squatters and police as a massive wave of punks and "alternative" folk had moved in (mostly from good but rather staid middle-class homes in West Germany), looking for a slice of exciting life in the new, fermenting Berlin. The scars of those conflicts were evident in the streets all around me. Occasionally punks would organise spontaneous free concerts in disused and abandoned parks in the neighbourhood. They would thrash around in the mud, make the most obnoxious noises possible and hit each other with anything they could lay their hands on. I witnessed those end-of-the universe scenes and wondered whether my life was worth living. I was well depressed anyway; this was pushing me over the brink.

But Berlin, thankfully, did not consist only of *Friedrichshain*. Closer to the middle of Berlin, in the aptly named district called *Mitte*, a vibrant cafe/bar/theatre alternative culture was developing at a fairly phenomenal rate. Stretching out north from there in the district of *Prenzlauer Berg*, the development was similar and this district was to become the first part of East Berlin to attract *Wessies* in the form of investors and residents. By the turn of the century it had been transformed, inhabited by trendy, young, professional people living in re-furbished, re-modernised flats with bars and restaurants offering every kind of cuisine imaginable. By the time I left Berlin in 2003, *Friedrichshain* had become the new

Prenzlauer Berg, gentrified almost beyond recognition. The contrast with 1993 was astounding.

Potsdamer Platz was the other massive development at the end of the 90's. It had been Berlin's central traffic junction before the war, became no-man's land during the Berlin Wall years and fallen derelict in the 90's. An enormous building project changed everything and by the new millennium, it had been completely transformed, looking like a mini Broadway with the German Railway Headquarters boasting its modest skyscraper in the middle. Most of the new government buildings were finished by the Millennium, complete with refurbished Reichstag, covered by a spectacular new roof and just over the road from where the high-tech Main Station was completed in 2005. Back in my district, a well-known bridge, the *Oberbaumbrücke* was re-opened in fine style, re-linking *Kreuzberg* in the West with *Friedrichshain* in the East. The new international airport was started by the end of the nineties. At the time of writing (December 2012), it is still not open. A project bedevilled by incompetence and faulty planning.

Basically, everything in Berlin was being pulled down, built-up, re-furbished, opened, closed, abandoned, re-discovered, re-built, etc. Choose a verb at the end of the previous sentence and it had been happening in Berlin since re-unification. A seething mass of constant change, transformation, ups and downs, social tensions, crises, scandals, cock-ups, conflicts and disasters. Berlin has always been all things to all men and more often than not with the word "too" in front of every adjective. Too plebeian, too pompous, too trendy, too dirty, too big. Too everything. Sexy but poor. Green on the edges, urban ugliness in the central parts. Seething social and racial tensions in some of the overcrowded central and western districts, disturbing, neo-Nazi tendencies in some of the sprawling eastern concrete estates, mixed with incorrigible communists reminiscing about the good-old days when the Wall still stood – for them the wonderful "protection wall" (German: *Schutzwall*) which defended the brave proletariat against the evils of capitalism. Berlin was (and still is) all these things and more.

And there was me in the middle of this pulsating mass of madness, trying to carve out a niche; a living; a life. *Cornelsen* had a sudden change of heart in 1996 and decided I should go back to being on the road all the time. I was out. I started writing and presenting for them instead and, in addition, teaching English to anybody who paid me a good enough hourly rate for my services. My private life was, let's say, interesting. Ranging from grim despair, through philosophizing contentedness, to triumphant ecstasy. But never normal and certainly never boring. For which I was truly thankful.

By 1997 I had moved to *Karl-Marx-Allee*, still in Berlin-*Friedrichshain*. The neighbours were nice, the view was good (sixth floor) and I relished the true sense of dramatic history living on this long intimidating avenue. In the thirties Alfred Döblin, author of *"Berlin Alexanderplatz"*, had his doctor's surgery a couple of houses away from me; Soviet tanks had rolled down the avenue to quell the workers' unrest in June 1953 and government officials had changed the street signs one night in 1956 to *"Karl-Marx-Allee"* after deciding that *"Stalin Allee"* was no longer appropriate after the then Soviet leader, Nikita Khrushchev, revealed what a particularly nasty fellow the "great" Stalin had been.

The road on which I now lived, officially called the B1, actually started in Königsberg, formerly in East Prussia, now belonging to Russia. It stretches across the full breadth of Germany, crossing Berlin at the Brandenburg Gate, continuing through Dortmund and ending in Aachen at Germany's most westerly point. I was living directly on the most central point of the road and this, I felt, in my romantic view of life, entrenched me firmly in the centre of 1000 years of German history. Whilst most Germans of my age and younger show a distinct lack of interest in history - the reasons for this are not difficult to understand - I have always felt an almost morbid, obsessive curiosity in it and the *Karl-Marx-Allee* years wonderfully fed this curiosity.

Talking about the massive expanse that once was Germany brings me to an "it's a small world story". In the building next door to me was a plaque on the wall advertising the dental surgery of a certain "M. Consmüller". I saw it every time I went to the underground station and the name rang a bell. After a year or so I realised this particular dentist had the name of the young student who had rescued me in deepest, darkest *Lichtenberg* about 20 years before (see p. 94). "No, surely not, I thought. This can't be true." I put it to the back of my mind until about six months later when my neighbour mentioned her dentist, who happened to be called Martin. I asked her to ask him if he remembered the *Lichtenberg* story with a lost Englishman. He did. It was him. We met, had a meal together and talked about that night and what had happened to us both since then. He related a steady tale of studying, working, bringing up children and surviving within the constraints of the East German system. The ten years since 1989 told a slightly more animated tale of establishing himself as a private practice dentist in the new Germany and making a good living out of it, thank you very much. He listened interestedly to my mixed-up story of new and false starts, highs and lows and laughter and tears in East and West. I am not really sure who envied whom; we had both experienced a lot in the twenty years since that summer night in Berlin-*Lichtenberg* and had both lived to tell the tale. Which is the main thing, I suppose.

Berlin generally offered rich pickings for a history-obsessed weirdo like me and my greatest weekly pleasure was a Friday afternoon walk through Berlin streets. I walked (or in good weather rode my bike), observed, reflected, imagined, pondered and marvelled. The most magical moments occurred when I stumbled upon places revealing the history of famous or not so famous people. This happened one Friday when I was strolling around the *Schöneberg* district of West-Berlin and spotted a plaque commemorating the fact that Christopher Isherwood had lived in the house I was standing in front of. The early thirties, the Third Reich just around the corner, Cabaret (the film and the institution), sexual and moral decadence in the air: my imagination ran wild as I stood there, staring at the building in front of me.

On another Friday I procured a Berlin street map from the thirties and attempted to trace the perambulations of Döblin's characters from his novel "*Berlin Alexanderplatz*". I walked around with a permanent "frisson" tickling my senses. I read in the local newspaper that unexploded Russian shells had been found on the tracks of the "*S-Bahn*" (local railway system) near the *Hackescher Markt* station. The Soviets had been projecting shells towards the Reichstag in the final days of April 1945 from an archway above a cafe I had often frequented on Fridays before starting my weekly "tour". Lucky me and lucky commuters who had been happily rattling over these unexploded shells for fifty years. There were a hundred years of Berlin history on my doorstep (and in this case above my head) and I was as happy as a pig in shit discovering as much as I possibly could on those Friday afternoons.

I was also re-tracing my own personal Berlin biography. One Friday afternoon I stood for a few minutes outside the registry office in the district of Berlin-*Lichtenberg*, which was literally around the corner from me, recollecting that June day when Silvia and I married. I was interrupted by a suspicious employee from within who emerged, enquiring whether he could help me. I didn't quite know what to say. The place where we had our reception, the famous "*Palast der Republik*" had been closed since 1990 due to dangerous levels of asbestos. It was eventually demolished after I had left Berlin. The street where Beate and Lutz lived was still there, of course, now minus the Wall. I wandered along to the building in *Knaackstrasse, Prenzlauer Berg* , where Lutz moved to after his divorce from Beate, but couldn't find his name on any of the doors. My romance with my wife to-be had started properly behind one of those doors many years previously. The brewery opposite, which I remember staring at out of the window the next morning, was no longer there; only the massive brick building which used to house it, now a thriving Cultural Centre.

Not everything in Berlin was to my liking. Berliners themselves, for example, are an acquired taste. Hectic and impatient by nature, they can get you to the same level of fidgety nervousness in next to no time. They sometimes appear to want to start an argument with virtually every utterance they make. They can be loud, domineering, with the sophistication and diplomacy of a rhinoceros. They are renowned for their humour, but you have to be in the mood for it: the borderline between joke and insult is sometimes wafer-thin.

Having said all that, the Berliners I know well do have a big heart. Reiner, the Berliner I mentioned earlier, possesses most of the negative characteristics I have just listed but has been a solid rock of support and shown compassion, warmth and generosity over 30 years that have gone far beyond the call of duty. The same goes for his wife, former in-laws and numerous other Berlin friends I have made over the years. But if you are unlucky enough to meet a particularly gruff Berliner in the post office one day, you might wonder whether they possess a heart at all.

In the spring of 1998 I was able to obtain a two-year contract working as a teacher at the University of Applied Sciences in Brandenburg on the river Havel. A 90-minute journey by tram and train from *Karl-Marx-Allee*. I have Gudrun B. to thank for obtaining the position. A true Saxon *Ossie* of the best kind: a communist, a friend of the ancien regime who worked in the former GDR education department under Margot Honecker (Erich's wife, with whom she was on first-name terms) and somebody who put solidarity into practice. She must have liked me.

Most of my colleagues in Brandenburg were also East Germans, showing many of those Eastern qualities I have already praised: showing solidarity and flexibility wherever necessary, always willing to pass the time of day with you and always helpful. The town Brandenburg itself was fairly nondescript; a few interesting historical buildings with a lot of work still to be done on most of them. And a veritable ghost town at night. I never contemplated moving there, happy to endure the three-hour daily commute back and forth from Berlin. Most of the people on my train were either West-Berliners or *Wessies* who obviously felt the same way.

Under the guiding hand of a new girlfriend I got to know Potsdam better in the final years before the Millennium. *Babelsberg* park, the location of the Potsdam conference, Frederick the Great's palaces and the seemingly endless stretches of forests and lakes were a true delight. In both towns, however, the catching-up process with comparable towns in the West seemed to be a painfully slow one. Unemployment always seemed to be double of that in the West and most families had relatives and friends heading West or already there. There were, quite simply, not enough jobs to go round.

My circle of friends consisted of *Ossies*, *Wessies*, Brits and Americans, mostly from the world of education in the broadest sense of the word. Berlin tended to wash up an eclectic mix of people who didn't fit in anywhere else - I was slowly coming to the conclusion that I myself was in that category. I had pretty well given up the hope of leading the orthodox life that other people had fallen for or drifted into; I had fallen into situations and places all my life and as long as I had enough to live on I felt pretty grateful for the ride. My flat in *Karl-Marx-Allee* had had a makeover and Berlin was an exciting place to be. The gentrification of *Friedrichshain* had begun and people were starting to believe that one day Berlin

10: The famous Berlin alehouse "Zur letzten Instanz" (1993).

11: The Deane twins at their favourite underground station in Berlin. My dad's the one on the right (2002).

12: Three generations of football fanatics in Westfalenstadion. Me, dad, Achim, before a Dortmund-Hertha Berlin match (2005).

13: The German Beatles story started here in Hamburg (2012).

would be finished. Things were ticking over quite satisfactorily.

My two-year contract in Brandenburg had been extended by another year, but I still didn't have a permanent job. Then I did a rather old-fashioned thing: I saw a job ad, applied for it, obtained an interview and got the job. Unfortunately not in Berlin (I had tried), but at another University of Applied Sciences in Wernigerode in the *Harz* mountains in the new federal state of *Saxony-Anhalt*. The good news was that it was permanent. The bad news was that I would have to semi-move there as the distance would not allow a commute à la Brandenburg. I would travel there on Mondays and return on Thursday afternoon; in the teaching-free periods I was able to stay in Berlin. At least my Friday afternoon Berlin history tours were safe.

Wernigerode was a more-up-and-coming East German town. 30,000 population (by contrast, the district I inhabited in Berlin, *Friedrichshain*, was Berlin's smallest with a population of 120,000), 15 minutes drive to the former border with West Germany (always beneficial), a fast-growing tourist economy (hiking and history), small and medium-sized industry (*Hasseröder* Beer, car component manufacturers) and a booming university (where I was about to start working). There was a vaguely cheerful and optimistic feel to the place compared to Brandenburg and unemployment, by East German standards, was relatively low. My colleagues were predominantly *Ossies* and an interesting bunch of non-Germans.

A fairly positive picture of my new working life, then. There was only one problem: Wernigerode was as boring as whale shit. Parochial, bourgeois, everybody knew everybody, nothing to do in the evening and even the queasy feeling that there was a nasty right-wing undercurrent at work somewhere (I wasn't far wrong, as I found out later). As in Brandenburg, I never seriously considered moving there permanently. The commuting was doable, I still had my long weekends in Berlin and with a portion of extra free-lance work, facilitated by the purchasing of a small economical car, I was able to finance the extra cost of accommodation in the form of a bedsit at the foot of the *Brocken* Mountain, North Germany's highest elevation at 1028 metres.

Travelling between two German worlds, quaint, pleasant, sleepy

Wernigerode and brash, chaotic, ugly and exiting Berlin was exhausting but also exhilarating; I was able to enjoy both worlds all the more because I lived in both: I looked forward to the hectic drone of Berlin and then the sleep-inducing tranquillity of Wernigerode. Work and sleep in Wernigerode, live and buzz in Berlin. I knew, however, that it could not go on forever. At his 40th birthday party a former *Cornelsen* colleague told me of a vacancy at his place of work, the University of Duisburg-Essen in Essen. I applied and just as a dyed-in-the wool *Ossie*, Gudrun B. had helped me into a job in Brandenburg, Markus R. an equally dyed-in-the wool *Wessie*, helped me into a job in Essen. He must have liked me, too. It was initially a two-year contract with realistic chances of it becoming permanent. I was willing to take the chance.

Goodbye Harz mountains. Goodbye Berlin madness. In many ways Berlin had given me everything I wanted, but since I had left *Cornelsen* a permanent job in the new capital city never seemed likely. I had left Liverpool, a place I loved, to get a job and I was leaving a sort of second home for the same reason. When I left Britain, I was 22. I was now 46. It is a truism, but after 50 you don't get jobs anymore. I wanted to avoid that from happening at all costs. I was sad to leave Berlin, but knew there was no choice and I knew in my heart of hearts that it would be my last professional move.

Essen, Germany, October 2003 to the present day

I've been in Essen ten years now. My job became permanent in 2005, in the same year as Liverpool FC became European Champions for the fifth time. The longest I have lived in any German city has been 10 years and six months (Berlin). So at the time of writing I am in danger of breaking my own record, something which bothers me little. I love my job, find Essen, its people and the Ruhr are generally pleasant and there's plenty to do. Culture is writ large (it was European Capital of Culture in 2010); there are half a dozen interesting towns that can be reached within 30-45 minutes using the excellent public transport system. That is the average travelling time to get anywhere in Berlin, too, so things haven't changed much there. I own a flat, earn enough money and don't need a car as the tram stops virtually outside my door and takes me to my place of work in the space of 20 minutes.

All this sounds slightly boring after some of the things I have been relating about Germany over the space of 35 years. But things do change as you get older and your mind becomes focussed on a few core elements which need to be in place. I have, with the help of Germans and Germany now put these things in place. Obviously the question sometimes arises: would it have been different if I had stayed in Britain? Better? Worse? More interesting? I think the only adjective which is 100% valid here is "different".

Having said that, if I were ever tempted to use the word "better" with regard to life in Germany it would be in connection with the stable economy. Germany has always allowed me to lead a reasonable life in a socially cohesive, prosperous, modern, progressive country. Also sounds rather boring, but it is those factors which are the necessary basis for anybody developing him or herself as a balanced, contented human being in society. Anybody denying this is living in a dream world. The German economy has the pleasant habit of remaining remarkably resistant to major economic problems that regularly afflict other countries, Britain, of course, included. I was glad to be out of Britain at the end of the seventies and beginning of the eighties. I experienced three of Thatcher's eleven years in power (82-83/89-90) and I could have happily lived without them. I lost my job in Liverpool in 1990 as Britain busted after briefly booming at the end of the Thatcher era. As Britain is staggering again in double-dip recession (2012) I am happy to retreat behind that cosy German wall of economic stability which seems to protect me from that British disease, "Boom and bust".

Man, however, as the Good Book so rightly points out, does not live on bread alone. There are unique aspects of British (or more accurately Liverpool) life which I miss and rarely find in Germany: the friendly wink of the bus driver; the heart-warming "thanks, love" as the fruit and veg woman gives you your change; the hilarious banter about football in your local pub. People are tuned into each other in a way that would never be possible in Germany.

But, at the end of the day, you live where the work takes you. That has been the ever-present in my journey through Germany and in that respect I have a certain number of surprising similarities with a Turkish guest worker of the sixties and seventies. The big differences are that I came with a degree in German and I am not a Muslim. Apart from that, we both probably thought that living here would be a temporary measure; we were both here because of limited prospects in our home country; we liked the working conditions and social system we found here; we liked the money and we both thought Germany was a good country to live in. If you asked both of us the following two questions: "Do you love Germany?" and "Has Germany been good to you?", I feel sure our answers would be the same: "No" and "Yes" respectively. How a first generation Turkish guest worker would answer the question: "Are you going to stay here?" is something I could only guess at. I guess he might; I guess I will.

5   The challenges of living in Germany

*"GERMANS TEND TO GIVE YOU THEIR OPINION, EVEN WHEN YOU HAVEN'T ASKED
FOR IT. YES, THEY CAN BE OPINIONATED. BRITS MIGHT THINK SOMETHING,
GERMANS SAY IT."*

No PROBLEMS

In today's world, "challenge" and "issue" replace the negative-sounding word "problem" and for the title of this particular chapter, they serve their purpose well, for to claim that I have had problems living in Germany, or that there are problems about living here would probably be going too far. There are problems about living, yes, but that has nothing to do with Germany: you have them anywhere, ranging from losing the soap in the shower to having your leg amputated after a gruesome car accident. Both could happen in any country and are not caused by any particularly culturally-specific behaviour of the people from that part of the globe. Most of the matters discussed in this chapter are niggling rather than full-blown issues and none of the issues has ever remotely come close to making me want to leave Germany. I have been occasionally angry, bemused, amused, confused and puzzled by the way of life and thinking – but my feelings have never bubbled over into total exasperation or desperation. This chapter relates those moments which make life in Germany different, perhaps even a little difficult, but certainly never impossible. In other words, nothing I have experienced so far has ever resembled the cultural equivalent of leg amputation.

In fact, as the years go by, these "problems" affect me less and less as I become desensitized, or, perhaps more sinisterly, "Germanized". I intend, therefore, to tackle the issues chronologically as they have hit me in the course of the last 30-odd years, starting with initial misunderstandings, and building up gradually to the aspects of German life that I still struggle to accept. Culture shock traditionally confuses you most in the early phase of any stay in a foreign culture, which means, in my case, the late seventies and early eighties and there were a number of incidents in that period which shocked me then but shock me no more. I will begin with them and an apparent banality: *Sauerkraut.*

The thought of trying foreign cuisine used to fill parochial Brits with fear and loathing and I must admit I approached my first forkful of *Sauerkraut* with some trepidation. Even the name worried me slightly – sour cabbage. I had never been a big fan of cabbage and the thought of it being sour hardly allayed my fears; to give my forebodings that extra layer of unpleasantness, the *Kraut* part of the word had been used during and since the war to describe Germans, and not in any particularly positive sort of way. As I munched on my first morsels, all my worst fears were confirmed as I wondered how on earth anybody could eat the stuff. So, you're thinking, he didn't like *Sauerkraut*. So what? Well, the "*Sauerkraut* moment" - and the ensuing "*Sauerkraut* episodes" in my German cultural discovery programme – created the model for most of the cultural integration attempts I was to undertake in the following 30 years or so.

The first portion of *Sauerkraut*, you see, was not my last; anybody who wishes to get used to something, needs to try that something more than once. Do you give up bike riding because you fall off the bike on your first attempt? Do you never drink again because your first pint tasted dreadful? No, you try again, and nine times out of ten you get used to it, get to like it, or even to love it. And those three states of being sum up, in simple terms, how a foreigner eventually feels about things that were initially new and different in the foreign culture. I tried *Sauerkraut* again and very slowly I got used to it and even got to like it. To bring the *Sauerkraut* allusion to its logical conclusion, I will now categorically state that there is nothing I like more than a portion of the stuff with accompanying meat and potatoes. Something I would never have imagined after that first, faltering forkful.

The general conclusion, therefore, is that the stranger in the foreign culture has to bring with him a basic desire to give that culture a chance. Certain aspects of a foreign culture will take getting used to: either you make an attempt to like it or you leave it. If the will is not there, you may well leave the foreign culture altogether. I was talking to a Portuguese barman in Lisbon recently who had lived and worked in Britain for a couple of years and actually quite enjoyed the experience. He claimed he came back to Portugal because he just couldn't bear the food and weather any more; he had tried to get used to it, but realised it wasn't going to work. Fair enough. As the weather in Germany is fairly similar to Britain's and the food, in fact, actually better, those two factors were never going to force me back home. The culture gap, as I said, has never been too wide to bridge.

A PRECAUTIONARY LIST

The following list contains a mixture of annoying habits many Germans have, things (in my experience) you should or should not do and various descriptions of concepts a non-German might find hard to grasp. The list illustrates factors which once represented initial (and in some cases lingering) cultural niggles in my life in Germany but which I hardly notice now. Others are simply pieces of advice for a smoother passage through daily life. They will be useful, however, for anybody planning or starting out on a longer-term stay in the country.

- There is a general "pushiness" to life, which manifests itself when getting on and off trams, trains and buses; the use of elbows to get what you want is not frowned upon to the same extent as it may be in Britain.
- In the same way, Germans have ambivalent feelings towards queuing and deep down believe it's for pansies (although things are getting better).
- On buses, trams and trains, Germans will always occupy the seat closest to the aisle, thus making it doubly difficult for anybody else to get onto the free seat next to the window. My theory is that they are hoping that this difficulty will deter you from attempting to occupy that free seat, thus providing them with more space. If *they* are sitting on the window seat, they will put their bag on the aisle seat, daring you to ask them to move it. If you don't dare, it means, again, that they have more space. Two different tricks, same result and same unsocial attitude on public transport.
- Germans like to get to the point quickly, which may come across as being impolite and abrupt as small talk is either missing

completely or plays at best a minor role; they are generally not great conversation-builders and answers to questions aimed at getting the conversation going can be one word or even monosyllabic. Don't expect questions from them to get the conversation going.

- They like to be honest, so expect an honest answer if you ask them whether they like your new shoes and don't burst into tears if they give you the truth. "Honesty is the best policy" is a phrase I learnt at school, but it can, however, produce clumsy, undiplomatic comments in Germany.

- Germans tend to give you their opinion, even when you haven't asked for it. Yes, they can be opinionated. Brits might think something, Germans say it.

- They smile less than other nations and certainly far less than Brits. Being smiled at, therefore, can produce looks ranging from bemusement to outright hostility. Caution in this activity is therefore the order of the day.

- ALWAYS take a little gift if you are invited to a person's home (even if you have only been invited for the smallest of beers).

- Most Germans like to have an image, so accept their own individual choice of image and act accordingly. If they project the idea of being a dynamic, successful business type, mention that you think high taxation is stifling business development. If you are in the presence of a green-oriented, alternative-thinking, mid-thirties person, don't bitch about having to separate your items when disposing of waste. If Germans are denied identity because of their past, they need to replace it by something else, and that is often an image. It might even be a way of covering up some profound sense of insecurity; we could go into this subject in more depth but this would require more pages than I have at my disposal for this book.

- By the same token, never ask a German man whether he has a car (unless he seems to be a radical version of the environmentally green character I just described in the previous point). Asking this question is tantamount to asking him whether he has a penis or not. An extra tip: if you see a German man in a small car, don't dare to hint that it may be **his** car. It must be his wife's, girlfriend's or daughter's: German men don't drive sissy little cars.

- Always wait for everybody to raise their glass when drinking in company. Adhere to the strict codex of saying "*Prost*" (translation: cheers). If there are only two of you, look into the person's eyes during the ceremony of saying *Prost.* Germans are also sticklers for waiting for everybody to be seated and ready before starting to eat; Brits seems to be more lax in both areas of drinking and eating etiquette.

- On first encounters, Germans often appear withdrawn and even slightly cagey. Do not expect a bright open smile and hearty, ice-breaking banter.

- When making requests, Germans generally start their sentences with "I". This can sound presumptuous and even bossy. Compare the English "Can/could I have more toast, please?" with the German language influenced "I want/would like more toast, please."

- Although first name terms are becoming ever more common, it is by no means as commonplace in Germany as it is in Britain or the USA. Erring on the side of caution before addressing somebody by their first name is therefore advisable.

- Personal questions such as "Have you got kids?" and "Are you married?" etc, are to be avoided until you know the person better.

- Humorous and frivolous banter is seldom the order of the day and can be seen as misplaced or inappropriate, especially in a business setting.

- Get used to being wished things like, "Have a nice day"; "have a nice evening"; "have a nice weekend"; "have a nice flight"; "enjoy your theatre evening/cinema evening/day off/working day" can start to irritate and the list of things Germans find to wish you seems endless; when they run out of things to wish you, they even revert to: "I wish you something" (German: *Ich wünsche Dir was*). In other words, they are asking you to think of something you're going to do and they will automatically wish you all the best for that particular something. Odd, but I suppose, pragmatic and logical. Or just a bit of harmless German fun?

- Spontaneous questions and suggestions such as "Fancy a drink (after work)?" or "Pop round to my place next time you're in the neighbourhood!" are best avoided: they are not expected and rarely provoke a positive answer. Both ideas are possible but rarely mooted without prior, firmed-up arrangements being made.

- The woman efficiently serving you your rolls in the bakery on Saturday mornings will never become your friend. This is also true of women who work in butcher's shops, supermarkets, tobacconists and florists. If you get the briefest of conversations going about the weather you are doing well. If you are George Clooney or Brad Pitt, other rules may apply.

- Expect scepticism and doubt to be raised at any opinion you express and arguments to be immediately developed to oppose your opinion. We call it "argumentative", Germans regard it as an important aspect of conversation and relationship building; we can misconstrue it as being "aggressive", Germans see it as proof that the relationship has some substance, can withstand the pressure of controlled conflict and, probably most important of all, is developing beyond the level of superficiality.

This last point in the above list (number twenty, if you were counting) is moving into a different league to points one to nineteen and is one that still causes me a certain amount of difficulty, distress even. The problem is that you don't always feel in the mood for discussing the ins and outs of any given question, whereas Germans invariably do. More importantly, they are often determined to argue their point until they are proved to be right, and in some cases, even if it takes all night. The language used in such discussions proves how seriously Germans take them; whereas we tend to choose harmony-seeking linguistic devices such as "Hmm, you may have a point there", or "I suppose you're right", or "Do you really think so?", the Germans prefer to fight to the death with such combative phrases as: "Absolute rubbish!", "I totally disagree!" or "You're wrong there", and battle on with all the argumentative rhetoric and self-belief they can muster. The general problem is that Brits prefer the easy-going approach, whilst the Germans seem more often than not to be up for the fight. It's no coincidence that the German adjective *"harmoniebedürftig"* (needing harmony) is almost seen as a form of abuse.

The potential for clashes between easy-going Brit and truth-seeking German is, therefore, always lurking and I have been a part of these "let's-have-a-heated-discussion" scenarios for many years now. I generally try to keep out of them as I dislike the idea of getting stroppy with people I actually like and often feel the strong, but perhaps cowardly British compulsion not to "cause a fuss." Germans see this differently and regard a good row as a sign of taking relationships onto a more profound, and therefore (in their eyes at least) superior level. In fact, the German might regard what we call an argument simply as a meaningful discussion. After the terrors of Nazi totalitarianism, Germans, seem loathe missing an opportunity to express their opinion how and when they want. The '68 generation, and the generations that followed, were also determined to keep the heated debating society alive and to benefit from the principles of freedom of speech that their grandparents did not enjoy (or perhaps even went to concentration camps trying to exercise). This applies also, of course, to East Germans, who experienced even more recently overwhelming restrictions on their ability to express what was on their minds. These are points we need to bear in mind if we sometimes have the feeling that Germans are perhaps arguing for argument's sake.

One positive effect of this debating culture (the Germans call it "*Streitkultur*") is that one actually learns to argue better as a result of being right in the middle of a culture which doesn't shy away from a good argument. There are still, however, moments in seemingly interminable arguments about God knows what, when I revert to an idiom I actually learned from the Germans themselves and turn to my debating partner with the ultimate words of capitulation: "*Du hast Recht und ich habe meine Ruhe.*" (You're right and I have my peace and quiet). This proves, perhaps, that even a German has sometimes had enough of arguing – a reassuring fact.

Another source of tedium in some discussions is the tendency for participants to peddle the politically correct viewpoint on almost all the burning issues of the day; perhaps this is my own fault for having friends, colleagues and acquaintances whose roots are in enlightened, well-educated, socially-aware families who represent decent, progressive, modern-thinking Germans. This is all well and good, but if you know what these people are going to say before they say it, it's hardly worth discussing anything in the first place. This is not to say that I will soon be joining primitive-thinking, beer-swilling discussion groups in low-life pubs any time soon so I can experience a real sweaty, barn-storming debate on the future of Germany without foreigners or why rapists should have their testicles removed without an anaesthetic; but at least then I wouldn't fall asleep, which is a legitimate risk when well-meaning, thoroughly decent people churn out predictable, impeccable, politically-correct arguments over and over again in discussions.

A further problem with the politically-correct, cosy liberal types is that they tend to start many discussions with the classic line: "You can't/shouldn't generalise". My counter-question is: Why not? If you don't generalise, it's actually quite difficult to have an opinion at all. I believe it's quite legitimate to generalise as a starting point for any discussion, before moving on to a more differentiated analysis of that particular point. I also believe that the general consensus is more often than not (although of course not always) an acceptable point of view; the fact is that the majority of the population is neither in favour of corporal punishment in schools nor in favour of capital punishment for murder, something that can be seen as real progress towards a more humane and violence-free society. I am quite happy, therefore to generalize and say: "Corporal and capital punishment is wrong." So what's the problem?

It is actually difficult to strike up a relationship with a German without him or her wishing at some stage to peddle their views on any topic ranging from how and where to dispose of your plastic bottles or the nuclear threat posed by North Korea. Germans have an argumentative streak in them (well, almost all the philosophers come from Germany don't they?!) and generally wish to argue points for far longer than the average Brit does (there I go, generalizing again). And the average Brit (i.e. me) often finds this a challenge, to put it mildly, or on some occasions, extremely boring. A bit like chewing on chewing gum, long after the flavour has disappeared. Of course, I understand the need for a thorough debate of any topic, and the success story of post-war Germany has proved that attention to detail has produced the goods for them; but the problem is that it can spoil an otherwise pleasant Saturday night when you may be more in the mood for banter and nonsense than serious, long-winded debate. There is a time and a place for everything, as they say, and Saturday night is often not the right time.

TV chat shows reflect the nation's apparent insatiable appetite to debate topics which have been doing the rounds for as long as I can remember. An all-time favourite is the question of pensions; the question of whether we will actually get one seems to have been gnawing away at Germans since Bismarck first mooted the idea before we even entered the 20th century. Only a couple of days ago on TV I witnessed a group consisting of an economics "expert", a member of the government, a member of the opposition, a worried pensioner and a loquacious young woman from a new fringe political party all droning on endlessly about the topic of pensions. In such debates, normally the only person who believes that our pensions are safe is the person from the party in power at the time. All the others are convinced that the system is doomed unless, of course, measures propagated by them are implemented immediately. At the end of the day, you simply have the feeling that everybody's happy as long as there is a topic which gives everybody a chance to shout at each other for an hour or so. This has been the pattern for as long as I have been in Germany; there are other recurring topics, such as the integration of immigrants in Germany, the environment, the welfare system, education, the role of women in society and Germany's image abroad. All evergreens which refuse to go away and recycled endlessly in the media and private circles.

Any non-German who wishes to be fully integrated would do well to gird up his loins and enter such discussions with well-structured and thought-out arguments and generous portions of stamina. You don't necessarily need to win the arguments (that's very difficult anyway with Germans), but just staying the distance will win you respect. The alternative is to use the method preferred by Churchill when he sensed tedium approaching: "I made the usual excuses, bade my farewells and went home."

CONVERSATION GERMAN STYLE

While we are on the topic of talking and communicating generally, it is also worthwhile knowing the rules of conversing in Germany, as they are rather different than those used by Brits. The lack of turn-taking is the most irritating; Germans fight for their right to talk and as a consequence, conversations, especially those involving more than two people, can be dominated by those who are the quickest, loudest and most dominating and you might have to be on the top of your game to get a word in edgeways; monologues can hold sway and in the worst-case scenario, the whole discussion can degenerate into a series of unconnected, dogmatic bursts of excitable opinions during which most people have stopped listening. In other words, a German discussion evening can become stressful rather than relaxing.

A regular occurrence in my world of work clearly illustrates Germans' weakness at turn-taking. I can be chatting amiably, intensively or otherwise with a colleague in the corridor, in my office or in the cafeteria when another colleague arrives, wishes to speak to me or my conversation partner and simply bursts in with a question or comment, killing the original dialogue on the spot. No waiting discreetly and patiently for an opportune moment, no apologetic request to speak.

Just straight in with no hesitation at all. It is often breathtakingly impolite.

Any discerning reader will have noticed that the way Germans communicate appears to be the biggest problem for a non-German. I would agree with this and put forward the general thesis that communication is always going to be the main problem of anybody living in a foreign culture; learning the language is one thing, learning how to communicate effectively in it (and with it) is another. The difficulties of adapting to the taste of *Sauerkraut*, the weather, the temperature of the beer and the colour of the phone boxes (and any of the twenty points mentioned in my initial list) fade into insignificance in comparison to the challenge of understanding the way human beings in that foreign culture communicate with each other. And Germans, to put it in a nutshell, communicate with each other differently than we do and getting used to it is the key to functioning properly in their company.

Digging deeper

Some fairly deep digging already took place in chapter 3 as we floundered around in the nether regions of the German soul and I wish to continue investigations as we move from the trivial annoyances to more fundamental yet wide-ranging issues with our investigative spade still active. But what do I mean by "digging a little deeper"? Sounds ever so slightly sinister, but in fact I simply want to make a couple of major observations about something lingering deep in the German soul which ultimately prevents them from actually being (or at least seeming to be) happy. And if anybody ever asks me for one major German characteristic which applies to most Germans and which generally casts a generally dark cloud over life here it would be the German tendency to see things negatively, which leads them to expect the worse and never be quite happy with anything. To put it into an even smaller nutshell, they often do not seem to be happy to be alive. Now, the word "*Lebensfreude*" does exist in German (translation: joy of living), Schiller wrote a poem about it called "*Ode an die Freude*" (translation: Ode to joy) and Beethoven even produced extremely moving and beautiful music to accompany the poem in his 9th and final symphony. So Germans, presumably, must have some inkling about what it is and how important it is. The problem would seem to be that they have difficulty getting it into their lives.

Let me give you a few examples from real German life. When I was living in Mannheim, I used to give one-to-one tuition to a retired dentist. I would drive to his place on Wednesdays at 2 p.m. and we would chat for 90 minutes to keep his English up to a sufficient standard for the regular holidays he was now enjoying in various parts of the world. On the day of one of our meetings I had just purchased a new car, so I thought I would start our conversation rolling by telling him the good news. He thought carefully about his answer and before he gave me it he asked me the English word for *Unfall*; I told him it was "accident" and he eventually responded to my announcement with the following solemn statement: "I hope you don't have an accident in your new car". Almost thirty years later I am still not quite able to understand the connection between my statement and his statement; instead I hold up my hands and say: "There are certain things that happen in the German mind which I do not really comprehend".

A similarly peculiar utterance was heard round about the same time when I was talking with a class at a large international company in Mannheim. The topic was holidays and one young woman talked about hiring a boat with friends and sailing round a selection of Greek islands. I encouraged the others to ask her some questions about this. The first question to emerge was: "Did you see any sharks in the water?" Sharks in the water?? What sort of mind produces such questions? Well, presumably the same sort of mind that produces the statement about having accidents in new cars. Both cases illustrate that Germans are able to see the negative, while I would take an educated guess that other nationalities would see the positive. Young woman in white bikini on boat in sunny Grecian sunshine fills me with definite feelings of joy; a German, on the other hand, thinks of shark-infested waters. A new car means for me modern, efficient comfort on an open road with the brand new stereo system blasting away. What does the German think about? A nasty collision, your new car a write-off (including injuries to you and your fellow travellers) and your car insurance premiums going through the roof. Although these examples seem like extreme ones (not to mention my tongue-in-cheek comments on them), they were preceded and have been followed by many others in my time in Germany. Share with a German friend your plans to start your own business, and he will probably list a number of reasons why it is doomed to failure. Express any ideas to try something new, slightly adventurous or different and the reactions are generally sceptical, urging caution or, in some cases, filling you with the fear of God. The Americans, of course, are the exact opposite in such situations, encouraging you with positive advice, expressed in almost congratulatory tones. By contrast, the Germans could be labelled the ultimate wet blanket: pointing out problems rather than possibilities, dangers rather than chances.

Some, however, are perhaps right to argue that such an attitude is far from being a bad thing; a healthy dose of scepticism can save many tears later and throwing caution to the wind can bring disaster. And anyway, doesn't the German success story prove that such an approach reaps dividends? They may well have a point, but being surrounded by people who seem happy to tell you that things are not possible and even fraught with danger can start to make you as pessimistic as they themselves appear to be. If adapting to a culture means taking the attitude: "If you can't beat them, join them", then you may want to start thinking the German way. Despite the fact that I am happy to adapt to the Germany way of life as far as possible, I don't believe I could ever accept that the two examples mentioned represent a healthy way of thinking.

IN THE GENES?

It is of course of academic interest to people of an academic bent to ask why the people mentioned made the comments I have quoted. The superficial, no-nonsense but slightly derogatory answer might be: "Germans are angst-ridden, so what do you expect?" (See references to "Angst" in Chapter 3). Other more deep-thinking and well-meaning souls might proffer the following explanations: "The retired dentist was expressing his sincere hope that you would drive carefully; he simply did not wish to see you having an accident. The comment about the sharks was a well-meant message of caution intended for anybody planning a boat trip off the coast of a Greek island." Another interpretation, resting somewhere in the middle of these two, but based on other characteristics linked to the Germans, could read as follows. "A German, never wishing to appear superficial in good company, decides to give an unexpected, more thought-provoking answer to the statement/question," i.e., not "Oh, what type of car did you buy?" and "How big was your boat?" The aim, therefore, is to avoid superficiality (although more cynical observers might just call it people trying to be clever).

My final piece of advice to non-Germans on the receiving end of such statements would be not to take it to heart; try and remain positive by consoling yourself with the maxim: "They mean well." Germans are renowned advice-givers and we can assume that advice givers have the interest of their advice receivers at heart. Rounding off the subject of advice-giving, I'd like to refer the reader to an example from the real life of a fellow-Brit (a fellow-Scouser, in fact) who has lived in Berlin as long as I have lived in Germany. After reading this chapter of my book, he related the following example in an e-mail to me (I quote verbatim, the brackets are mine): "I always cycled to work (in Berlin) irrespective of the weather, all the year round. One winter, I was slowly and carefully cycling though packed snow down a small side street. The on-coming bin lorry stopped. The driver leant out of the window and told me in no uncertain Berlin terms that I should not be on my bike, it was far too dangerous, I was nuts. Then he drove on. For me, so typically Berlin and to an extent typically German. This would NEVER happen in Britain. So, the question is why do they think they have the right to give their unsolicited opinion on anything and everything? The incident still makes me smile".

His question is an interesting one and the fact that he smiles about it today shows he has grown accustomed to those sorts of comments and has developed over the years a laudable degree of cultural understanding. The Berlin binman's tone of voice and vocal delivery is also mentioned, a factor which surely further tested my friend's tolerance and it is easy to see how conflict can quickly ensue. If intercultural harmony is to be ensured, it is always useful to bear in mind that we should always be endeavouring to give the other culture the benefit of the doubt, something my friend was doing in exemplary fashion by not twisting his bike round this *apparently* aggressive Berliner's neck. It is probably the case that the binman was wholly unaware of causing any offence. He was offering advice in, as my friend puts it, "Berlin terms" - probably the only terms he knows. Neither should we forget that they (Berlin binmen and Germans generally) may well be making the same effort not to be shocked, disturbed or offended by the things *we* say or do.

GENERAL MALAISE

One more aspect of life in Germany which still weighs on me heavily after over three decades in the place is the Germans' apparent inability to relax. In many ways it is linked to the problem of general pessimism I have described in the previous paragraphs: they seem to be in constant stand-by mode, fearing that something is going to go wrong at any given moment and that we should all be prepared for the next big disaster every moment of our lives. It also has something to do with the Germans' desire to get things right. It is no coincidence that they often use the English saying "Nobody's perfect". I have the distinct feeling, however, that any German worth his salt has the ultimate aim of debunking this defeatist theory. "Take it easy" is another idea which Germans like but don't believe in their heart of hearts is really doable.

The effect of this attitude on the general feeling of everyday life in Germany is easy to imagine. After a few moments back in my hometown in Britain, I feel more relaxed, less worried and generally at ease. And the reasons are quite clear: people care less, look less anxious and are generally more tolerant of the things happening around them.

As all amateur sociologists/anthropologists/philosophers/economists will tell you, there are, however, also negative consequences resulting from this attitude. Being more relaxed can also mean dropping litter where it shouldn't be dropped, not cleaning public toilets as well as they could be cleaned, not preserving infrastructure to the standard it could be kept, etc. I could extend the list to fill the rest of this book. The conclusion might be, therefore, that the German desire for getting things right produces a spick and span environment where things work, but where people feel less at ease. The British easy-going attitude to almost anything is good for your blood pressure and general well-being but sometimes produces an environment characterised by shoddiness and sub-standard quality.

The summing up at the end of that last paragraph is, of course, an outrageous generalisation but describes my general mood when I make my regular sojourns to and from Britain. The fascinating question remains of course: could we

146

have a more relaxed Germany and still have the efficiency and quality? I am pleased to report that such a development may already be in process and an experience I had in the mid-eighties (back in Mannheim again) seems to provide evidence that it was already present then. I was in the basement of Karstadt (a major German department store) doing my shopping in the food hall when I spotted a poster promoting "Coffee from all over the world". "Aaah", I thought, "a free sample of coffee. Why not?" There was a spanking-new coffee machine set up; plastic beakers, milk and sugar all ready. Half a dozen or so shoppers with the same idea as me had gathered in that particular corner of the supermarket, looking forward to sampling. Unfortunately, the promotion lady was nowhere to be seen. One brave man decided to help himself and started pouring out coffee. Others followed suit, passing each other milk and sugar, chatting, mingling and generally enjoying the spontaneous get-together around the source of free coffee. It was Friday afternoon and the scene was an example of people behaving at their best: relaxed, helping each other and just generally chilling out with a smile on their face.

This all changed dramatically when the lady in charge of the promotion (and, more importantly, in charge of the free coffee) returned from wherever she had been. We were all unceremoniously admonished for our audacity, told to replace the coffee immediately and wait for her to serve us. It was her job to dish out the coffee and nobody else's The spell was broken. People shuffled off sheepishly, the smiles disappeared and everybody guiltily dispersed on their separate paths, reassuming the default setting of anonymity and post-modernist isolation.

I see this incident as proof that Germans are just as keen as any nationality to be spontaneous, warm and compassionate. The problem in Karstadt was the voice of authority which put an end to a warm, uplifting happening. Somewhere along the long and complicated path of German culture over hundreds of years one question has set root in any German's mind: "Am I allowed to do this?" The question per se is not a bad one, and gives us a moral compass without which we would live a life of barbarism and chaos. Problems arise, however, when rules and regulations (and the inherent fear of them) hold us back from being what we should be, i.e. human beings. The promotions lady was only thinking of rules and

147

regulations (not to mention the little power kick she was personally enjoying) when she tore into us with such negative glee on that Friday afternoon.

The problem for the promotions lady was that the customers had dismantled her framework, which required *her* (and only *her*) to serve the free coffee. The customers themselves would also have been aware of a framework which also required them to wait to be served *by her.* The customers had guiltily broken the framework and were enjoying the mischievous glee which went with it and the spontaneous chatting and good feeling created took their mind off their misdemeanour. The promotions lady's broken framework was, however, one step too far - hence the outburst. A framework is what we might thus call the German security blanket; the teddy bear clutched by the toddler in the dark bedroom or the script in the sweaty palms of the actor who is not yet sure of his lines. If I have learned anything about the Germans after over thirty years of living amongst them, it is the importance of that framework. If it's there, they are as close to being as relaxed as they're ever going to be; if it's not, things can get, let's say, interesting. In other words, relaxation comes neither easily, nor spontaneously; it's constructed for structure and to prevent anybody having to leave their comfort zone. In other words, ensure that the framework is there and you'll be dealing with a relatively relaxed and easy-going German; take it away and life can become much more difficult.

My guess is that the promotions lady in today's supermarket might not need the framework to the same extent as her colleague from that earlier generation. She might very probably have reappeared with the words: "Oh, I see you're helping yourself. And I don't blame you! Lovely coffee, isn't it?" The incident also shows that the customers in that food hall were already ahead of the pack; the people in power – represented in this case by the outraged promotions lady – were actually defying a welcome new trend in Germany towards a more relaxed, flexible and open society. One is reminded of the iconic call of East German demonstrators in 1989: "*Wir sind das Volk!*" (We are the people!).

There is still one major aspect of the German mindset which any non-

148

German living here for any serious length of time will have observed and will need to accept: the Germans are a hard folk to please. This manifests itself in the general attitude that seems to be expressing the opinion that one doesn't count up the things one has, but the things one doesn't have (and would obviously like). The German (as I mentioned in a previous chapter) is unhappy that the German national football team "only" reaches the final of the World Cup; he is unhappy if, after starting on an academic career in higher education, he doesn't become a professor. And he is, for example, unhappy if the train is 10 minutes late. The German generally does not think: a) Wow, what a great achievement that my team got to the World Cup final, b) I am in a permanent well-paid secure job at a university, even though I am not a professor and c) the train has arrived and that's the main thing.

The desire for the best is, of course, no bad thing. Many would in fact again argue that this desire is the very engine of the German success story – I wouldn't disagree with that. However, one would sometimes appreciate a touch more humility and sense of proportion; the saying "you don't know how lucky you are" frequently enters my mind when I observe people complaining about things which are quite simply not worth complaining about. A further disturbing development is how quickly East Germans warmed to the idea of "only the best will do". In the GDR days a bar of West German chocolate was enough to send most East Germans into a paroxysm of elation; a few years later the same people were already bored by most of the delights the West had to offer. Indeed, satiation may also be part of the general problem today: the attitude of "seen it, done it, been there" is rife and it's hard to see where the next kick is going to come from.

The complaining mentality is, therefore, an irritating by-product affecting people living in a country with the highest standard of living in Europe. Bearing this in mind, the apparently constant need to complain is something difficult to understand for somebody hailing from countries with lower standards of living. Unfortunately it also has echoes of the German proclivity to see the world negatively and their inability to relax that I have already mentioned. I could sum up this malaise in Germany by saying that life is, generally speaking, more tense than in other places on the planet; it's something you get used to, learn to live with and accept.

AN UNACCEPTABLE ASPECT OF GERMAN LIFE

Which brings us neatly back to my premise at the beginning of the chapter when I stated that you try the new things the foreign culture has to offer, you get to accept, like them or even love them and get on with your life. Everything I have mentioned so far in this chapter has been subject to that process. People have often asked me (and I have sometimes asked myself) whether there are any aspects of German life that I find wholly unacceptable and still cannot get used to. The answer is "yes". Germans stare. Be it kids, pensioners, teenagers, respectable middle-aged couples, tramps, students, alternative types or beautiful women, they all have one thing in common – they all stare. On the tram, train or bus; in the supermarket; in restaurants; at bus stops; on any street; anywhere; everywhere, they stare at any time of day, they stare from dawn till dusk. They stare non-stop. They are quite simply a nation of starers, and it is something I hate, have always hated and will always hate about life in Germany. It's rude, irritating and grossly impolite and if I ever do get into a fight in Germany (which hasn't happened yet), that will be the reason. I have lost count of the number of times that I have been so close to asking an offending starer: "Excuse me, what the _ _ _ _ are you staring at?"

Interestingly, when I mention this trait to Germans I know, they often deny everything. They have noticed nothing, I am only imagining it, it's not true, they protest! But it is. More interestingly, other non-Germans agree with me, whether it's fellow Brits, Americans, Irish, Turks or Russians. Russians, for example, are inveterate non-starers who have mastered the art of non-eye contact over generations; I always recognise them on the tram in the morning because they are the only white people not staring at me. I dread to think how they cope under the German "staring regime". Perhaps we can form a self-help group to help us cope.

This German habit has, apparently, also bothered groups of young Turkish citizens. In a number of comedy shows in Germany a few years ago there were frequently send-ups of irritated young Turkish chaps on German streets in which they shouted aggressively at startled Germans: "*Was guckst du?*" (What are you looking at?). There are actually T-shirts with this "slogan" printed on it and which has become a sort of parody of vaguely aggressive and cocky young Turkish men. It proves, however, to what extent many Turks have also found the staring habit a particularly annoying one.

Asking where the staring habit comes from is probably futile. My own theory is that Germany's patchwork of states over centuries has created nervous communities who needed to know who was entering their patch of land, village or town at any given time. Anybody unknown had to be weighed up quickly to establish whether he was a friend or foe. A good way of doing this is to have a good look at the person in question; staring, of course, is one way of doing this. Another theory, and clearly a less pleasant one, is that Germans tend to be rather wrapped up with and focused on themselves; so much so that they don't actually know they are staring. This would also explain why most of my German friends and colleagues deny that Germans stare: they are so immersed in their own internal world to notice that they or anybody else is doing it. Whatever the reasons, it's damned annoying and I wish they would stop it.

ALLES NICHT SO SCHLIMM

This chapter was originally going to be entitled, "Let's have a rant!" The closer I got to actually writing the chapter, the more I realised that I didn't have much to rant about; the final section on the subject of staring is the closest I have actually got to one. The word "challenges" was as critical as I could get when summarizing any difficulties I have (had) with German culture. The way of life here is very different to the British one, but there is really nothing that would make it impossible for an open-minded person to live here; once the language is mastered to a reasonable level, most other things look after themselves. That is not to say that there are no difficulties, but I hope the chapter has offered a balanced overview of things to watch out for as a newcomer to Germany, whilst also offering an entertaining and enlightening guide to my own individual process of integration and, ultimately, assimilation.

The wonderful thing about living in a foreign culture is that you can cherry pick: taking the best aspects of the new culture while giving the less palatable ones a wide berth. The old joke comes to mind about heaven being a place where all the policemen are British, all the cooks French, all the engineers Germans, etc. As globalization steams ahead we are already able to have virtually anything from anywhere at any time we want. This allows me to have a wonderful chat with a delightful and charming Turkish female student at university, then devour my tasty Italian pizza while chatting happily about football to an equally charming Turkish waiter and read my favourite British newspaper on my smartphone. I can then stand at pristine German urinals and call myself a very lucky man. If it wasn't for the dour German staring at me on the tram going home, I really could call it heaven. But as German efficiency ensures that the tram is in immaculate condition and spot on time, I will even forgive him that because, as no German wants to admit: "You can't have everything". Not even in Germany.

6.   East and West Germany – forever disunited?

"Marriages of convenience don't traditionally generate sensual happiness, spontaneous joy at being alive or relaxed, smiling faces."

The East-West relationship before 1989

To understand anything about the Germans who emerged from the German Democratic Republic (aka GDR or East Germany) in 1989, it clearly makes sense to know how life was there before the Berlin Wall eventually fell on November 9, 1989. And therein lies the main problem: how many people actually know what life was like behind that infamous construction? Well, apart from the 17 million East Germans who lived there themselves, very few. East Germans, of course, are quick to point this fact out whenever West Germans pontificate about life in the former GDR. East Germans' main argument is that only somebody who actually lived there can give an authentic picture of East German life. It is hard not to agree with such an obvious statement.

West Germans' knowledge of East Germany was limited. Many made a one-off visit to East Berlin on a day visa. Those who had relatives in the GDR might have spent a few days at a time there. But generally speaking, it was a place that most West Germans didn't visit. If you didn't have relatives there, there was little to attract you to the place: boring food, dodgy environment, generally unspectacular scenery, crumbling architecture, poor quality roads, unpleasant, snooping border guards and shadowy bureaucracy. You even had to exchange a minimum amount of money for every day of your stay there (25 Deutschmarks per day in the eighties, plus administration fees). Clearly, if you had the choice of driving down to the romantic, picturesque regions of Italy or the south of France to spend your holiday in glorious sunshine or of negotiating a hazardous trip to a ramshackle, grey, mousey place like the GDR, it was fairly obvious which choice you were going to make.

And apart from anything else, West Germans didn't feel exactly welcome there. Weren't they supposed to be the class enemy? Nasty bourgeois revisionists who were, together with their equally nasty NATO imperialist allies, hell-bent on starting a nuclear war? Weren't they from a country which was actually keeping the tradition of fascism (their word for National Socialism) alive by providing refuge for former Nazis? Such was the general tone of the one-dimensional propaganda war which the GDR authorities had been relentlessly waging since the two German states had been founded in 1949. The official GDR take on things almost certainly did not represent the population's views as a whole; but as the population's views weren't known anyway, it didn't really matter.

The average West German's views on the GDR were hardly any more positive. For most it was a country dominated by a regime which kept its citizens virtually locked up in one massive open-air prison, surrounded by an 866 mile long wall made impenetrable by barbed wire, self-releasing guns, mines and border guards with orders to shoot on sight anybody attempting to get to the West. It offered no consumer goods to talk of, there were long queues for even basic commodities, no freedom of speech and the secret police were never far away.

It is not surprising, then, that when reunification actually came about, two sets of Germans harbouring a whole series of negative images and feelings about and towards each other came face-to-face with rather sheepish looks on their faces. The road to real togetherness was going to be a long and difficult one. And this was before anybody was to fully grasp the mammoth costs that would be involved in completing economic unity and its possible ramifications. The Germans have a saying: "*Bei Geld hört die Freundschaft auf*" (Friendship ends when money is involved - my translation). In this case money was going to spoil any initial post-unification party plans and complicate the already difficult German-German friendship before it even started to get off the ground. This chapter primarily aims to offer insights into how this difficult process of coming together has been progressing; before moving on to that, I would first like to give you some of my own personal impressions of life behind the Berlin Wall.

EVERYDAY LIFE IN THE GDR – PERSONAL IMPRESSIONS

Despite admitting at the beginning of this chapter how difficult it is for anybody from the West to describe how life was in the former GDR, I have taken it on myself to try. After reading Chapter 4 of this book, you will know that I spent considerable amounts of time there in the seventies and eighties and was once married to a citizen of that now defunct state. I have made a rough calculation of how much time I actually spent there between 1978 and 1989 and it amounts to approximately 120 days. Enough time, I believe, to be able to paint as accurate a picture as any other non-East German could.

The overall picture was a fairly bleak one. You experienced poor and often unfriendly service in virtually every retail outlet you frequented, found no goods or services which could even remotely be described as luxury or of superior quality, were faced with a constant lack of varied foods and were both dismayed at the generally shabby and run-down appearance of everything, be it roads, flats and houses or the internal fittings of such buildings. Entertainment was provided by mainly lacklustre cinemas, theatres, pubs, restaurants, all in short supply and all providing extremely limited capacity if any of the aforementioned were offering anything out of the ordinary (i.e. something from the West). There always seemed to be shortages of everything; hence such jokes as: "What would happen if they brought socialism to the Sahara?" Answer: "There would be a shortage of sand".

It is, however, important to differentiate between the 120 days I spent in the GDR and actually living there as a GDR citizen. The crucial difference was that I was always able to leave the place after experiencing a few days of this "interesting" but frugal and minimalistic life. My GDR friends weren't so lucky. The other major difference was that I had experienced life in the West, which, of course made life in the East seem even worse. They were used to the life they were used to and had come to accept it; moreover, despite all the shortcomings described above, the people I met there seemed reasonably content in a stoical, black-humoured sort of way. And the fact that there were so few material pleasures to be had meant that life was more focused on relationships with other human beings. This involved talking to them, drinking with them (booze, at least, was always readily available and affordable) and laughing, dancing and sleeping with them (these activities were free of charge, of course). In my experience, East Germans often survived the GDR by pursuing such pastimes with an intensity their opposite numbers in the West didn't – they, on the other hand, were simply busy amusing themselves with the latest consumer items East Germans couldn't get their hands on. Or travelling the world. Or doing dozens of other things East Germans could only dream of doing. If I had one good thing to say about the GDR, it would be that people were more tuned into each other because there wasn't much else to be tuned into. Simple things such as being with people you liked and making the best of those times together is something I think back fondly to. They were people constantly battling against shortages; this created a society characterised by grim solidarity, forming a myriad of informal self-help groups which lent, borrowed and bartered to alleviate the overall sense of helplessness. Laudable and compassionate actions abounded in the face of general shortage and many older East Germans today talk about it with an understandable sense of pride and affection.

More cynical observers might point out that it's all very well my waxing lyrical about boozy, fun-loving East Germans displaying generous portions of solidarity, spending quality time with each other and generally making the best of things, but what did I really know about the grim reality of life there? How was life at the workplace? How did you get an appointment with a specialist doctor? How long was the waiting list to buy a car? What about possible run-ins with the authorities or with, perish the thought, the STASI (short form for "*Staatssicherheit*", Secret Service)? I knew nothing about such ever-present everyday challenges because I wasn't facing them on a permanent basis. And this brings us back to where we started - only those who lived there can ever give us the full, unadulterated picture. For this reason we have to take their word on anything they tell us now.

As a frequent visitor I could only ever relate snapshots, depressing impressions or amusing tales and anecdotes about the "other Germany" when I returned to the West. A Germany cut off from the Western world – unless you were one of its very few privileged citizens, such as high-ranking party officials or top sports people who were the only ones allowed to travel west; add to them people of pensionable age – women over 60 and men over 65 who could come and go as they pleased (if they stayed in the West it was one less pension to pay and somebody could have their flat). We're talking here about an exceedingly small minority of the population. Add to that figure people of pensionable age – women over 60 and men over 65 could come and go as they pleased (if they stayed in the West it was one less pension to pay and somebody could have their flat). Although restrictions were relaxed in the course of the eighties and a restricted number of East Germans were allowed to travel west for weddings, birthdays and funerals of close relatives, for the rest it was a case of making the best of a pretty poor deal: you just didn't have any alternative.

I could see with my own eyes that everybody had a job, a place to live and enough money to survive comfortably on. In that respect there was a sense of absolute security. But I could also see that you couldn't buy much of value with that money; many people's flats had outside toilets, primitive plumbing and fitments and offered little or no comfort. Anything vaguely representing quality could only be paid for with Western currency; if you had friends or relatives in the West prepared to give you some, you were lucky. If not, you were living in a country which presented a picture of ordered grimness. A country where people did without, improvised and kept their mouths shut about the system they were undeniably suffering under. And not even East German citizens were aware at that time to what extent the Stasi were busy checking how often those East German mouths were not remaining shut.

THE IMMEDIATE AFTERMATH OF REUNIFICATION – THE NINETIES

The euphoria during and immediately after the fall of the Berlin Wall soon gave way to the sobering wake-up call caused by the costs of reunification and the size of the reconstruction task ahead. Billions of Deutschmarks were pumped into the East German economy in the years following reunification on October 3, 1990, sparking off a general mindset in West Germans that they would be paying for the costs of reunification in the form of higher taxes and social security payments for a long time to come. The resulting increase in the national debt also worried West Germans, proud of their traditionally good housekeeping practices. Their prejudices grew, stemming from their homespun observations of life in a Communist system – East Germans, they proclaimed, were afraid of hard work. Provocative quotes such as, "Working as under the Communists and living as under the Capitalists is impossible" (1998 Edinger/Nacos: 21) further fuelled the flames of antagonism.

More bad feeling was caused by the cost of financing East German pensions. In the years following reunification, generous pensions were paid out to East Germans who had worked for as long as 45 years under the GDR regime but who had paid not one penny into the West German pension system which was providing the money they were receiving. (In some cases, those same people were getting more money from the system than West Germans who had paid into the system for many years). This was particularly true of women who had been in work for most of their life in the GDR and were, consequently, receiving substantially larger pensions than most women of pensionable age in West Germany.

This was just one example of numerous bizarre anomalies which were driving East and West Germans ever further apart in the nineties. West German resentment was understandable, but both East and West had to face up to the fact that if reunification was to be a success, they would have to try and pretend that there had never been two Germanys; all Germans had the same rights to any benefits they were entitled to, regardless of where and when they had lived in either of the two states between 1949 and 1990. This was a pretend game which the reasoned, matter-of-fact German mind had real problems playing.

The relationship between East and West Germans in the immediate post-unification years might be summed up by these following opposing viewpoints: the *Ossies* were sick and tired of having to show eternal gratitude for being helped out of the economic disaster once-called the GDR; *Wessies* were equally peeved at the unending amounts of money the whole process seemed to be costing. The *Ossies'* apparent unwillingness to be patient in their desire to achieve Western levels of prosperity also irked. Eastern ingratitude, Western arrogance. Western ignorance, Eastern lack of grasp on reality. This emotive and unproductive slagging match rumbled on through the nineties; only people with their head deep in the sand would claim that it is still not rumbling on to some extent today.

Regardless of how attitudes were in the nineties, East Germans actually did have the lion's share of problems to deal with: the East German workforce had been reduced from almost 10 million to 5.7 million by 1994 (cf. Edinger/Nacos 1998:18), a staggering blow for people used to guaranteed employment. Deep down, the threat of unemployment had always been the East Germans' greatest fear and when it happened it had devastating psychological effects on many. The mantra fed to them for 40 years in the GDR had been: "Only here are you guaranteed job security for life". Those who lost their jobs in those years started to long for that guarantee again.

Many West Germans seemed to have little sympathy for the plight of East Germans at this time, some eager to blame them for lack of initiative after 40 years of socialist fairy tales. An image of heartless, cruel, capitalist *Wessies* was emerging, further fanning the flames of East-West conflict. Unscrupulous West German insurance agents and dodgy financial consultants also made rich pickings during this time as they promised naive and inexperienced *Ossies* fast-track schemes to mouth-watering prosperity.

East Germans were subject to bad press in the nineties as a result of a large number of incidents of racist violence in the new federal states. It is a fact that East Germans, through no fault of their own, had little experience of foreigners living in their country. With the exception of Vietnamese, Cubans and Africans from socialist states living and working there for fixed periods of time as a part of bilateral work exchange agreements with the former GDR, foreigners were a rare sight. Neither did all GDR citizens accept the heavy burden of responsibility caused by the Second World War; they were raised to believe that they were in fact fighting the Nazis in the Third Reich. No guilty conscience there then. Unlike the more sensitive, conciliatory and tolerant approach to foreigners showed by West Germans down the years, some East Germans saw foreigners simply as threats to their livelihoods in the harsh economic reality post 1990. Hoyerswerda and Rostock remain painful reminders of this mindset when homes for foreign refugees and émigrés were set on fire in the early nineties. (Similarly shameful incidents were also happening in West Germany at the time – in Solingen and Mölln Turkish citizens were falling victims of cowardly arson attacks, proof that racist-fuelled violence was not only a sick pastime of East German extremists).

Such incidents, the relative strength of far right-wing parties and the consistent electoral successes of the fairly extreme left-wing PDS (regarded as the successor party to the all-powerful SED) played into the hands of West German pundits who wanted to believe that East Germany was only playing lip-service to the idea of democracy. West German embitterment, tinged with that *Wessie* sense of smug arrogance, reached new heights as sayings such as "they've learnt nothing" did the rounds in the West. The fact is, however, that outrages against foreigners were not, and are still not, restricted to East Germany - as subsequent events have proven.

Government policy of introducing lower pay scales for public service workers in the East further increased East Germans' sense of injustice. Ostensibly to counter lower productivity in the East, it simply seemed like straightforward exploitation and discrimination to many East Germans. Their pay was to gradually reach western standards in the coming years, but its effect was to make East Germans feel like, for the time being at least, decidedly second-class citizens.

Further bad blood was caused by West Germans claiming property rights on buildings they had to abandon when the two states were created in 1949. East Germans were receiving letters from lawyers in West Germany informing them that the house or flat they had been living in all their life actually belonged to "Heinz Schmidt" in Hanover. Understandably, a nasty shock to the system, especially as the heartless principle of *"Rückgabe vor Entschädigung"* was enshrined in the constitution, meaning that the East Germans involved in such cases had to hand over "their" property to West Germans without being entitled to any compensation. Cries of "colonization" rather than "unification" (1998 Edinger/Nacos: 22) were starting to be heard in the East and for the first time the term *"Ostalgie"* (being nostalgic about the former GDR) was banded about.

Ostalgie was partly a reaction to the myriad of nasty surprises raining in on East Germans at this time, but also a shot at the rather arrogant West German assertion that everything connected with the GDR had been a waste of time. By doing so, of course, West Germans saying that East Germans' lives had been a waste of time. Quite an odious assumption to make and something which East Germans shrugged off as a statement from people who had never experienced life in the GDR. East Germans were daring to say that some aspects of life in the former GDR had actually been quite good; some went even so far as to say that some things had been better. Disbelieving head-shaking was the order of the day in West Germany.

It might well be that East Germans had in mind the kind acts of solidarity and the general atmosphere of camaraderie at their stress-free work place when they were indulging in these acts of *Ostalgie*. They might also be referring to the comprehensive provision for small children if their mothers wanted to go back to work. Otherwise it's very hard for a non-East-German to imagine anything else they could be feeling nostalgic about. When you have lost your job in your late 40s, however, with little prospect of finding another one, *Ostalgie* might well have been the last pride-salvaging refuge remaining.

East Germans' feeling of nostalgia seemed even more out of place and incomprehensible when it gradually became known to what ends the Stasi had gone to snoop on them in the GDR. The "Stasi files" were being opened by the "Gauck authorities" (Gauck is the current President of the Federal Republic of Germany and former East German human rights campaigner) for anybody who wanted to see them. This time it was the *Ossies* shaking their heads in disbelief as they discovered who had been spying on whom. The number of loyal citizens engaged in these activities, whether on a free-lance basis or as a permanent state employee, was truly staggering. There were actually a number of cases of married couples informing on each other – grounds for divorce, I wonder? Many East Germans experienced the shock of their lives when viewing their Stasi files, which produced feelings of anger, amusement and downright disbelief.

One of the results of these revelations was that East Germany itself was becoming a divided country, consisting of those who had been doing the spying and those who hadn't: the snoopers and the snooped upon. There were further, divisive subdivisions caused by other developments: there were those who still believed, in an evangelical and frighteningly dogmatic way, in the principles of the old regime (the incorrigibles) and those who, whilst welcoming the change, still saw some merits in the old system. Then there were those who had done well out of the change and those who actually believed they had become worse off since 1990. There were East Germans who had left East Germany since the change, mostly now permanently or semi-permanently settled in West Germany, but still making visits. And finally those who had done well before the change (thanks to party membership, privileges, etc) and who were doing well (or perhaps even better) now, too, but disavowing their former political beliefs (or perhaps not). In the years after 1990, the East Germans were not only having to process the vast amount of changes in their society but also having to witness the creation of a large number of different, "new" East Germans, all endeavouring to find their feet (and then a place) in the brand new world they found themselves in.

The ten years leading up to the millennium, then, had made the East-West relationship more difficult than it already was. East Germans spent these years constantly attempting, for better or worse, to learn what the new system was all about. Their relationship with West Germans was an unequal one right from the start: their only teacher and role-model was the rich and sometimes contemptuous and smug older brother in the West. Learning about the economic system meant learning from West Germans; being able to rebuild and revamp the whole country depended on West German finances and know-how; the lesson about how democracy worked was to be copied from 40 years of near-impeccable West German governmental practice. East Germans were having an inferiority complex fitted into their psyche free of charge and the resentment and animosity resulting from it was getting under their skins with a vengeance.

THE LOST CHANCES AFTER 1990

What could have been done differently in these years to have alleviated some of the problems I have just described? Economically, probably very little; most economists were in broad agreement that the former GDR needed restructuring and massive help, which was always going to lead to high unemployment and increased debt. On the human level, however, I feel the West Germans could have shown more diplomacy and compassion at critical moments in the years following reunification. The constant regurgitating of the usual clichés about ungrateful *Ossies* was an eternal irritant; prejudiced snipes galore about a country of which they generally knew nothing and the hurtful rubbishing of every East German's biography was bound to turn even the most western-oriented *Ossie* into a *Wessie*-hater. Even I hated *Wessies* sometimes and I wasn't even an *Ossie* – how must they have felt?

Let me give you an example. I was enjoying a beer on a beautiful summer's evening in the market square of Wernigerode, a relatively prosperous East German town, in the early years of the new millennium when I got talking to a middle-aged West German couple spending a few days touring the Harz mountains. "We thought we'd come and see what they were doing with our money in the East", they joked, observing the beautifully restored buildings all around us. Even 12 years after reunification, the Wessies still seemed to think that the only thing the East Germans were doing was spending their money. I presume they were trying to be funny, but such "many-a-true-word-spoken-in-jest" comments reminded me again of how slow and arduous the road to one Germany was going to be.

Western heavy-handedness also helped create divisions in the political culture of East Germany. I am convinced that the left-wing party called "*Die Linke*", the successor party of the PDS, who in turn had succeeded the former GDR's all-powerful SED (Socialist Unity Party), would have received considerably less support if West German politicians had showed a touch more diplomacy and understanding when appealing to potential East German voters in those early post-change years. The mad rush to elect Helmut Kohl and his easy-to-understand form of CDU free-market policies in the first free elections was simple to predict; when the enthusiasm for Helmut Kohl had subsided again, however, the SPD could have appealed more effectively to left-minded East Germans in the elections after that. The West German tendency to talk down to East Germans estranged many of them and over 20 years after the fall of the Wall, they regularly retreat into the cosy warmth of a "real" East German party in the form of *Die Linke* (or much worse, indigenous right-wing extremist parties). Many East Germans still believe that only a party which has its roots in the former GDR can truly understand and represent East Germans and few West German politicians have convinced them that this is not the case.

And so the term "*Die Mauer in den Köpfen*" (The wall in your heads – my translation) was coined. The physical wall had fallen, only to be replaced by a psychological wall, ensuring that East and West Germans remain at arm's length. Despite possessing the same culture and speaking the same language, there had been a divided past and 17 million Germans had spent 40 years living under a totalitarian regime which allowed its inhabitants little freedom, stifled individual expression and imposed an economic system on its inhabitants which gave them few or no fruits from their undoubted hard labour. The West German historical narrative had been a five-star economic success story, unparalleled in post-war European history and all played out in freedom. Should anybody be surprised that the people from these two states were going to need a long time to even become acquaintances again, never mind be truly united? The problem has been further exacerbated by the financial burden created by the costs of reunification and the accompanying (and continuing) economic and social problems. The champagne corks popping at the Brandenburg gate and the raw and genuine overflowing of joy on November 9, 1989 was the easy part of the ride – what followed was going to be full of sober Monday mornings.

THE SLOW PATH TO UNITY CONTINUES: THE NEW AND OLD FEDERAL STATES OF GERMANY SINCE THE MILLENNIUM

The preceding paragraphs hardly make joyful reading, despite the fact that German reunification, and the ending of the Cold War was a cause of genuine joy. The fact that a nation could be peacefully reunited after being separated for decades by barbed wire, a wall and two diametrically opposed East-West power blocks was a true cause for celebration. And, most important of all, it all took place without one shot being fired. Money, I suppose, really does ruin everything. Every West German in the years after the change became very aware, very quickly that their long-cherished prosperity was at risk, and the fall of the Wall was one of the big reasons why. And every East German was worried they were going to be too late to get a piece of the cake. These two factors, and the other factors described in the chapter on the nineties made that decade, for some, a painful, joyless one.

As we enter and progress through the second decade of the new Millennium and approach the 25th anniversary of the fall of the Berlin Wall, the problems remain. East and West Germans are still different; West Germans have a self-awareness and self-confidence born of virtually uninterrupted prosperity and tremendous opportunities since the late fifties. For many, the world was their oyster, their plates full of the rich fruits of economic power. Making the best of a botched job was the maxim of the majority of East Germans in the 28 years between the construction and deconstruction of the Berlin Wall. The people that emerged were a depressed, battered lot, desperate to catch up as quickly as possible with the Germans who were just lucky enough to be living in a non-Soviet zone after the war.

Many East Germans have retained many of the positive characteristics I personally admired in the pre-Wall days: simplicity, flexibility, eagerness to help and share, a deep-seated desire for social justice and a natural approach to relationships. They openly and honestly talk about private matters and friendships are maintained even when people move apart geographically (I have much evidence of this from personal experience). In conversations with East Germans, I have noted these are also some of the characteristics they miss in many West Germans.

If this doesn't sound too patronising, 40 years of socialism GDR-style might have produced something worthwhile after all (if you don't include the East German design of the "Little Green Man" on pedestrian traffic lights now in operation across the whole of Berlin). The East Germans' reluctance to disown and disavow everything they had lived with in those 28 years understandably remains and so does their anger at West Germans' condemnation and mocking of everything that was the GDR. Their pithy argument (aimed at West Germans), "Don't judge, you didn't live there", is also a powerful one. But the basic West German attitude remains and, it has to be admitted, prevails: without West German economic power and clout that was brought into the reunification equation, none of the revamped or sparkling buildings and prosperity most East Germans now enjoy would be possible. Would the Russians have packed up their things and gone so quickly without that huge West German pay-off (see Chapter 1)? The unequal relationship remains.

There is now, of course, a new generation of Germans. No East German under 30 has any recollection of life in the GDR and those young people remarkably resemble their West German counterparts in any aspect you care to mention. There are few traces of the shabbiness of the former GDR in any towns in East Germany and whilst unemployment has remained stubbornly high in many of the new federal states, few people there would claim that reunification has not brought them a satisfactory degree of prosperity and a vastly improved lifestyle.

Further western resentment has been fuelled recently as certain disadvantaged regions in the old federal states (i.e. West Germany) have complained about lack of support to some of the towns also suffering from the effects of deindustrialisation: numerous examples can be cited in the Ruhr area. Increased support for the new federal states seems to have resulted in shortfalls in help for regions in the West which are facing equally stiff challenges in the form of rising unemployment, ageing population and migration. The "*Solidaritätszuschlag*", introduced as a temporary measure after 1990, literally a "solidarity surcharge" deducted at source as a percentage (5.5%) of income tax paid, is earmarked for projects designed to boost the economy in the East. The "temporary" measure is still in force almost a quarter of a century down the road and many are pessimistic about it ever being withdrawn. Disillusioned *Wessies* are expressing the desire that some of these funds could now be directed to projects to help poorer regions in the West.

For me personally, one of the sad consequences of reunification has been the way many East Germans have become used to prosperity; the sad and predictable cycle of possessions not producing peace of mind can be observed in many people's lives. This could also be another reason for regular outbursts of *Ostalgie*; the memory of that strangely tasting Bockwurst, washed down by a bottle of equally dodgy local beer with your colleagues on one of those riotous, socialist works outings might linger longer in your memory than the visit to the posh Italian restaurant where you don't feel quite at ease. Spreading Nutella on your toast holds no thrills now; when the parcel from the West arrived thirty years ago and Nutella was included, the thrill was indescribable (or so older East Germans tell me). East Germans naturally signed up for consumerism when they put the GDR behind them and for many the thrill has simply gone. There is, as the old cliché reminds us, a price to pay for everything. Or as the Muslims say: take what you want and pay for it.

Final thought: Where's the joy?

As time passes, people forget; sometimes they even forgive. The East-

West conflict I have described was raging hardest in the decade following reunification and an uneasy truce has since settled over the country. And economically speaking it is not all doom and gloom. The German economic success story has, generally speaking, continued with East Germany lagging behind, but doing quite nicely, thank you very much. The standard of living in the East is lower, but we are comparing it with one of the highest standards of living in the world, so it's all relative. And do East Germans compare their current standard of living with that of their former socialist brothers and sisters in the Czech Republic, Poland, Hungary, etc? Methinks not.

And the horror scenarios that kept West Germans awake at night when East Germany joined them in 1990 have not happened. At the time of writing (end of 2013), German pensions remain the highest in Europe, inflation is moderate, unemployment under the European average and Frau Merkel (an East German, by the way) is applying West German housewife principles to budgeting and keeping the national debt under reasonable control. Economic observers will point to an ever-increasing gap between rich and poor in Germany; the East-West divide is a constant reminder of this trend and proves the pessimists right. But the fact is that German reunification was not the major reason for this trend: it has been going in that direction all over the world since neo-liberalism started finding its feet and becoming the familiar medicine in the wake of Thatcher and Reagan in the eighties.

As a modern, successful, economic unit with a top infrastructure and fully-functioning system of government, the five new federal states which used to comprise the German Democratic Republic are something every German can be proud of, unrecognisable from the country on the brink of financial, moral, economic and infrastructural ruin over twenty years ago. Yet this chapter makes somewhat depressing reading, which is actually peculiar considering we are talking about something which Germans had dreamed about for many years: a unified Germany in freedom. They got it, yet I seem mostly to have related stories of anger, disappointment, resentment and distrust. It would be easy to gleefully jump to conclusions and make disparaging remarks about the gloomy and pessimistic German psyche, seeing the glass half empty rather than half full. But I believe that there is more to it than that.

The fundamental differences in the development of two sets of Germans for forty years have been described in some detail in this chapter; these differences led to the very difficult birth of this new German state. The staggering changes facing the former inhabitants of the former GDR, particularly with regard to the economy and social system, guaranteed that their initial years in the new Germany were going to be a crash course in everything pertaining to the tried and trusted West German system, ending either in unemployment, disillusionment and despair on the one hand, or employment, a good standard of living and a satisfactory degree of contentment on the other. 17 million East Germans will have 17 million slightly different stories; all of them, however, will have had one common denominator: economic survival depends on adapting to a system which is totally strange to you, but which is not going to go away. With your mind firmly on making a living, there isn't much time left for celebration.

Marriages of convenience don't traditionally generate sensual happiness, spontaneous joy at being alive or relaxed, smiling faces. And so it was (and perhaps still is) with the new Germany. They are together because politically and economically it makes more sense than not being together. It's a little bit like two pensioners marrying to save on the heating bills and securing a reasonable pension for one of them when the other one passes on. Little or no romance attached, but it does make good sense.

Neither has the romance of patriotism lit up German eyes since 1989. "We don't do patriotism", could well be the maxim of both German states since 1949. The GDR stood by the motto of International Socialism while West Germany believed in the solidity of the Deutschmark as its guiding light; believing in the fatherland had been off the agenda since Hitler wrote his last will and testament in 1945. There are never scenes of Germans hugging each other because they love each other as Germans. In the West, flags were kept firmly out of sight until World Cups and European Championships when the occasional hug was allowed and East German flags only flew when there was some mass demonstration for a worthy socialist cause. Football appears to be the only time Germans allow themselves nationalist emotions.

The long history of regionalism in Germany (see chapter 3) means that if

Germans show patriotism at all it is towards their local area or region; which probably goes some way to explaining why they are not particularly taken by the idea of being part of a huge entity called Germany. The joy of being part of one big "one" doesn't really move the average German. A merchant sailor from Rostock has little or nothing in common with a baker from the Black Forest; in the same way, a docker from Liverpool has little or nothing in common with a farmer from North Devon. The difference is that the latter are linked by an English kingdom going back 1000 years which they are, in a strange, inexplicable way rather proud of. Asking a German whether they are proud of anybody or anything from German history will probably provoke a long, puzzled silence, followed by a blank stare. The Americans, Italians, and Spaniards, for example, have few qualms about egging the emotional, patriotic pudding despite having far from perfect pasts. Germans, on the other hand, are far more reticent about displaying anything like love for their own country; the grim nature of their past seems to top everybody else's and its paralysing effects are still plain to see.

The reunification was first and foremost an economic coming together of two states which hadn't been together for forty-four years. Before that they had been in the middle of a barbaric world war (1939-1945), preceded by six years of totalitarian dictatorship preparing for that war (1933-1939). There had only ever been 14 years of a rather shaky democracy in the form of the Weimar Republic (1919-1933) whose latter years produced a virtual civil war scenario between right and left-wing warring factions. Before that there was the First World War (1914-1918) which was preceded by an outdated Empire with a positively non-democratic Kaiser at the helm (1870-1918). In other words, reunification meant, in historic terms, going back to a state associated with the "bad", rather than the "good" old days (although Germany had never previously existed within the same post-1990 borders).

Germany had been divided for centuries: left and right; revolutionaries and non-revolutionaries; capitalist and non-capitalist; Prussian and non-Prussian; Catholic and Protestant; clerics and non-clerics; pro-Napoleon and anti-Napoleon; democratic and non-democratic. The list is a long one and the latest German state, embedded in the centre of Europe and within the borders fixed at the Potsdam conference in 1945 and which came into existence on October 3, 1990 was attempting to make these symbols and slogans less relevant. Democratic, tolerant, European, open-minded; these are the new generation's watchwords in their new Germany. Willy Brandt's famous saying, when referring to the coming together of the two former states, *"Jetzt wächst zusammen, was zusammengehört"* (What belongs together, is now growing together – my translation) presupposes that Germans belonged together in the first place. As long as the growing is in an inwardly direction, nobody is going to be complaining, least of all East and West Germans themselves.

GOODBYE MADNESS

Whether passionate love between East and West Germans ever blossoms is highly debatable; too much has happened in the past for the relationship to be anything more than an uneasy friendship between two people(s) steadfastly refusing to take any blame for that uneasiness. People of a pragmatic bent often create a principle from the truism that some things are best left unsaid and that will probably be the best way forward for the people of this reunited Germany.

The not-yet-born generations of East and West Germans probably won't fully understand what all the fuss was about anyway. The Cold War, the threat of nuclear war, the *"Stasi"*, *"Ostalgie"*, the Berlin Wall, Eastern inferiority complexes and Western insensitivity will all be issues they might stumble across in history books and which might generally puzzle them. Presumably they will be so immersed in the social media of the day and the delights of the latest consumerist trends that the monumental events engulfing Germany in the last decade of the 20th century will seem as distant from their reality as the French and Industrial Revolutions seem to ours. *Wahnsinn* (madness) was on everybody's lips on that November night in 1989 when the Berlin Wall ceased to have a purpose any more; ironically, what had been going on before that date in Cold War Europe had been the real madness. What has followed is normality: democracy, free elections, free market, freedom of speech and freedom to travel. This normality has also created challenges for a large number of people, and the East Germans have clearly had the lion's share to contend with, as hopefully this chapter has pointed out. As Germans

170

in East and West switch out the light every night, close their eyes and take their leave from another day in their new marital bed called "Germany (sort of) United", they might not all be humming Phil Collins' 1989 hit, "Another day in paradise", but most will surely have to admit that things have turned out quite satisfactorily since that November night in that fateful year of 1989.

7   The state of the nation at the beginning of the 21st century

"THE "ECONOMIC GIANT, POLITICAL DWARF" ROLE FITS LIKE THE PROVERBIAL COMFY SHOE AND NOBODY IS IN ANY GREAT HURRY TO TRY ON ANY OTHER."

A   THE ECONOMY

Fair weather or foul?

With thirteen years of the 21st century completed, there would appear to be few clouds on the German horizon. As far as the economy is concerned, it is where it has been since the economic miracle revved up and moved through the various gears, sweeping all before it: at the top of the European Economic Champions League. Germany's political institutions have been a paradigm of stability, allaying any fears of relapse into bad old ways. The re-unification process, despite the enormity of the task and the costs involved, was, by and large, pulled off with admirable German efficiency and aplomb and the new, expanded fatherland is everybody's friend, settled peacefully in the middle of Europe. Germans seem to be living in a society in which social tension is negligible. No London-style riots here. No massive youth unemployment, as in Spain. No financial meltdown à la Greece. No Italian political anarchy and high-jinks. If this was a school report, the teacher would probably be writing: "Keep up the good work". Should I then, say everything is rosy in the German garden and move straight onto the final chapter of the book? Well, not quite.

Germany's reputation as a country where quality and high standards are writ large is a strong one. My book so far tends to reflect this - apart from chapter 5 (and parts of Chapter 3, perhaps) the book is laudatory rather than critical; in contrast to Marc Antony at Caesar's funeral, I have come to praise rather than bury. But discerning readers (which I assume you all are, especially the German ones) will want the "warts-and-all" approach on the state of a nation. In other words, I believe you wish me to go the extra mile. This chapter, therefore, needs to go beyond the remarkable achievements of a nation which was as good as dead nearly 70 years ago and will also focus on a few of the darker shadows. During the extra

172

mile, therefore, I intend to address topics which I believe we can call burning issues and which could well turn into grey clouds, threatening heavy rain. If I may milk the meteorological metaphor once more, I would add, however, that the rain will probably be showery rather than constant.

Germany needs to face up to the ubiquitous challenges thrown up by the 21st century: globalization, the need to co-operate with partners world-wide to combat terrorism and rogue states and to help co-ordinate an ever-expanding European Union, to name but three. Closer to home, an increasing gap between rich and poor, an ageing population (with ever-decreasing rates of birth) pushing its generous social system to its limits, problems integrating foreigners (or citizens with a migration background) into German society are all issues continually making their presence felt. Clearly, the disturbing list of matters to be dealt with above can more than likely be found in most countries of the developed world. So how is Germany's scorecard?

STILL THE ECONOMIC GIANT?

The economy is still the strongest link: export-driven with renowned products in the automobile, chemical, pharmaceutical, engineering and electronic industries; a modern infra-structure with high-tech plant and machinery; a well-trained and responsible work force; a population benefitting from 40 years of continuing affluence, generous pensions, ample amounts of inherited cash and property and a well-established, stable federalized system of government whose declared aim is that prosperity should be spread as equally and fairly as possible nationwide. All these factors have put the country in a stronger position than most to cope with the challenges listed in my introduction. Generally speaking, therefore, Germany has been more than coping.

I was watching a lecture on YouTube recently by the acclaimed literary academic, Terry Eagleton. He maintained that anybody glancing into a general history book on any country in the last couple of hundred years will find the middle class doing well and prospering, climbing impressively up the social ladder and amassing wealth and influence, despite the problems other classes might be experiencing. A generalised statement it may be, but there is a good deal of truth in it. The middle class has more often than not been in the right places at the right times in history to make the most of business and professional opportunities and this has certainly been the case in Germany where shrewd use of amassed capital and further progress up the ladder in the fifties and sixties helped to create Germany's most successful middle class ever. In fact, Tony Blair's assertion at the turn of the century that in Britain "everybody's middle-class now" would be more valid for a country like Germany rather than for his own. Germany has always had a strong middle-class and that class has further thrived and expanded since the end of the war, displaying the strength and solidity to survive any of the minor or major economic crises which have emerged since then. A combination of no-nonsense middle class values and German attention to reality and detail gave birth to a particularly potent version of bourgeois prosperity. Sensible investment in property, a disciplined approach to money, a deep aversion to credit and a desire to make sure their children learn something useful for the purpose of finding gainful employment has been the backbone of Germany's economic success since the fifties.

This widely established class in Germany is still doing well; I have already mentioned that very few people in this country ever seem to have to do without anything. The problem with the statement, of course, is that I have been mixing primarily with people since 1978 from that very class and various economic crises (and there have been a few in the past thirty years or so) seem to have simply bounced off them. I have generally been struck by the ease with which people afford holidays, cars, new furniture, clothes and virtually anything that takes their fancy. So is there anybody in Germany today who is really suffering in a period which most people would agree is far more economically challenging than ever before?

"It's all relative", would be the most useful truism to use in this connection. What an average middle class German family might regard as a "normal" house, holiday or car could well be seen as sheer luxury by a middle class family in my home town. Defining what middle class means is a notoriously difficult remit, such terms being infamously slippery and cross border comparisons are even more difficult; certain media reports of the middle class in Germany being squeezed are difficult to take particularly seriously by anybody who is able to make the comparison between Britain and Germany. When Germans complain, I am reminded of the Liverpool Football Club manager, Bob Paisley when he said: "Mind you, we had a bad season a few years ago: we came second". He was being ironic; the Germans are normally being deadly serious.

We need to get down to the nether regions in Germany before we start seeing anything alarming. As already stated, by keeping your eyes open on the streets you can see that there are more homeless people and more down-and-outs and beggars than ever before. Official statistics back this up and reports from various watchdog agencies regularly publish reports of more and more people slipping through the social net and most people are in agreement that this trend began in earnest when a new, rationalised method of calculating social benefits was introduced at the beginning of 2005, known popularly as "*Hartz 4*". The much discussed reforms of that period ushered in a new approach to the problems of social welfare and the fact that they were introduced by an SPD-led coalition indicated that they were not the ideas of some right-wing, neo-liberal government à la Margaret Thatcher. There was a general consensus that Germany would have to streamline, toughen up and face economic reality; this has meant, as is often the case in such shake-ups, that those at the bottom of the pack feel the most pain from such "reality checks".

NEO-LIBERAL BREEZES AND "*HARTZ 4*"

The expression "*Hartz 4*" is the term used for the level of social benefit unemployed (or unemployable) persons receive after they are no longer entitled to unemployment benefit. The *Hartz 4* benefit is no longer based on a percentage of the claimant's last net income, but rather on what the state deems to be sufficient for individuals or families to exist on. Its introduction was seen, and is largely still seen in some quarters, as a draconian measure. Unemployment benefit, after the introduction of this change, was to be paid for only one year (18 months if you were over 55). Its recipients are also obliged to disclose their savings, property and cash to the authorities when applying for such benefits; in other words, they are means-tested. The idea behind this is that potential recipients are expected to use up their own resources before receiving anything from the state.

The impact of this new system initially sparked off waves of protest and outrage within German society, and not only from the expected sources, i.e. left-wing politicians and activists, trade unions and social services. Heiner Geissler, from the conservative CDU party, was equally up in arms, pointing out that a man in his fifties, unemployed for the first time, could, as a result of the new system, be on the bread line within a few years, savings and property gone. Is this social justice, he asked? Men or women at that age tend not to find employment again and the new regulations were going to make life particularly hard for that category of people. It was, quite simply, the biggest break Germany had yet made from the traditional concept of the state looking after its citizens from cradle to grave.

Traditional SPD, worker-friendly members of society are still shocked that it was instigated, planned and introduced by an SPD-Green coalition government (Peter Hartz, whose name gave the scheme its popular labelling, was the SPD mastermind behind the whole thing). Subsequent right-of-centre governments have gladly adopted the reforms and protests gradually petered out. However, as is customary in Germany, the debates in the media during this period were relentless. There were (and still are) two camps: those from the more neo-liberal, conservatives who argued that the over-generous social benefits system had encouraged a dependency culture which was preventing Germany from entering the real world of highly competitive global markets. The traditional left, together with some middle of the road, socially-minded conservatives in tow, such as Heiner Geissler (see above), foresaw a new and dangerous poverty trap with the inevitable social problems trailing in its wake.

So how is "post-*Hartz 4* Germany" as it pursues a more streamlined social welfare system, in keeping with the neo-liberal climate dominating most of Europe? A scientific text would now delve into a myriad of detailed statistics proving or disproving a number of theses about how Germany is faring after such reforms. The intelligent observer need go no further than the nearest quality newspapers, journals and reputable websites which constantly report on a widening gap between rich and poor since 2005. Media reports and statistics reflect a generally disturbing drift towards more people living on the breadline and more and more people heavily burdened by debt: a further curse for those who have slipped into the murky waters of *Hartz 4*.

The *"Bundesagentur für Arbeit"* /statistik.arbeitsagentur.de/ regularly offers a comprehensive overview of official unemployment figures in Germany. A brief look at the reports contained therein indicates that the majority of *Hartz 4* recipients stay unemployed longest. As they are clearly receiving less than before the restructuring, and have, in some cases lost much of their own personal savings before being able to claim these reduced benefits, you don't need to have a degree in economics to realise that those at the bottom of the social ladder are getting seriously poorer. This process was completed a few years later under a further overhauling of the social welfare and benefits system by the Grand SPD/CDU Coalition. This reform came to be known as *"Agenda 2010"*. The aims of the overhaul were to cut costs, streamline the system and provide incentives to stimulate industry and trade in order to modernize Germany for the 21st century. Many see *Agenda 2010* as the ultimate sea change which favours employers, those with capital and those happily settled in the category "middle class". Others, on the other hand, see all these reforms as being long overdue and argue that if an SPD Chancellor initiates them, we should finally accept that the free market is in the ascendency and should have its way. The new CDU Chancellor, Angela Merkel, together with her FDP coalition partners, were more than happy to work with Schroeder's reforms when they took over power in 2009; protests have also subsided as Germany shook off the effects of the financial crisis at the end of the decade with the economic ship being relatively steadied in the years thereafter.

The unemployment figures in the last few years also give cause for mild optimism. In 2009, the percentage of persons unemployed stood at 8,1%; as I write this in May 2013, it stands at just under 7% - a real but not earth-shattering decrease in four years. The big question is: has this been a result of the reforms, i.e. are more people making more effort to find a job because it's worthwhile finding one? Possibly, but that could be one factor of many. Other factors include the inescapable truth that temporary, short-term contracts are on the increase in Germany and that, as a consequence, people are becoming more flexible in the labour market; the perennial strength of the German economy and the increasing number of new (and not particularly well-paid) jobs have been created in service industries; the traditionally sensible approach of trade unions (as is often the case) in pay deals is also helping to keep Germany competitive.

Germany remains one of the few EU countries not to have a minimum wage on the statute books and the absence of minimum pay legislation is also lauded by the neo-liberal factions of society as another reason why German unemployment figures are the best in Europe. This argument is a debatable one. The number of East European workers and illegal and half illegal immigrants working long hard hours for next to nothing is a shameful trend and has nothing to do with competitiveness but everything to do with unscrupulous, ruthless profiteers. It is not hard to imagine that certain numbers of *Hartz 4* recipients may also be working in illegal jobs offering a pittance; it is, however, hard to imagine any such recipients breaking away from social benefits to take up such jobs.

THE GERMAN MIDDLE CLASS

And that brings us back to the middle classes and those in quality employment, with a good education and training behind them and earning an average or above average income. They are also more than likely the sort of people awaiting the next batch of inheritance money to be passed onto them; it is quite simply a fact that those parents who made it in the heyday of the fifties, sixties and seventies have generally passed on the mantle of prosperity to later generations who now make up the majority of today's comfortable middle class. They are precisely those people mentioned in the history books Mr. Eagleton was referring to at the beginning of this chapter; those beavering away, keeping their noses clean, minding their own business and washing their cars on Saturday. In other words, the average face of "Middle Germany" (doesn't quite have the same ring as "Middle England", but it serves the purpose reasonably well). They represent the backbone of society and are the majority; more liberal, easy-going, tolerant, trendy and progressive than their forefathers, but still a solidifying influence on the modern Germany we see today.

It is hard to criticize this state of affairs and it is also important to point out that Germans generally remain critical and socially aware, even when they are sitting pretty. Their critical approach to all things is a given, and the principle of social justice drives much political thought and action, even amongst those you would imagine to be staunchly conservative. The watchword of the fifties and sixties, "Prosperity for all", coined by the CDU finance minister, Ludwig Erhard, has left a lasting mark on many generations of Germans. The results of a survey by the renowned *Allensbach Institut* were highlighted in the *Westdeutsche Allgemeine Zeitung* on 15 February, 2013 when 69 % of the Germans questioned believed that property and income were "unfairly distributed". 64% also believed that social justice was "on the retreat" in Germany. Over 50% also believed that it was the job of the state to create fairer economic conditions.

The teaching of history in schools may also have played a decisive and positive role here. If there is one message that does get through to young people, it is that social divisions, economic inequality and the resulting actions of opposing, extremist parties lead to the calamity of National Socialism. This is the big lesson, the one that teachers of all political persuasions are always eager to impart. The general desire, therefore, to achieve a balanced society in which everybody has a fair crack of the economic whip, remains a strong driving force in the modern German psyche. The "I'm alright, Jack" philosophy often prevalent in Britain, largely a result of the policies of a certain Mrs Thatcher in the eighties, will remain an alien one to most Germans. Thatcher's statement, "There is no such thing as society, only individuals and families", for example, would be an absolute non-starter in middle class German circles and often outrages my students when I quote it in British cultural studies seminars. They always think I'm joking: I always wish I wasn't.

A disturbing trend which has been evident for twenty years or more in Germany is the phenomenon called *"Politikverdrossenheit"*, meaning "disenchantment with politics": the highly politicised late sixties and early seventies are now but a distant memory. There are a number of obvious reasons for this: the scandals and shenanigans of politicians and the general consensus that they are "only in it for their own interests" seem to have done irreparable damage to their reputation; as the middle class expands and the main parties attempt to appeal to an ever wider mass of people, their policies tend to become very similar to each other; many people seem content with their lot, some have just simply become complacent and are not particularly interested in changing anything. The role of the economy is always uppermost in people's minds and many people believe, perhaps rightly, that big business rules and multi-national concerns rule the roost anyway, particularly with their powerful lobbies. In other words, politicians are seen largely to be in the pockets of such interest groups. It is a trend that can be seen all over the world and the reasons for it are presumably similar. However, turnouts at generally elections remains relatively high (around 70%), so perhaps we shouldn't worry too much.

Environmental issues can also stir Germans into ferocious action – the atomic reactor catastrophe in Fukushima, Japan in 2011 was the main factor in enabling the German Green party (*Bündnis 90/Die Grünen*) to obtain a 100% increase in votes from 12,5% to 25% in the Baden-Wurttemberg state elections in the same year. However, the fact that more and more people see politicians as people just wanting to make a cosy living from politics rather than people who want to change things for the good of society must give cause for concern. Leaving decisions that can change our lives to such people can hardly be good for democracy and the German fear that it is being undermined by this trend is understandable. My own students' general disillusionment with politics is particularly strong and if the trend continues, the threat to democracy will start reaching dangerous proportions. Perhaps the most disturbing aspect of this condition is that people no longer talk about it; it is an accepted fact that politics leaves most people cold and nobody is particularly interested in getting involved.

Thankfully, however, there are still plenty of people getting involved in grass-root politics and we should take heart from the fact that the tradition of the German middle classes getting involved in local issues and campaigns to solve all sorts of problems, ranging from freeing pavements from dog shit to preventing international airports damaging their immediate environment is still strong and definitely worthy of praise. They are called in Germany "*Bürgerinitiativen*" (citizens' initiatives) and are seen as an excellent way for "ordinary" people to exert their rights on matters that directly affect them. Their meetings allow everybody to express their opinions, discuss them openly and thoroughly with other citizens, take decisions and democratically vote on the next steps to take. This tradition has no signs of dying out as recent demonstrations in Stuttgart to protest against the expansion of the main station there have proven: TV pictures of middle-aged folk and pensioners taking part in (largely) peaceful, but agitated and prolonged protests for weeks on end cannot fail to impress. No violent, chaotic, young extreme, anarchistic nut-cases attacking the police and behaving like animals; rather professional, cultured folk passionately letting their voice be known by turning up every day and seeking dialogue and sensible solutions. And they were largely successful, as plans for the expansion have now been put on ice after a number of meetings with the powers-that-be.

GERMAN CHAVS?

But what of the rest, the long-term unemployed, the eternal under-achievers, the problem cases? Have they become what we call "Chavs" in Britain? There are currently (2013) three million people unemployed in Germany and it would seem that approximately half of them are long–term unemployed. Whether they have become the same as the much maligned "Chavs" in Britain is open to debate, but the term "*Hartz 4 Empfänger*" (*Hartz 4* recipient) is now widely synonymous with people who have low aspirations, constantly watch daytime TV, buy unhealthy food from low-cost supermarkets and spend any spare money they have on booze and cigarettes (and, increasingly, drugs). The general inference is that they don't want to work, are quite happy where they are and will milk the welfare system whenever possible. I would not suggest that they are subject to the same level of vicious abuse as their "counterparts" in Britain, but they are still a soft target for better placed members of society; if such people attack the target with a wry "only joking" look on their face, they can usually get away with it – a sad scenario also pointed out by Owen Jones in his excellent book, Chavs. *The demonization of the working class* (2011), in which he describes how the British working class has gone from (as the back cover of the book explains) "salt of the earth" to "scum of the earth". It generally suggests a hardening of attitudes towards people lingering at the lower levels of society and, consequently, a general acceptance of the law of the jungle principle that at the end of the day it's "every man for himself".

De-industrialisation, which has admittedly not taken place at the frighteningly fast and vicious pace as in Britain, has also changed the face of the working class for ever in Germany. Mining, steel working, heavy industry, shipbuilding and mass production factories have almost disappeared from the landscape and with them the old-fashioned values and characteristics of the working class: solidarity, collective aspiration and strong communities. By the eighties the beginning of the end was in sight and those men and women who had spent twenty, thirty years or more years with the same companies were now making do with low-paid security work, shop work, or temporary, menial jobs. As the twenty first century emerged and *Hartz 4* and the need to be flexible became the order of the day, Germans were forced to develop a new aura of dog-eat-dog individualism. The fact remains, however, that many present *Hartz 4* recipients are in that situation through no fault of their own, which makes the cheap jokes at their expense all the more cruel and unfair.

Germany's general economic strength, high pensions and sensible and generous social planning has, by and large, spared its people the searing pain and hardship suffered by their British counterparts at the hands of Mrs Thatcher in the eighties during her mass de-industrialization programme and systematic dismantling of the trade unions. The blows were also cushioned by the well-organised German dual training system, effectively combining practical in-company training with vocational college attendance, a system which has consistently been able to offer a future to many young working class people who were still able to learn traditional trades such as electrician, plumber, mechanic, carpenter, joiner, welder, painter and decorator, cook, etc. For the less technically-minded, there is a large number of training courses to qualify people to work in commercial fields such as banking, insurance, public administration or in general administration in companies large and small. The hard-to-dispute German belief that if you get a qualification in something, you'll always make a living has never gone away, and continues to support the existence and flourishing of small to medium-sized enterprises by providing a consistent supply of quality trained staff who take pride in their craft.

It is wrong to claim that in Germany the old working class has simply given way to a feckless "Chav" rump. Owen Jones claims in his 2011 book (see above) that major parts of the British media has already accepted this as the truth in Britain, hence their ruthless stigmatization of this new form of underclass. The term underclass (In German: *Unterschicht*) has, however, reared its ugly head in the German media in recent years and is meant to describe an unemployable section of the lower classes who are lost to society owing to poor education, poverty-stricken social backgrounds, chronic health problems, alcohol and/or drug dependency and an extreme anti-social attitude. In other words, a dependency culture so fossilized that the people enmeshed within it might only be creating costs for society for as long as they live. The exact percentage of the population deserving of this disturbing description in Germany can only be guessed at, but recent figures from an article entitled *"Armut und Reichtum: Die Unterschicht verfestigt sich."* (Poverty and wealth: the underclass takes root – my translation) from the business/economics section of the renowned German newspaper, *Die Frankfurter Allgemeine Zeitung*, of 07.02.2013 suggest that 20% per cent of the population can be said to be part of this underclass, particularly with regards to income.

The article also points out that the problem is exacerbated by the increasing number of single households. Such households have often been created by separation and divorce, making it more difficult for the persons in them to move up the social ladder as the possibility of sharing costs no longer exists. Mounting debts incurred by such individuals add extra burdens that some never overcome. Single mothers are particularly disadvantaged as the possibility of finding employment becomes more difficult as child-care can be costly and not always available; if people in such situations experience emotional problems such as depression, leading perhaps to alcohol or drug dependency and (long-term) unemployment, permanent poverty is the unavoidable consequence. Such scenarios are becoming increasingly common in Germany and are liable to be a lasting consequence of these socio-economic trends.

The main message of the article seems to be that whilst the number of people now part of an emerging underclass is not increasing at a particularly alarming rate, the chances of getting out of it once you are in it are decreasing. In other words, it would seem to be saying, the underclass is here to stay. The structure of families has changed radically as the idea of the traditional "nuclear family", consisting of mummy, daddy and 1.3 kids becomes ever less commonplace (although, presumably, still the norm). These new structures are making lives more complicated and those at the bottom of the heap living in such structures and with such added complications will increasingly have their work cut out making even a moderate success of their lives.

The German working class and the break with the past

So where does the "new" working class come from? Well, they are still the same people that have always started apprenticeships and trainings in the sort of professions we imagine non-academic school children from non-academic families always take up. Yet small to medium-sized German companies are still searching for young people to fill traineeships in the skilled tradesman fields, such as plumbing, carpentry and car mechanics. Simply put, Germany can't find apprentices. The working class professions are still there, but fewer and fewer people fancy doing the traditional working class jobs, or for that matter, being working class. And there is little prospect of today's German middle class families sending their children into the breach to solve the problem: parents' aspirations are growing all the time as they expect their children to go to university and enter the classic professions such as lawyers, doctors, dentists, architects, teachers and professors. As the middle class expands and more and more people feel part of it, they have taken to the consumerist life-style and are embracing it passionately; like their working class opposite numbers, fewer and fewer of them want to get their hands dirty. Not that there are many dirty jobs left as de-industrialization and high-tech working practices now dominate; the traditional muscle wrenching work in factories, mines and steel mills is largely over.

As in most countries, flexibility on the labour market has become the byword in modern Germany. Getting used to this new way of thinking, however, has not been easy. Loyalty given to and provided by companies, where people often worked all their lives, was a major source of social harmony in Germany and contributed to employees' motivation, increased efficiency and general well-being. In a shake-up at the University of Duisburg-Essen a few years ago, it was decided that many non-academic jobs previously done by employees of the University would be outsourced. This meant that our long-established porter at reception, a witty, down-to–earth, local chap who had been there all his life, and liked and known by everybody, was replaced after his retirement by a rather bland person employed by an equally bland security company. The bottom line, of course, is that his successor's contract will be more cost-effective as the social benefits of working in public service disappear overnight: job security, extra public pension, to name just two. The fellow working for the security company will be noticeably worse off in every way and the general deterioration of the standard of living of people working in the lower ranks of society thus continues.

This example of outsourcing in public services can be observed all over the country as cash-strapped local authorities seek any means of making savings to fill gaping holes in budgets. The Agenda 2010 reforms have also made it easier for employers to terminate contracts, an area seen as a cornerstone of German employees' rights down the years. As a consequence, more flexibility is also demanded by those employees now working in traditionally volatile fields of business such as call centres, direct marketing and security. "Jobs for life" as a philosophy is dead and buried; "hire and fire" is "in" and Germans have had to, very much against their own traditions and beliefs regarding cradle-to-grave provision, bite the bullet. Moving from job to job, and perhaps even from place to place in the pursuit of employment does not blend well with the general German desire for security and familiar frameworks (see chapters 3 and 5). After the ultimate victory of the free market since the fall of Communism, the runaway train of private enterprise has been sweeping away everybody before it. The credit crunch and accompanying financial crisis reminded people of the dangers of an extreme capitalist free-for-all; the consequences of that free-for-all, however, have been that more savings have had to be made in the public sector to pay for the mess left behind. The super-rich can speculate and the lower class has to foot the bill – the number of financial institutions which were bailed out in the years after 2009 are testament to this fact.

Conversations with people working in companies and fields of business exposed to this new and uncomfortable wind of flexibility and unfettered markets confirm that life is tougher, and the general working climate is contaminated by unease about job security and the future. The atmosphere created has obviously increased tension, distrust and a large number of stress-related illnesses and medical and psychological complaints related to the workplace. The fact that relationships outside the work place are consequently negatively affected by this probably doesn't even need to be mentioned. Such developments remind me of the ever-repeated words *"Die fetten Jahre sind vorbei"* (The fat years are over – my translation) that have been doing the rounds since I arrived in Germany (see previous chapters). And, generally speaking, the statement is true.

At the risk of repeating myself, however, we still have to employ the old truism, "It's all relative" when attempting any analysis of the economic state of the German nation as we move through the early years of the 21st century. A number of important questions need to be raised in this context: "How fat were the years between 1955 and 1980, before unemployment became more like mass unemployment?" Answer: At the level of obesity. How much of a bolster were Germans able to amass in those "fat years"? Answer: An extremely large and generous one. "How has the level of state pensions been in this country in all these years, particularly in comparison with other European countries?" Answer: High, leaving most other Europeans standing. "How has the inflation rate been in these years?" Answer: Moderate, with no huge swings. "How much cash, property and assets have been inherited during the past 50 years?" Answer: Staggering amounts. "How fast have rents and the price of property risen in the same period? " Answer: With the exception of areas in and around Cologne/Düsseldorf, Munich, Hamburg and Frankfurt, very moderately, thus leaving a considerably larger amount of money in most people's pockets than in countries like Britain, for example. And one last question, which rounds off this section with an important, personal insight. "How many people have I met in the last 34 years in Germany who has ever had to do without anything?" Answer: I can count them on the fingers of one hand.

As in keeping with the general approach of this book, I have not backed up all of the above assertions with a mass of statistics. I firmly believe, however, that a brief but precise sift through any publication or reliable website will confirm that the statements I have made are generally true. And on the final statement, you can quite simply take my word: most people in this country very rarely have to do without. Germany, despite new challenges ahead (see the rest of this chapter) and a more cutting economic wind, is still an economic giant. And even if further setbacks occur in the coming years, the inherent strength of the economy and the general sensible approach of the people in it and running it should ensure a continuation of the German success story, albeit with more modest growth rates. And if more severe times emerge, the generous harvest yield of those famous fat years will keep most people happy for a considerable time to come.

B   GERMAN SOCIETY TODAY – LESS GERMAN?

THE ROLE OF FOREIGNERS IN TODAY'S GERMANY

In a discussion with some of my students recently they claimed that the new working class in Germany is made up mostly of foreigners. Walking around the University in Essen during the early hours of the morning strongly supports their assertion: you only hear foreign tongues in the rooms and corridors as the cleaning ladies go about their work. Presumably every public or commercial building in Essen is cleaned by teams of foreign cleaning ladies on every working day of the week I have never seen a German cleaning lady at our university; either they feel such a job is beneath them and have better jobs to go to or they simply don't need to do such jobs. This, clearly, does not apply to most female foreigners of working age.

Just this week our university had its bi-annual window cleaning. The window cleaning team assembled in front of the lifts waiting to be assigned their tasks: an eight man team and not a German in sight with the exception of the fellow explaining the rota for the day (presumably the boss). Foreigners tend to do those sorts of jobs and are also your taxi drivers, bus drivers, refuse collectors, delivery men, people selling you all manners of drinks, snacks and meals in all manner of catering outlets ranging from exclusive Turkish restaurants to your simplest snack bar. 80% of the early morning trains to Düsseldorf airport are full of men and women of non-German origin; they don't have suitcases with them for their trip to the sun - they are ensuring that the airport functions for another day.

Like many airports in Germany, indeed like many of its towns, Düsseldorf would cease to function without their foreign labour force. Again, they do the less glamorous jobs, but they are still jobs that need to be done. It is hard to deny the fact, therefore, that many of the grandchildren of the original guest workers from the early and mid-sixties are still doing the jobs the "Bio Germans" do not want to do (Bio Germans are those born in Germany of German parents and grandparents). The original demand for guest workers was caused by a chronic shortage of labour; today's picture is, of course, totally different with almost 3 million people unemployed. But it is true that most Germans never really re-accustomed themselves to doing the "dirty" jobs and in the course of time it has become a given that it is generally non-Germans that do them. A customary, simplistic and ultimately primitive call from the Right has always been to "send the foreigners home", thus solving the problem of unemployment at a stroke. A perennial, malicious suggestion the German Right is often at pains to point out is that guests (as in "guest" workers) are expected, sooner or later, to go home.

One of the major challenges facing Germany today is to help transform this workforce into integrated citizens, people who want to live here as well as work here and feel, as far as possible, at home here. The Italians were the first to come in 1955, followed by Greeks and Spaniards in 1960, Turks in 1961 and Yugoslavs in 1964. Portuguese, Moroccans and Tunisians completed the influx of "Guestworkers" by the end of the sixties and beginning of the seventies They were hard-working pioneers in a foreign country who had little or no desire to stay longer than it took to perhaps save enough to buy a plot of land back before returning with a decent sum of Deutschmarks. Many stayed, particularly the Turks, had their wives follow them and had children, whose children now form the third generation. Since that time more foreigners have moved to Germany: settlers from Poland, Russia and Romania with German forefathers entitling them to German passports and residency in Germany. In more recent times asylum seekers from failed nations and conflict ridden war-zones have also settled, adding an extra cultural mix to a country which has, in the meantime, become used to accommodating foreign cultures.

Foreigners in Germany – The basic numbers

To facilitate comprehension of which and how many non-Germans are now resident in Germany, the *Federal Statistical Office Germany* offers the following overview (figures refer to 2010):

Total population of Germany:

81.715

Population in Germany with a migration background:

15.746

The expression "with a migration background" is an important one to understand: it basically means any foreigners who moved to Germany after the founding of the Federal Republic in 1949 **and** all citizens who have foreign parents, grandparents and great grandparents who moved here or who have been born here since then. Just to make things slightly more complicated, such citizens who have since then taken up German citizenship are Germans with a migration background. The largest group of foreigners in Germany is the Turks with approximately 1.607 million inhabitants. However, you can almost double that number by the same amount to account for Turks who now have German citizenship. In other words, just over 3 million Turks live here either as foreigners or German citizens with a migration background. For the sake of statistical analysis, however, both groups are citizens with a migration background.

Categorizing Russians, Poles and Rumanians who have moved to Germany since 1949 is also a slightly tricky business, depending on whether they had German forefathers before they left their homelands. If they did, they became German citizens on arrival. However, they still bear the name citizens "with a migration background". Such people coming without this claim to citizenship are simply referred to as foreigners. The other large foreign groupings in Germany reflect that initial surge of foreign immigration in the sixties in the form of "Guest workers". The 2010 figures look like this: 550,000 from former Yugoslavia; 520,000 Italians; 283,000 Greeks; 115,000 Portuguese and 110,000 Spaniards. New influxes have been witnessed in recent years by Poles (now standing at 468,000), Rumanians (160,000), Bulgarians (94,000), Hungarians (82,000) and Slovakians, Slovenians and Czechs (totalling approx. 90,000). These countries have all recently become EU members and their citizens have moved West in considerable numbers in search of a better life.

Other cultural groupings have moved to Germany in the wake of political upheaval, war and political persecution all over the globe; in other words, asylum seekers. Afghanistan, unstable (North) African states, Asia and The Middle East (notably Iraq), the former Soviet states and a host of other countries have been spewing out refugees, the homeless, the persecuted upper and middle classes, professional classes, not-so-professional classes, down and outs and various motley crews in recent years, all of whom have been landing at German airports in ever-increasing numbers in the past twenty years or so relating various tales of persecution and seeking a new start here. Citizens from more stable states of Europe and North America include 100,000 Americans and a similar number of British.

Foreigners in Germany – The doom and the gloom view

One politician-turned-writer who has made himself unpopular (but also rather rich) in recent years by pontificating on the underclass and foreigners in Germany, is a certain Thilo Sarrazin with his controversial book, *Deutschland schafft sich ab* (Germany is doing away with itself - Sarrazin's own translation of the title), which appeared in August, 2010. By the end of that same year, it was reported that over 1 million copies had been sold in Germany's bookshops, with final sales figures reaching 1.5 million. Retailing at almost 23 Euros per copy, it proves that hard-hitting, populist polemic, backed up by a myriad of carefully selected statistics and debatable Darwinist-influenced theses can make you a millionaire in a remarkably short space of time. In preparation for my own book, I decided, with a heavy heart, to invest 23 Euros of my own hard-earned cash to see what all the fuss was about.

If Germans bought the book because they liked the sound of its contents, then we should be slightly worried; if those same readers agree with the contents *after* reading the book, we should be getting really worried because it means that about 1.5 million Germans feel the same way as Sarrazin does about the state of the nation; namely that *Hartz 4* recipients are happily milking the system across the

190

board and having as many children as possible to increase their social benefits. The children they bear will, just like their hapless parents, also be rather stupid and place even more of a burden on the country's social system by being unemployable whilst bringing down the overall level of national intelligence. Sarrazin's analysis of foreigners' contribution to Germany today is an equally negative and depressing one: like the German underclass, Muslims' propensity to breed troubles him greatly and this, combined with their lack of academic achievement, aspiration and reluctance to accept and be fulfilled by the "German way of life", is, in his view, condemning Germany to a dire future. This is clearly reflected in the subtitle of the book: "How we are putting our country at risk."

Projecting population trends, Sarrazin predicts that the Germans are going to be outnumbered by predominantly Muslim foreigners within the next 100 years, a thought filling him with dread. Chapters 7 and 8 of his book explain that the only way of avoiding this is by "encouraging" intelligent, middle class Germans, preferably younger than thirty – and one assumes the Aryan variety would be his favoured choice of mating couples – to produce at least two or three children to redress the imbalance of having too many dopey, lazy foreigners and/or *Hartz 4* recipients claiming financial support they simply don't deserve and producing as many economically unproductive children as possible. To redress the imbalance, he argues, we simply have to revamp the benefits system so that having children no longer guarantees financial windfalls for the lower classes. And we can always find some interesting tax alternatives to help the better off produce superior German stock to keep us economically competitive. In other words, we have to be selective, a word guaranteed to send sickening shivers down the spine of anybody with a rudimentary grasp of modern German history.

Sarrazin's creepy obsession with such ideas was the main reason why he had to endure so much violent criticism in Germany after the publication of the book in 2010. He just avoided being thrown out of his own party, the SPD, but lost his lucrative job at the Germany Federal bank as a result of such socially divisive, pseudo-Darwinist, insidious ramblings. Indeed, it is particularly surprising, and for many disturbing, that such ideas can emerge from a member of a party which purports to have the interests of the working class at heart. Or is it simply another example of a general right-wing drift and a less compassionate Germany in which people are more tuned in to the limits of how much help the state can and should provide?

Sarrazin takes up many of the theses supported by conservative politicians in Britain in his criticism of what he sees as an emerging dependency culture in which people have got used to being provided for, seemingly sapped of any desire to show self-initiative to escape from their lethargy to find some sort of job and make the first step towards self dependency and a gradual climb up the social and economic ladder. He also makes valid points that people in such situations should, for example, be obliged to do something in return for the benefits they are receiving, either by taking jobs that don't immediately appeal to them or completing training programmes efficiently and well before being allowed to continue receiving support.

Any such reasonable suggestions he makes, however, quickly lose their appeal and credibility as you soon realise that his sincerely-held belief is that no unemployed persons or Muslims from the lower classes have the slightest intention of working - his generalizations in this respect verge on defamations and can only be based on prejudice and lazy judgements. That is not say that such people *don't* exist, but any intelligent human being would demand hard evidence to prove that they *all* behave that way. Sarrazin's continual criticism of Muslims' life style and attitudes can only be seen as an irrational form of weak-minded racism. Are no other groups with a migration background guilty of some of the anti-social behaviour Sarrazin accuses the Muslim cultural groups of? He thinks not, but I feel sure that any clear-thinking individual would see this as a grossly unfair generalisation.

The main problem of his book is its almost psychopathically rigid focus throughout on Sarrazin's principal theses: Muslims refuse to integrate and learn the German language; they do not wish to abide by liberal laws and rules of German society and by and large live in parallel societies; are happy in their dependency culture, suppress women in their families around the clock; only produce children to improve their families' financial situation by making them eligible for ever more social benefits; show little or no interest in their children (particularly their daughters) doing well at school and completing professional training and produce macho male teenagers who later devote themselves to a life of petty (or not-so-petty) crime and violence. He makes similar claims about the lower German classes, without, of course, the extra portion of religious and racial bigotry. The neo-liberal solution he offers, i.e. removing or drastically reducing basic social support aimed at preventing any citizen falling into the poverty trap, will convince few Germans accustomed to the state providing a safety net for survival. Neither will Sarrazin's constant refrain "In the USA they do it differently" have won him many friends: I have not met a German yet who is even halfway convinced that the radical American way of tackling economic problems is the right way for Germany. The more he pushes these theses, the more you are convinced he can only be packing the book with this never ending-list of prejudices to provoke intelligent readers into closing it and bemoaning the loss of their 23 Euros. Or perhaps he is simply attempting to goad dangerous dimwits into taking the law into their own hands to solve the "problem."

Foreigners in Germany – The example of Neukölln, Berlin

Sarrazin's arguments do not appear from nowhere, however: all of the claims in the last paragraph can certainly be levelled at **certain** members of the foreign community in modern Germany and **certain** members of the indigenous German lower classes. The fact that he has pointed it out and spoken out is the first step towards starting a public debate with a view to solving those very problems; however, the bull-in-a-china shop, one-sided, dogmatic, generalized, almost offensive approach destroys most chances he might have had of presenting measured and reasonable arguments to find appropriate answers to those very problems. Heinz Buschkowsky, SPD mayor of the *Neukölln* district of Berlin, which boasts the highest proportion of foreigners in any area of Germany, describes in grim detail in his book, *Neukölln ist überall* (2012) ("*Neukölln* is everywhere" – my translation) some of the scenarios Sarrazin hints at.

In some ways, Buschkowsky's book is even more depressing than Sarrazin's. With his finger firmly on the pulse of what is really happening in *Neukölln*, having been born, bred and buttered there, he relates the consequences of what he believes to be foreign families' reluctance or inability to adapt to German society and describes a world of high unemployment in which young men happily drift into a world of drug dealing, crime and violence. Many of these men, he claims, are themselves emerging from backgrounds where domestic violence is the order of the day. According to Buschkowsky, the main problem for young women from the *Neukölln* foreign community is the fact that they are denied any chance of bettering themselves professionally and socially because their main aim in life is to marry and have children. Buschkowsky's survey of local schools is particularly depressing as he claims that many pupils and teachers are terrorized by young, aggressive, disrespectful, uninterested Turkish and Arab men whose language skills in their native tongue or German are limited to disconnected unintelligible, threatening grunts. And all that taking place in parts of *Neukölln* which have long since become no-go areas with poor housing and little or no sense of community save gangs of bored foreign youths looking for trouble and usually finding it; parallel societies where indifference, squalor, isolation and fear made any form of integration an impossible goal long ago.

At least Buschkowsky does not seem to believe all is lost; education is the answer, he repeatedly claims, but reports that the foreign communities in his area of Berlin seem not to want to take offers of training and education seriously enough to kick start their lives towards a better future. He, like Sarrazin, bemoans apathy and even a certain belligerence among such communities towards the society they find themselves in. Working hard and being good at school, he argues, does not appeal to the macho, tough image of many young North African, Middle East and Turkish males and lost generations are the result with the obviously disturbing consequences for the economy and society in general.

Both Buschkowsky and Sarrazin are at pains to point out that the most serious problems are caused by a new type of foreigner streaming into Germany for the last 25 years or so, the majority of whom come under the guise of asylum seekers. There is probably some truth in their arguments that some of these asylum seekers simply came for the chance of improving their life style at the expense of the German welfare system (although it is always difficult to offer hard evidence for this). Families who followed have often been at the lower end of the social strata, further exacerbating the social problems of the German towns sheltering them. Add to this criminal elements from nationalities originating from war-torn parts of the globe, and you can see the sort of massive problems people like Buschkowsky have to try and keep a lid on.

Prostitution, drug dealing, knife crime and mafia-style machinations, according to Buschkowsky, has become a life style in certain areas of *Neukölln* and large sections of immigrants in these areas see this life style as perfectly acceptable: doing a normal job (if they can get one of course), would be positively boring and probably nowhere near as profitable. Most Germans have moved away anyway, he goes on to report, leaving the field clear for ghetto areas to flourish in a grim world occupied by lazy, directionless immigrants. Violence takes place almost exclusively between the foreign warring factions, Turks and Arabs hating each other with the most zeal and exhibiting this hatred by regularly staging mass brawls. All this would be bad enough without Buschkowsky and Sarrazin claiming that this is all taking place while these very same people are cashing in benefits while securing and boosting that seemingly endless supply of cash by making their submissive wives pregnant yet again.

Clearly, neither book is making much of a positive contribution to social and racial harmony in Germany today. Reading Buschkowsky's book evokes the impression that in his district of Berlin the only scroungers, criminals, uneducated citizens and trouble makers are those with a migration background from the lower classes - at least Sarrazin distributes his venom equally across the lower classes and regularly brings the "Bio German" rabble into his line of fire as well. But even the most politically correct Germans must admit that they have brought up real issues from a darker side of modern Germany. Moreover, such problems are not going to go away by themselves. One can disagree with the way both authors address the problems - and in particular with some of Sarrazin's more dubious suggestions for solving them – but it is of great importance that somebody is starting to talk about them. Freedom of speech is a cherished concept in a country longing to give the impression of being open-minded and tolerant, so why shouldn't such commentators also be given a fair crack of the whip? Sarrazin, after all, claims that all he ever wanted to do was start discussions moving on such subjects. Cynics would claim he was just clever enough to find a ready market by fuelling the flames of discontent amongst conservative Germans who always had a hunch that Southern Europeans were never to be fully trusted and certainly never as hard-working as they themselves. Either way, he has produced a nice money-spinner to take into his retirement.

Both authors claim that they are simply bringing topics to light which most Germans in high places have been carefully avoiding for too long. Their books, therefore, may well open the floodgates to a new era of no-holds barred authors sparking off debates on topics which have almost become taboo. Some would see this as a good thing: are Germans supposed to keep quiet for ever on uncomfortable phenomena of modern German society Heinz Buschkowsky describes in such grim detail? Is it not possible to criticise foreigners in Germany without immediately being branded a racist? Although the title of Buschkowsky's book is a trifle inflammatory, it is not hard to imagine that many of the scenarios described can be witnessed the length and breadth of the country where large sections of towns have predominantly immigrant residents. The problem in Sarrazin's book (and in most parts of Buschkowsky's) is that the minority immigrants *always* get the blame for virtually *everything*. And his astounding generalizations that they all behave the same way, i.e. badly, have all the hallmarks of racist prejudice that you can hear in any beer bar when the young, impressionable lads or the wizened old boys are airing their aggressive views on a Saturday night. These types of Germans solving such problems "by other means" is the last thing Germany wants.

After reading both books, you come to the disturbing conclusion that both authors believe that there would be no problems if foreigners and the lower classes were not here. A simple, Stalinist view: "A human being, a problem; no human being, no problem". Sarrazin, in particular, supports the view that reducing benefits would do the trick, forcing the lazy into any job in order to survive. In fact, if there were no benefits, he argues, many (Muslim) foreigners would think twice about choosing Germany as a "safe economic haven"; or, even better, they might go home. Buschkowsky is short on solutions to the many problems dragging his district into the dirt, but mentions that throwing money at the problem is not one of them.

Programmes to ensure that foreign children attend Kindergarten and school regularly and the introduction of all-day schools (also supported by Sarrazin) are concepts he firmly believes in with a view to improving integration and thus bettering the chances of such children. However, you still have the impression that he believes that things are simply not going to get better because the mentality of the foreign citizens trapped in economic lethargy paralyses the initiative needed to get out of it. While reading his book, however, I had the impression that Buschkowsky, the jovial, likeable SPD mayor was more a man of the people, mixing with people on the streets of his troubled district to find out what was really going on. His general commitment to integration is also unquestioned and his hands-on approach to tackling the very real problems that do exist is admirable; for these reasons alone I find his book has some degree of credibility.

Civil servants in Germany – The last bastion of the privileged

The personality of the rather aloof German civil servant, Thilo Sarrazin, (b. 1945), is rather different. After obtaining his PhD in 1973, he became a civil servant and basically stayed one all his life. The economy and balancing the books of municipal budgets have been his main areas of work, notably in the Berlin Senate during the difficult years following re-unification in 1990. It is difficult to imagine him getting out onto the street to find out what is really happening. I wonder how many *Hartz 4* recipients he actually knows? Or foreigners, generally? Or is he just another well-educated, middle class know-all who has done well for himself, read a few books, concocted a few ideas based on statistics and half-baked baked prejudices and who observes the problems he sees around him from the comfort of his well-furnished study? And then write a book about them, securing six-figure royalties which will make his life considerably more comfortable than it already was. And yet his book seems exclusively concerned with the costs of providing for those who are unable to look after themselves. If we take Oscar Wilde's definition of a cynic as "Somebody who knows the price of everything and the value of nothing", we may take Herr Sarrazin as the ultimate cynic; and his speciality seems to be foreigners who, quite simply, cause costs.

My words are polemic, driven by negative emotions and can hardly be considered as balanced writing; this is precisely the problem you have after reading a book like Sarrazin's – you tend to react in the same tone and manner he employs. The book covers topics which need to be covered, but the way they are covered is unlikely to produce balanced, differentiated discussion, free of emotion. If Sarrazin focuses on what the less fortunate in today's Germany are costing the system, we are surely allowed to ask what he is costing that same system. Here I am referring to the fact that he is, to use the German word, a "*Beamter*"; the usual translation is "civil servant", but the position in Germany differs from the British equivalent in one major aspect: a *Beamter* pays neither unemployment contributions - as they have jobs-for-life - nor pension contributions. When they eventually become pensioners, however, they receive an enhanced pension. If that is not privilege, I don't know what is. There is also the question of the debatable economic principles on which such a system is based – getting a bigger pension as a reward for paying **no** contributions towards it has a ring of madness about it, which I think even our economic wizard Sarrazin would find difficult to justify. No fear of unemployment, an above-average generous pension without paying for it – I wonder how many of the people Sarrazin spends 408 pages lambasting can benefit from such state indulgence? For me, it simply heightens Sarrazin's hypocrisy when he talks about certain sections of the population milking the system when his own professional status (i.e. being a *Beamter*) means the state has lost hundreds of thousands of Euros since 1973 when he first entered the civil service and will continue to do so until he and his wife (also a *Beamte*, by the way) finally go to meet their maker and cease to be "a burden on the state", a concept he happily frightens us with throughout much of his book.

Sarrazin is, of course, not the only *Beamter* in Germany and it is not his own invention, but it is one of life's mysteries that the powers-that-be have not concluded that such a system is unfair, socially divisive, uneconomic and thoroughly outdated. The problem is that 90% of the powers-that-be are themselves *Beamte*; and if you're a turkey, you don't vote for Christmas, do you? The fact that Germany still has them at this stage of its history also leads me to the conclusion that it believes it can still afford them; this, in turn, illustrates, I believe, that talking of economic crisis in Germany is misplaced: as long as Germany can afford *Beamte*, we must assume there is sufficient cash under the mattress to avoid anything approaching economic meltdown.

Which leads us to some fundamental questions at the end of this section: Are the two authors reflecting modern Germany societal reality? Do the books in question and the willingness of both authors to tackle uncomfortable questions reflect a more realistic, less taboo-ridden Germany or is it simply an uneasy lurch to the Right? Are they justified in predicting doom and gloom scenarios for parts of Germany with a high proportion of foreigners? How many Germans today share these views? Is the integration of foreigners also part of the general German success story or rather a serious blot on its copy book? Is Germany doing away with itself and is *Neukölln* everywhere?

"Yes" and "No" could be the answer to all the above questions. I have partially answered some of them in this chapter so far. Sarrazin and Buschkowsky have focussed, I believe unfairly, on the negative impact of foreign cultures on modern Germany and I would like to redress that balance by giving my own experience and views before ending this section. Before doing that, however, I believe it is important to offer some final words on the two authors who have dominated much of this chapter as I believe their views, biography and past say much about how their generation's view of Germany has been forged by their respective post war lives. Finally, I wish to provide some insights into how opinions are expressed and formed in a Germany still struggling to escape from its grim pre-1945 past and attempting to build on the general success story of its post-1945 past.

C   GERMANY TODAY AND TOMORROW – THE MAIN CHALLENGES

Sarrazin and Buschkowsky – Troublemakers, realists or just nostalgic ramblers?

For modern Germany, striving has been focussed on leaving the shadow of the past behind it and becoming a "normal" state. As the word "normal" normally provokes endless debates as people desperately (and usually unsuccessfully) attempt to define what the word actually means, I will reduce it, in this context, to a state which allows itself to show pride in its achievements and the things that define it. It is also the right of the citizens of that state (and here I specifically mean "Bio-Germans") to express their opinion on how life in their country should generally look. Messrs Sarrazin and Buschkowsky are making use of that right when expressing their opinion on the state of Germany today. They show a deep nostalgia for a Germany which no longer exists, but which they still believe to be superior. They represent, if you like, a bridge between the economic miracle years of the fifties, sixties and seventies and the more complicated recent decades. For this reason, they illustrate effectively where Germany has come from since 1945 and where it might want to go in the future.

Many have accused them of racism and lack of respect and understanding for people at the bottom end of society and I wouldn't deny that there is evidence in their writing to support that accusation. Many of these authors' more radical statements, however, may be more a sign of anger and frustration at the passing of a time in German history when hard work, discipline and the completing of apprenticeships and trainings ensured a good, steady job in a society where people knew their place, were happy with their lot and made sure their children had enough to eat and were well-behaved and worked hard at school, showing respect to older people in positions of authority, such as teachers, parents and police. I am, in other words, describing Germany in the fifties and sixties - the very years during which Sarrazin and Buschkowsky were making their way in a post-war Germany heading towards genuine and lasting prosperity and full-employment. Buschkowsky tells us of his mother, who was number eleven in a family of 12, and his early years of great modesty and no little deprivation. As he points out, everything he got he worked for; his parents' pearls of wisdom were always:"*Willste was, machste was, dann haste was*"(Buschkowsky 2012:33), (If you want something, do something, then you'll have something - my translation). Words which irritated him at the time, but ones he believes would help younger people today to free themselves from a dependency culture some of them have cosily drifted into.

Nor was Thilo Sarrazin born with a golden spoon in his mouth. In his book he relates with pride how, in the fifties, he learned to read and master his school subjects in an independent and disciplined way. He shared his living space with seven other people; they didn't even boast a radio, never mind a TV and he raises the legitimate question as to whether he would have done so well at school if he had spent most of his waking hours playing computer games, as is the modern phenomenon. The German discipline of sticking to a task till it is successfully completed seems to be the virtue he believes is lacking in today's generation. Both authors seem to be longing for the "good old days" when people kept their noses to the grindstone and were rewarded accordingly for their hard work and efforts. The modern comforts of modern life were not available: central heating in every dwelling, mobile/global communication, Internet, flat screen TVs and convenience food, to name but a few. But life was certainly less difficult in the sense that there were fewer choices and not the myriad of new challenges which face modern German society today.

These truisms should remind us that Buschkowsky and Sarrazin are to some extent applying the principles of yesteryear to solve the problems of today. They are principles which many of their generation in Germany today still find appealing and which few people could have any objections to. What's wrong with being disciplined, hardworking, learning a trade or profession and keeping to your task whilst being modest and content with the hand that's dealt you? Answer: nothing. Moreover, the best parts of both books for me are when they suggest, with a certain innocent sincerity, that those at the bottom of the pack take these principles to heart. The big modern picture, however, is a far more complex one, where modern society demands far greater flexibility, endurance, qualifications and soft skills to climb the ladder as quickly as earlier generations did. And this in a period of consistently high levels of unemployment which now stands at 3 million, the level it has almost always been at since reunification.

Neither did earlier generations have to cope with de-industrialisation, automation, globalization and the ever rising costs to the social system caused by an ageing population, low birth rates and the aforementioned reunification. Hundreds of thousands of job-seekers from new EU countries in the East are also making competition for jobs even fiercer. The bottom line is that while there are consistently three million people unemployed in the country, the problems described by any social commentators are likely to be around for a long time to come. To sum up, the principles lauded and adhered to by Sarrazin and Buschkowsky may have guaranteed them and their generation a job and a decent, secure future in their day; in today's competitive Germany they would only be a useful starting point.

The main weakness in the argument of any commentator wishing to lambaste the unemployed and people receiving benefit is the fact that the vast majority of those people are not in that position because they want to be. At the end of the day, it is a simple fact that there aren't enough jobs to go around. This is true in Germany today and probably in every country on the globe; it is, as Edward Heath, former British Prime Minister, once proclaimed: "The unacceptable face of capitalism". Unemployment, put simply, is a problem which has never been solved and Germany, whilst doing better than other countries, has not found a real answer, either. And despite the impressive sales figures for Sarrazin's book, I doubt that many people in this country favour many of the measures he recommends.

Freedom of opinion?

The fact that both Sarrazin and Buschkowsky were vilified in no uncertain terms by large sections of the population after publication of their books was a sobering reminder that Germany is not quite as mature as it would like to think it is: reasoned, cultivated arguments expressed in a civilised manner tended not to be the reaction. Rather there were uncontrolled, noisy, threatening demonstrations at their readings, including a number of death threats. While already admitting that some of Sarrazin's book has distinctly provocative elements, the reactions of some sections of the population did not reflect the flowering of a liberal democracy based on Churchill's maxim: "I disagree entirely with your opinion, but I will fight to the death to ensure you have the right to express it".

We are, in this context, back to the problem of taboos in Germany and the German love affair with political correctness. This has lead, in my opinion, to the dictatorial tendency of large sections of the left-of-centre, trendy establishment to lay down very strict guidelines concerning what you are allowed or not allowed to say. My views on gay couples' rights to adopt children were treated with such vilification recently by students and colleagues alike that I have now decided to keep them to myself in the future. I regard myself as centre left (or maybe even just left), yet the reaction of some people to my views made me feel like a reactionary, homophobic Tory. "It's OK to express your opinion as long as it's the right one", seems to be the current philosophy in Germany. Minorities, for historical reasons, enjoy an almost mythical level of protection; outrage, therefore, is the normal reaction when even the merest breath of criticism comes their way. This probably explains the reactions of that establishment when books like *Neukölln ist überall* and *Deutschland schafft sich ab* appear, but hardly illustrates a healthy attitude to the forming and discussing of opinions. Another interesting point is that most people have not even read the books in question!

A book by Henryk M. Broder, *Kritik der reinen Toleranz* – ("Critique of pure tolerance" – my translation) published in 2009, spends 223 pages pointing out that there is a down-side to being tolerant. By page 71 at the latest, you have got his message: making "being tolerant" your modern-day religion can lead to dangerous levels of over-tolerance where damaging patterns of behaviour are making our modern world a more dangerous place to live in and where we are on the greasy, dangerous slope to chaos and a world of "anything goes". He has a point. He just labours it for 150 pages too long, severely testing, indeed, the reader's own levels of tolerance.

The interesting point that Broder makes, however, is that we have almost become conditioned to be tolerant to religious and cultural minorities, come-what-may. The "come-what- may" part of the sentence is the dangerous bit, according to Broder. And, verily, he has a point. An important level of normality will have been reached in this country when a German can express his opinion based on what he truly believes, rather than his desire to make the world think that he is a "good German", which is tantamount in the current climate to being a "tolerant German". Others may argue that Germany's misdemeanours in the past make political correctness its ideal bedfellow - a relatively small price to pay for 12 years of terror and barbarism. This particular argument is still bubbling under the surface and will no doubt continue to bubble for the foreseeable future.

Foreigners in Germany – My outsider's view from the inside

The question of foreign integration remains the biggest burning issue in Germany today and I have already presented in some detail the way in which authors such as Sarrazin and Buschkowsky see the situation. In this connection, I believe I have made my own views clear on how they see things. In the following section I wish to develop my own ideas and describe my own experiences over 30 years.

At the beginning of section B of this chapter I proffered the thesis that foreigners have become, to a large extent, the new working class in Germany and I gave examples backing this view. There are, however, sizeable numbers of foreigners in Germany who are doing considerably better. In fact, many of my immediate contacts with people with a migration background prove this point. Many of my students have such a background and are now studying to become teachers or for a degree which will enable them to enter the free markets in a large number of promising positions. Many Turkish students, for example, have parents or grandparents who first came to Germany in the early sixties as manual labourers. It fills me with particular pride to see the professions of the parents of such students on Curriculum Vitae when they apply, for example, for university places in Britain: "Fork lift truck driver"; "Miner" (retired); "Shop assistant in a bakery". So much for Muslim parents not being interested in their children's education, Messrs Sarrazin and Buschkowsky! Clearly, like any German parents worth their salt, they were anxious that their children should have a better standard of living than they had.

Approximately 30% of my students at the University of Duisburg-Essen have a migration background. If they have got as far as university, clearly somebody has been doing something right in their upbringing. This sort of success story is not only restricted to university students: my Bosnian neighbours from the first floor of the building I live in are a pleasure to live near. Husband, wife, two lovely kids with impeccable manners who are being brought up to be fully integrated members of society while remaining Muslim Bosnians in their hearts. The husband is a trained electrician who has worked at the same company for the best part of twenty years since he completed his training; his wife, who joined him considerably later in Germany shortly after the civil war in former Yugoslavia, works also as a cleaning lady to earn extra money. The family is generous, kind, helpful, tolerant and pretty much what you would call perfect neighbours. Sceptical readers would point out that I'm probably just lucky. Very true, but I believe it also points out that cultural background has little bearing on whether people behave well or badly; their cultural background will influence certain aspects of their behavioural patterns, none of which bother me in the least. The husband, for example, seems to take the view that housework is something a woman does: he goes to work, comes home and everything is done for him. My limited knowledge of Muslim culture suggests to me that this could well be the trend in similar households. Does this give me the right to knock on his door and remind him of the fact that the modern German (or British) man generally shares household chores these days with his wife? Hardly. Have I the right to force a beer down him when he drops into my flat on the grounds that every German or Brit loves to have a beer after a day's work and therefore he should do the same? I presume he drinks very little alcohol because his religion does not favour such practices. My neighbours speak Serbo-Croat on their terrace below of which I understand nothing: Does this bother me? Why should it? This is actually multi-culturalism in action: different communities living side-by-side in peace whilst pursuing their own customs. As long as their customs don't impinge on my life in any detrimental way, and vice-versa, we can all do what we want. And it is my firm belief that the vast majority of Germans see it the same way.

And this is, by and large, the way life proceeds in multi-cultural Germany. Angela Merkel, the current Chancellor sporadically proclaims that "the multi-cultural project has failed". The everyday reality of life in Germany points to her being wrong. "*Multi-Kulti*", as the Germans call it, is reality, the way things are. Germans do their thing, foreigners do their thing, and occasionally they meet in different social settings where they have common dealings with each other. And in those settings they generally treat each other with respect. To ask for more can quite simply upset the multi-cultural equilibrium. It is far easier for an Anglo-Saxon like me to stand at a beer festival bar, slugging back beer and schnapps with an equally convivial German, arguing about whether Geoff Hurst's shot did actually cross the line at Wembley in 1966; to ask a Turkish fellow of my age to do the same is a cultural bridge too far for him to cross. Yet time and again, foreigners in Germany are being requested to "integrate". The problem is that nobody ever really knows what the word means. The concept of culture is being questioned anyway as "Transculturality" gains momentum and individuals of all cultures in every country are subjected to an overwhelming variety of influences in this globalized, shrinking world (see also Chapter 3).

When all the rhetoric, polemic, sermons and declarations have done the rounds in Germany and every talk show, book and Internet forum has chewed over and analysed all aspects of the subject of integration from every possible angle, it would seem to me that most people agree that foreigners living here should be able to expect the following things from the government and citizens of Germany: tolerance of their religion and their rituals of worship; sensitivity towards acceptable customs emerging from their cultural traditions and religious beliefs; freedom from discrimination in the labour and housing market and protection against racism in the form of verbal insults or physical threats. By the same token, I believe Germany can expect the following from its foreign citizens living here: adherence to the laws of the land and the constitution; the willingness to learn the German language to an acceptable level of fluency and accuracy to facilitate social integration and improve job prospects; and finally, the understanding that education is ultimately the key to integration. These are common sense demands for each "side" to take to heart and put into practice; I defy anybody to claim that any are unreasonable or impracticable.

The above framework is already being adhered to by most of the majority and minority population, which is why I would hesitate to suggest that integration has not been, generally speaking, a success. Even in the Sarrazin and Bucshkowsky books, their demands on foreign communities rarely stretch beyond the ones I have suggested. It is, as the old truism teaches us, the extreme minorities that spoil it for everybody else. By "extreme minorities" I mean the criminal, Mafiosi-style elements of foreign communities and more recently arrived economic refugees determined to milk the system for all its worth while engaging in a staggering number of illegal activities, including prostitution, human trafficking, blackmail, extortion, money-laundering and drug-dealing. Extreme minorities also exist on the German side of the equation: that ever-present, latent racism of nationalist Germans, who, deep down, sincerely believe their country would be a better place when the German "*Leitkultur*" (dominant culture – my translation) is firmly back in place and foreigners are no longer to be seen. Outbursts of horrific violence against minority groups, mainly Turks, do sporadically occur and are invariably carried out by neo-Nazi groupings, which unfortunately refuse to go away. As I write this, a large number of members of such a grouping (NSU - *Nationalsozialistischer Untergrund*) are on trial, accused of the systematic murders of 10 Turkish citizens over a period of ten years. While such extremist tendencies are still at work in this country and until the appalling behaviour of those involved has been banished forever, we have to conclude that the problem of integration remains an urgent one and debates on the subject will not be abating anytime soon. The school report, therefore, would have to include the immortal words: "Generally good, could do better".

A new generation of foreigners

As already mentioned, a new generation of well-educated and well-trained foreign citizens has emerged who have also, like their fellow German citizens, pursued and attained a more prosperous existence than that of their parents and grandparents. As a result, a more confident, modern type of foreign citizen can be seen all over modern Germany today: in good positions, driving quality cars, wearing stylish clothes and living in well-furnished apartments and houses - a far cry from the first wave of Turkish, Yugoslav, Spanish, Portuguese and Italian "Guestworkers" who shuffled out of trains in various railway stations the length and breadth of West Germany in the early and mid-sixties to be temporarily housed in nothing more than barracks to solve the problem of labour shortages and push on the Economic Miracle to greater heights. Hundreds of thousands of foreigners arriving for what seemed at the time for them to be a short-term "fix" during which they were to make as much money as possible and to return home at the next available opportunity.

As mentioned earlier in this chapter, many low-paid jobs are still performed by foreigners, but those who have realised that education and training is the real key to getting on have moved up the ladder, forming a new foreign middle class spawned from all the nationalities of those 60s guest workers; an additional dose of entrepreneurship has hoisted other foreign businessmen into relative prosperity or even top positions in society, light years away from the first stuttering steps of their guest worker forefathers in the sixties. The biographies of foreigners in Germany are varied and often fascinating, with equally varying levels of success. 50 yards up the road from where I live is a take-away pizza business which, people tell me, has been there for twenty years, owned by an Afghani. The whole building next door to me belongs to a Turkish family; the husband and father of two children runs a second-hand car business and rents out flats in the building to other foreign families. Funnily enough, I never hear a word of Turkish from his lips. His brother, whose German is of a reasonable standard but by no means perfect, owns the ground floor of the building I live in and rents the premises to a General Practitioner, a German, who happens to be my doctor and is a season ticket holder at the local club, *Schalke 04*. Just to finish off this hotch-potch picture of multi-cultural local variety, I should add that my Bosnian neighbour's wife cleans the premises of the doctor's surgery. We all get on rather well.

Despite their differing backgrounds and the different tales they all have to tell, the one thing all would probably claim is that they are better off in Germany, economically at least, than in their native country, regardless of whether they are selling coffee in a bakery at the station or running a thriving travel agency or second-hand car business. So, what is the problem, then? Or let's go one step further and even ask the question: "*Is there* a problem?" If we leave aside for a moment the problems we have discussed which beset any individuals or sections of society with little or no education and training, I believe that the main obstacle to integration is a psychological one which has its roots in recent German history and the development of the Turkish communities here since those first guest workers arrived. To put it bluntly, they weren't supposed to be staying very long; consequently, little effort was made in the first ten years or so by either side to integrate or be integrated. Guest workers were people who worked hard here, kept to themselves and were occasionally seen (primarily at the workplace) but very seldom heard. When their wives joined them, they rented accommodation in the less salubrious parts of town and continued to keep their noses clean. The men had enough German to allow them to do their jobs, their wives shopped in local Turkish shops sprouting up around the areas in which they lived or in supermarkets, which were anyway self-service.

Some would argue that this is a diluted and wholly unscientific picture of Turkish life in the sixties and early seventies in Germany; the description of the first generation is a general one, but their lives at that time can hardly have consisted of much more than bed-to-work, work-to-bed. In some ways the people involved were probably treated like a temporary site for building supplies and materials which was to be closed and cemented over when the buildings next to it were eventually completed. Economic expansion in West Germany in the sixties, however, continued at full throttle and once one project was completed, another began: there was always plenty of follow-on work for willing guest workers to continue with. Integration only started to develop with faltering steps when such families started having children and further integration continued as Turkish school leavers entered the jobs market, making Germany their second home. This second generation, backed up by improved fluency in German and modest but confidence-building prosperity, made their presence felt in a completely different way. No longer ensconced In barrack-like quarters, they were breaking into the society their fathers only knew as a place to make a living in and it is at this stage that we are reminded of Max Frisch's words: "*Wir haben Arbeitskräfte gerufen, und es sind Menschen gekommen.*" (We called for a labour force and human beings arrived – my translation). They were no longer people living to work but working to live and to create a life similar to the people whose country they had helped to reconstruct. Some Germans took an inordinate amount of time to realise this.

Second generation foreigners

If you place the second generation Turks into the time frame comprising the end of the seventies and start of the nineties, you are probably talking about the period when anti-Turkish discrimination was at its peak. Sensitization to and awareness of other cultures was not yet fully on the agenda in Germany and jokes ranging from unpleasant to downright offensive abounded in those days; it could be said that Turks were seen as second-class citizens who were still, by and large, doing the dirty jobs the Germans didn't want to do. The generation to follow were clearly eager to leave that shadow, but feelings of resentment and anger must have been present among many of them, leading to the developments of some serious inferiority complexes. With such feelings and emotions lingering, it was clear that many second generation Turks did not feel welcome. In view of these historical developments, integration was never going to be easy for this, the largest group of guest workers in Germany.

Turks, of course, were not the only migrant workers in Germany - Greeks, Spaniards, Yugoslavs, Italians and Portuguese had also been here since the early sixties. It would go beyond the scope of this chapter (or indeed of this book) to explain in detail why there were fewer problems regarding integration amongst these nationalities, but some obvious reasons spring to mind: non-Turkish immigrants were Christians; Turks weren't, so where were they supposed to pray? Turks presumably did so at home or in communities who organised makeshift mosques where non-Muslims were obviously not to be seen. Italians, Spaniards and Portuguese were able to go to a Catholic mass and were also likely to get to know Catholic Germans, or might even marry one (a not altogether uncommon occurrence). Greeks and many Yugoslavs, though not of the Roman Catholic faith (with the exception of Croatians and Slovenians), also had fewer problems practising their religion and getting into contact with the indigenous population, especially when their popular eating places, along with Italian pizzerias and restaurants, became more and more popular in the sixties and seventies (Turkish eating places became popular much later).

It has to be said that Turks tended (and still tend) to keep themselves to themselves, spend an above average time in the company of their extended families and marriage or intimate relationships with Germans was (and still) is relatively rare, whereas "mixed marriages" between Germans and other non-Turkish immigrants were (and are) more common. EU membership, which has finally come to most of the other states making up Germany's immigrant populations, has not yet been granted to Turkey, making those Turkish employees who have not yet obtained German citizenship feel more vulnerable and less part of the community. As unemployment rose in the eighties, certain right-wing parties gained support at various state and federal elections by putting forward their simplistic and racist solutions which consisted of sending Turks home and giving their jobs to Germans. Tension and mistrust grew again. Outbreaks of violence aimed at foreigners following re-reunification in 1990 further worsened the situation when a new and unpleasant generation of Neo-Nazis emerged out of the woodwork in the former East Germany to give fresh impetus to right-wing ideology and, more sinisterly, violent action.

Third generation foreigners

In the meantime, a third generation of Turks was making their presence felt as we entered the new millennium. It is a generation with a new and increased self-confidence in the light of continued upward mobility; some found the economic climate harsher while still able to maintain a reasonable standard of living and some dropped through the net as described in such detail by Herr Buschkowsky. The 2000+ generation all had one thing in common: they took further steps towards moving away from that 60s generation by presenting themselves as a fully established part of the German landscape as a community of people who clearly look different, behave differently, dress differently and who now represent Turkey in Germany in a unique way. One imagines that many of them resemble their compatriots on any street in modern Turkey: dressed to impress, with both the men and women taking great pride in their appearance, while others, particularly the women, wear more traditional clothes, including head scarves and veils. The families are generally larger and more excitable than German ones and most of them are now bi-lingual, with the exception perhaps of the first generation women who are now grandmothers and who might never even have learnt German then and have no need to learn it now. Add to this the ubiquitous presence of Doner Kebap snack bars and fruit and vegetable stores and older and younger Turkish men, hanging around chatting and passing the time of day together.

I am conveying a picture which is fairly typical of most large German towns today; in many ways it is a harmonious, almost idealized picture, one that most people have got used to in the past twenty or thirty years or so, but it is also an example of people from a different culture being themselves and proving that multi-culturalism is a viable option. It is, of course, not the picture you can readily witness in less salubrious areas of such towns where youth unemployment is high and money is tighter. The influx of foreign immigrants who have recently come to Germany as asylum seekers from all over the Middle East and Northern Africa is complicating the mix further in these areas; many such immigrants are also finding it very hard to integrate at all. Tension with Turks (and between each other) is common and the threat of ghettos springing up is real. "Bio-Germans" in such areas are a rare commodity. Yes, we are back in Buschkowsky territory again.

New identities and "Turkish ways of life"

The extra input of foreign immigrants in the past twenty years from a wider variety of different cultures and conflict-ridden regions has undoubtedly set back progress. Many did come with nothing and a number of them have stayed at that level and become long-term recipients of state benefits. The third generation of Turks, who still make up the majority of the immigrant community, have other problems: finding themselves in the middle of a difficult identity crisis is one of them. The inevitable questions they are asking themselves are the following: Am I now German? Half-German? Wholly Turkish? Half Turkish? When I ask my Turkish students these questions they inevitably state proudly that they are Turkish first and foremost. Further probing reveals that they generally feel quite happy here in Germany and couldn't really imagine living in the land of their fathers. They enjoy holidays there, however, and find life there warmer (and not just the temperatures) and generally more pleasant. They generally grow up here bilingually and may have more Turkish friends than German ones. They find other German students generally friendly and accommodating but still tend to socialize with Turks. The fact that much of their life is spent in a family setting is a given for them and is something that few would want less of or find in any way peculiar.

These descriptions do not represent a wide cross-section of the Turkish community in Germany. Neither have I organised such questions in a scientific manner; I have simply gathered impressions over the past ten years in informal contact on campus with third generation Turks. The answers I have received have been remarkably consistent over those years and I would conclude that the one issue that has not yet been resolved has been the one concerning identity: young Turks growing up here are aware that they are neither Turkish nor German, although their impulsive, gut reaction is always to claim the former. In some ways, I can relate to them, having the same ambivalent feelings after spending over thirty years in Germany: I am a British-German here and a German-Brit in Britain. Many Brits almost see me as a German; many Germans feel the same way.

Identities, of course, are not set in stone and new ones can be formed as cultural change marches relentlessly on. Social commentators observe a trend amongst younger Turks to seek new identities in religion and some have flung themselves into their Islamic religion in a big way: for some a solution to the annoying problem of not being accepted as "real" Turks at home, and not being fully accepted by German society. Thankfully, only a minority of young Turks seek the dogmatic, hard-core aspects of their religion and most approach life in a more open and liberal way. Some Turkish men have German girlfriends, have the occasional drink and straddle both sides of the cultural divide, floating between that divide in a relaxed and natural way. Some Turkish families have become less conservative in the course of the years in Germany, others have perhaps moved in the opposite direction in an attempt to rescue the principles of their religion and traditions. One has the impression that younger male Turks have more leeway and scope to push the boundaries of their family traditions and ties and find a way of life which allows them to be respected by their own community (i.e. in the family and home) and the German community (i.e. at work, educational institution and when pursuing leisure activities). It would appear that the Turkish female generally has a harder time of it if she comes from a more conservative family and wants to seek and adapt a more westernized, liberal lifestyle; it would also appear to me that few have German boyfriends, either by inclination (i.e. perhaps Turkish women quite simply prefer Turkish men) or to avoid creating friction in their families.

Clearly there is no one Turkish-German family: not every Turkish family follows every aspect of their religion to the letter and some have more liberal attitudes than others. Everybody, to use the mother of all truisms, is different and until a full-scale, comprehensive and reliable empirical survey is carried out, it will be difficult to really pin down what the "Turkish way of life" is in Germany. The closest I myself have got to finding out was when a female Turkish student gave a class presentation on the custom of Turkish females wearing head scarves. That part of her talk was interesting enough, but when she invited questions and it became clear that she was prepared to answer such questions openly and honestly, the other non-Turkish students showed a natural curiosity that proved to me how seldom they have the chance to find out about Turkish culture - and how genuinely interested they are when given the chance.

The student's descriptions of courting rituals in Turkish families, for example, were both enlightening and fascinating, despite the fact that all the German students found them so far removed from their own reality that they could hardly believe their ears. The same Germans, however, also seemed convinced by the Turkish student's assertions that such rituals were accepted by all parties and actually functioned rather well despite what some North Europeans might see as the interfering and decisive role of the respective parents in the partner selection process. The whole session was a lesson in learning about the way they do things in another culture by listening to a person from that culture without feeling the slightest pressure to do things the same way. One had the impression that such exchanges take place far too seldom.

Even without such fascinating insights, however, it is clear that Turks live a rather different home and family life to Germans. It is very unusual for Turkish people to live with their respective boyfriends or girlfriends before they are married; it is unusual for Turks not to marry Muslims and generally they marry other Turks; parental blessing of potential partners is important and not respecting the wishes of parents can lead to tension and disharmony and in some extreme cases, family tragedies. The murder of Muslim women disobeying the wishes of their parents in this respect has happened in Germany (as they have in Britain, of course) on, thankfully, a very rare number of occasions. We are talking about "honour killings", a murder ritual condemned by everybody, including the vast majority of Muslims in this country and ascribed to evil people who are acting on a wholly misguided interpretation of their own religion. Jasvinder Sanghera writing in the "Guardian", after such a tragic incident in Britain a couple of years ago, sums up my own feelings on this topic and I am convinced it is a view supported in every community in Germany today: "It is not part of anybody's culture to be abused".

It is worth remembering that the Turks are not the only Muslims in this country; the multifarious mix of cultures from the Middle East and North Africa further confuse the picture as more radicalized youths and young men arrive from such conflict zones. The radicalisation of Muslim beliefs can be observed mostly amongst these immigrants and asylum seekers and has in turn created fears in some circles that a tiny but dangerous minority are letting themselves be used by terrorist-style groups with murderous ideas. According to the German magazine *Focus* of 11.06.13, (http://www.focus.de/politik/deutschland/) Germany's Federal Office for the Protection of the Constitution reported radicalised Islamist groupings to have approximately 42,000 members, an increase on the previous year of 4.000. The danger of imminent incidents is presumably omnipresent.

Britain has already experienced such incidents in the form of a suicide bomb attack (7.07.05) in which 56 people died and 700 were injured and the grisly murder of an off-duty soldier (22.05.13). Both atrocities occurred on the streets of London and were carried out by British born Muslims; they were, therefore, "home-grown" terrorists, to use the common jargon. Germany has thus far been spared such attacks although in the past few years two or three planned terrorist bombs have only been intercepted and foiled at the eleventh hour. One has the sickening impression that one of them is, sooner or later, going to succeed. If "home-grown" terrorists in Germany do finally manage to pull off a similar atrocity, we will have a whole new list of problems to deal with in German society which may well make present concerns about integration seem inconsequential. The population braces itself for something occurring at sometime in the future, whilst hoping that radicalisation is not developing so fast that people involved will want to kill for their beliefs. Foreigners in Germany - and Turks in particular, who were the main victims of the recent series of NSU murders – may be inclined to point out that right-wing radicals are already killing for their beliefs. Neither can Turkish citizens feel happy about the Federal Office Federal Office for the Protection of the Constitution (http://www.verfassungsschutz.de/en/index-en.html) reporting that approximately 22.000 members of radical right-wing organisations are also in existence. One can speak therefore of an uneasy peace.

Visits to Germany by the current Turkish Prime Minister, Erdogan, do little to motivate his compatriots living here to integrate when he calls on them to reject assimilation into German society. In a speech to 20,000 of his Turkish compatriots in Cologne in 2008, he even expressed the opinion that assimilation was "a crime against humanity", hardly rhetoric designed to bring people of different cultures together, but rather fuel dangerous notions of nationalism amongst the Turkish community. Erdogan oversimplifies the question of Turkish identity in Germany by offering one simplistic option: be as Turkish as possible.

Such statements also give useful ammunition to members of German far-right parties and organisations who then argue that if Turks are not willing to assimilate, they should go home. They will also argue that if Turks are encouraged to be as Turkish as possible in Germany, why ever can't Germans be as German as possible in, what is, after all, their own country? At the end of the day, of course, we should all be endeavouring to be as human as possible; the consequences of such endeavours would certainly alleviate most of the problems emerging when people of different backgrounds and beliefs live together. On a day-to-day basis people of any culture have principles which allow them to get on with people they have to get on with and in most cases those people summon up sufficient supplies of patience, tolerance and understanding to make encounters peaceful and beneficial for both sides. By and large, this description accurately reflects the millions of encounters taking place between various cultures every day in this country and all over the world.

The problems of the "Leitkultur"

I have mentioned at various stages in this book that some Germans have a tendency to want (and seek) perfection; the advantages and disadvantages of such an attitude have also been discussed in some detail. Some of them would also seem to be seeking a similar sort of perfection in the integration of their fellow foreign citizens: they should be a paradigm of contented, fully integrated citizens and somehow naturally display the German virtues already mentioned before.

Heinz Buschkowsky, as we saw earlier, would apparently want them to develop in this way; in other words, just like "in the good old days". Sarrazin would be happy if they reduced the number of children they were creating and leave the country as soon as they are unemployed or old. Other conservative politicians believe that they should be following, as far as possible, the German *Leitkultur* (The dominant culture, i.e. the German one). The problem with this advice is that most Germans find it very difficult to define what their *Leitkultur* is; others even find the idea of a German *Leitkultur* reprehensible. Others believe that total tolerance is the way forward and find it equally reprehensible that Germans should even dare to offer any suggestions to foreigners on how they should lead their lives. At the other end of the spectrum, in the meantime, neo-Nazis sporadically persecute foreigners when they manage to get themselves sufficiently organised, with enough hate-filled members, to carry out murderous hit jobs as the NSU have been doing for the past ten years or so.

It is indeed a confusing world for foreigners and I am sure they must often ask themselves what Germans actually want. The basic framework of common sense and decency I referred to a few pages previously would seem to make the most sense and most people (foreigners and Germans) I know would be happy to make it their basic guideline. But another issue has regularly reared its confusing head throughout this book: what does it mean to be German? What is the modern German identity? This question also throws up a further issue in the complex subject of foreign integration in Germany: if Germans themselves have dubious feelings about their own nation and culture – yes, I am talking about the past again now - , foreigners will presumably feel encouraged to cultivate their own way of living in the country they - or their parents or grandparents – have chosen to live in. Other nationalities less burdened by the horrors of the past will quite happily live according to the guidelines, customs, traditions and ways of their own culture and many of the foreign nationalities residing in Germany are doing just that and causing nobody any hardships by doing so.

The problems of "over"-tolerance

Can we actually be "over"-tolerant? Well, I suppose we can be over anything and as the old saying goes, "Too much of anything is not good for you". I would make the case that modern Germany (for reasons already mentioned throughout the book) sometimes does itself an injustice as a result of showing tolerance when sometimes a short, sharp blast of intolerance might be the better option. The modern German reluctance to give any guidelines on "how we do things around here" creates the image of a nation unable to express what it stands for. The Basic Law makes much of general concepts of freedom, the right to express one's opinion and the inviolability of man's dignity but the vigour required to implement such laudable principles is sometimes sadly lacking. A case in question at my own university has recently brought this into sharp focus and illustrates that the integration process is indeed a two-way process.

A group of students in our Anglophone Studies department produced a series of posters based on the contents of graphic novels covering a wide range of cultural and social topics. These posters were exhibited in the university library after an official opening ceremony. After a number of weeks a couple of Muslim students felt that their religious feelings had been hurt by one particular reference on one of the posters. They also believed that another poster had given unfair preference to the Israeli side during an Arab-Israeli military conflict. The students cut out one part of the offending poster, handed it in and allegedly expressed their dissatisfaction in a threatening way to library staff. The Professor responsible for the exhibition had all the posters removed as a protest and an attempt to protect library staff during their day-to-day work.

This is the bare bones of the story and it threatens to become an unpleasant and long-winded affair. However, the reaction of the Rector of the University to these events says a great deal about the general desire of people at the top to brush things under the carpet, appear understanding of minority sensibilities and make clear that everything they do is seen to be driven by tolerance. Allegedly, the Rector's immediate reaction was to instruct that no reference was to be made to this incident to the media and that a group of Islamic academics were to be called in to examine whether the posters in question represented in any way an affront to the Islamic faith. Since then, more common sense university staff, including the Dean of the Department of Humanities has criticised this reaction and pointed out that the police should have been immediately informed of the damage to private property (i.e. the students' posters). In an interview to the local press, the Dean also pointed out that scholars should be able to quote from any appropriate sources in the pursuit of academic excellence without fear of censorship or threats. In other words, academic freedom had been infringed upon. In a more general sense, the right to express one's opinion had also been dealt a body blow.

In such matters modern Germany, therefore, can go in one of two directions. One based on common sense and the principles enshrined in the Basic Law (i.e. Germany's constitution) or one which allows itself to be dictated to by fundamentalists or extremists. The opposition to the Rector's "let's not cause a fuss and get bad press" line gives me cause for optimism as it proves that people have grasped that cowering to minorities which do not share these common sense principles will take the country into dangerous territory: the majority become estranged; further radical sections of minority communities are encouraged to force their doctrines onto that majority and German extremists also feel the need to take the law into their own hands. The efforts made since 1945 to learn from the past and transform the country into a paradigm of progressive tolerance have been laudable and, by and large, successful. Sooner or later, however, the obsession with tolerance can lead to paralysis and lack of direction. The case described above is a perfect example of this and reminds me of the simple question influencing much German behaviour since the end of the Second World War: what does the rest of the world think of us? A pre-occupation with this question can lead to a nation making decisions which are not their own and which are ultimately counter-productive.

"Prosperity for all" – The eternal slogan, the only solution

To sum up, Germany shares many of the concerns which occupy any country in the modern, globalized, consumerist, technology-driven world: the perpetual problem of balancing the books in the face of an ageing population with low birth rates; the need to produce job opportunities for large numbers of its under and over-qualified citizens in a post-industrialised age and to cope with the problem of emerging inequality and increasing lack of social cohesion. Increasing disillusionment with politics and the men and women purporting to represent the interests of the country (i.e. politicians) is not a problem only common to Germany. Like many countries in Western Europe accommodating foreign migrants, Germany also has its own particular challenges integrating such citizens. Germany is also sharing the European and global burden of finding solutions to wide-ranging problems such as terrorism, global warming and financial melt-downs.

I have gone into some detail regarding German strategies for coping with the economic challenges and, by and large, they have closely resembled the general global trend represented by neo-liberal thinking and belief in the free market. Messrs Sarrazin and Buschkowsky have been given generous coverage with their own provocative (Sarrazin) and doom-laden (Buschkowsky) look at the problems of multi-cultural and socially-divided Germany; Sarrazin's views in particular represent a distinct and disturbing break with the post-war German policy of making social peace a priority. Whilst understanding many Germans' anger at some of Sarrazin's more radical discourse, I still welcome the desire to tackle difficult subjects and condemn the general trend to stifle discussion by throwing the predictable cloak of political correctness over uncomfortable subjects. I believe it to be an essential part of Germany's growth to full maturity to develop principles based on the way things are rather than on what Germans think they ought to be.

This is particularly true with regard to the debate on the integration of foreigners; too high expectations, overdoses of tolerance and lack of clarity on what Germany believes in, have all contributed to some of the problems we are now experiencing. As economic times get hard, it is also apparent that disaffected and disillusioned young foreigners are likely to be the first to slip through the net. The explosive mix of cultures from North Africa, the Middle East and Turkey, often consisting of young men from such disaffected circles, is a further danger brewing in certain parts of Germany. Add to that the ever-present threat from German right-wing extremists and insensitive murmurings from Germans sympathising with some of the more radical anti-foreigner statements of commentators such as Sarrazin, and it is clear that much still needs to be done if the lofty aim of ensuring that the journey from "guest workers" into citizens is completed to the satisfaction of all concerned.

It is hardly likely, however, that such an ambitious goal will ever be reached; Germany is already a multi-cultural society in which large parts of the Muslim communities still lead lives which are rather different from much of the majority German population. Many social observers find the aim of full integration (whatever that actually means) a false one – people want to lead their lives they way they see fit and be left alone to do so. This probably reflects the general desire of many Muslim citizens and, come to that, of many citizens throughout the country who do not lead their lives according to some fictional "German or Muslim way of life", but rather pursue a number of different hobbies, pastimes and interests which our modern world offers in abundance. As long as we are not bothering anybody else by, for example, searching for truth by employing the latest Buddhist meditation techniques, by training homing pigeons or by doing Nordic walking every weekend, people's tolerance is barely stretched. Individuals or groups of individuals make sense of their existence in an endless number of ways and most of the ways employed have no negative effect on anybody else. As long as it's within the law, their own route to self-fulfilment is happily tolerated.

All these things will carry on in Germany as long as the 80 odd million people living here have enough resources to develop their lifestyles accordingly. So far the traditionally strong German economy has impressively papered over a number of small cracks and most people have been able to continue their prosperous life styles without serious interruptions; in other words, so far so good. In the midst of continuing prosperity for most sections of society, however, the risk of complacency is a real one. The German middle classes are perhaps not sufficiently aware of the growing gap between them and the less fortunate echelons of society below them and the gradual transformation from a society of the "haves-and-the-have-mores" to the "haves-and-the-have-nots". Challenges are emerging as the number of disaffected citizens of this country increases, be they *Hartz 4* recipients, single parents, patchwork families, foreigners or extremists of any persuasion or cultural background. Indeed, some observers would even place the likes of Sarrazin and Buschkowsky in the category of extremists. Such authors, however, only find an audience when the economic situation is creating unease and helplessness among the population. Regardless of your opinion of how they express their views, they are, after all, only writing about the difficulties emerging in Germany today which are caused by a complicated social and economic situation. Germany has reformed its social system quite drastically in the past decade to face up to this situation and it remains to be seen whether it is going to keep a populace with high expectations happy in the long term.

The economy and the demands of the future

The beginning of this chapter reminded us of the strength of the German economy; that strength and seemingly permanent robustness has been the glue which has kept everything and everybody together and kept all the problems I have discussed, relatively small and manageable. Despite the recent global financial crisis, nothing much has changed and the disposable income required to still their consumerist hunger can still be found without any overdue exertion. Others are feeling the pinch, although the average Briton (and I count myself as one of them) might well say that anybody who moans in Germany is moaning from a very high level; the high-level moaning, I fear, could be here to stay.

Will Germany continue to stand only as a bastion of economic health, efficiency and prosperity? The fact remains that most Germans are more than happy to regard their country first and foremost as a successful business venture, relieved not to have to flex any political muscles. They are happy to present a country which is tolerant, liberal and understanding of foreign cultures and they are continually trying their very best to be everything their forefathers quite clearly weren't in the years between 1933 and 1945. The "Economic Giant, Political Dwarf" role fits like the proverbial comfy shoe, and nobody is in any great hurry to try on any other. Quite simply, it is a country that wants to stay out of the headlines and try to portray the image of the good guy, perhaps even wanting to be loved from time to time. These are all understandable aims and desires which are going to remain deep in the German psyche for a long time to come. Expect little change there.

It is also true, however, that there are problems regarding foreign integration which require a firm stance on what Germany actually stands for. If moderate voices in Germany do not make a reasonable but firm stand and make clear what they imagine modern German values to be and how they are beneficial for all sections of the community, other more radical elements will do so, with all the concomitant dangers. I still firmly believe that there are enough decent Germans around to make their case and get everybody on board, regardless of ethnic background, race, religion, age or gender.

If the economy holds together, Germany holds together; that has been the case for the past 60 years and will continue to be the case in the rest of the 21st century and beyond. Heinz Buschkowsky quotes a foreigner from his beloved Neukölln who remarked to him: "*Heimat ist immer da, wo das Brot ist.*"(Buschkowsky 2012: 66), (Home is always where the bread is - my translation). This doesn't sound very romantic, and it doesn't show any real love for the country that person has chosen to live in. However, the statement and the sentiments behind it are probably only reflecting the general feeling Germans have about their own country. Patriotism and, even worse, nationalism are out but we appreciate the creature comforts a thriving economy offers and happily snuggle into a lifestyle not on offer anywhere else.

I quoted Terry Eagleton at the beginning of the chapter, who pointed out the meteoric rise of the middle classes in the past couple of centuries. Germany has made the best possible use of middle class industry and nous in its own particular success story, pushing the country forward economically and politically. As the old working class battle cries fade in Germany (and with it the SPD's chances of electoral success), and market-driven reforms are generally accepted by both major political parties and large parts of the population alike, right-of-centre conservative coalitions (CDU-FDP) seem to have almost become the natural choice of government. Ecological issues are still fervently discussed by the Green party, and irreverent, vaguely crack-pot minor parties (including extreme right-wing ones) occasionally reel in a flurry of protest votes, but the majority of the population remain middle class and happy to conserve the status quo.

The future, then, is very firmly in their hands. Whether Germany manages to make a success of integration, prevents the dangerous drift into a British-style "Haves-and-have-nots" society and succeeds in developing a balanced and mature identity depends on the movers and shakers of society represented by the burgeoning German middle-class. When their members obtained their first portion of the new Deutschmarks in 1948 they started investing sensibly and have been doing so ever since. The word "sensible" has played a dominant role in German society all these years and we can but hope that the German middle class, with the enormous economic clout it possesses, continues to influence, decide and innovate in a sensible way. In the space of sixty four years of German democracy they haven't made too many mistakes and judging by what I have seen and experienced during the last 34 years of that period, I hold the firm belief that they will continue doing the right things despite the complex nature of modern Germany. Whatever has happened in Germany since "Zero hour", they have always stuck to the sensible path, making extremism of any form their enemy. New complexities demand new approaches, some of which have been discussed at length in this chapter; I feel sure, however, that the sensible approach will prevail, and that they will make the right decisions again to ensure that Germany remains in the pole position it has been in for the best part of those 60-odd years. Terry Eagleton will be right again about the middle classes; it is, however, imperative that those same German middle classes take the rest along with them, too.

8   The final verdict

"GERMAN HYGIENE IS WONDERFUL, BUT MAN DOES NOT LIVE ON HYGIENE ALONE."

DIDI HAMANN, A LIVERPOOL TAXI DRIVER AND AN UNPATRIOTIC CONFESSION

Writing a book about a foreign country you have been living in for over half your life not only answers the usual questions about that country, but also automatically develops into a journey of self-revelation during which some fundamental questions about your own relationship to that country emerge. Has it become your home? Is it better than the country you came (and come) from? Do you still miss anything from your homeland? Will you end your days in the "new" home? Writing the book has helped me to conclude that "Yes" is probably the answer to all the above questions. This means that writing the book has been very useful, if only for this reason.

Whether it has been useful for any other purpose remains to be seen – I eagerly await feedback from anybody who has ventured to read it. Above all, I hope it has kept the promise contained in the title - "an outsider's view from the inside". Any reporting or analysis of German cultural standards and developments in Germany has been presented through the writer's eyes and that writer remains an outsider although his right to call himself that diminishes with each passing year. The attempt to offer a balanced view of all things has been a serious one throughout the book, but the omnipresence of subjectivity has hopefully given the book its unique attraction. The mere presence of such liberal portions of subjectivity disqualifies it, of course, from being a scientific text.

The British author, Jeannette Winterson, believes, however, that objectivity doesn't really exist anyway, and she states her case in her latest autobiographical work, *Why be happy when you could be normal?* : "When we are objective we are subjective too. When we say "I think" we don't leave our emotions outside the door. To tell someone not to be emotional is to tell them to be dead". (Winterson 2012: 211). Whilst not going quite that far, I believed that my book had to transmit the feeling and emotions connected to what actually happened to me during all those years in Germany; otherwise the words just become a tool for the

225

transmission of detached analysis and the book just another collection of facts about Germany. There is nothing wrong with that, but it just isn't that sort of book. Thus my opinions about everything that has happened during my time here have been formulated and expressed with only a thin filter of objectivity. If my book has proved Winterson's theory that it is impossible to have a thought without a feeling, then I can happily live with that fact; I would like to think that the book has benefitted from this approach.

After completion of the book, two main conclusions emerge in connection with my own relationship to Germany: firstly, whilst remaining in my heart of hearts a "Scouser", my approach to life has become increasingly German. What does this actually mean? Primarily, it involves approaching matters in a sensible, reasonable, structured and goal-oriented way. That all sounds a trifle boring and definitely not very rock and roll, but I will have to accept it as a phenomenon which has sneaked up on me over the years and gradually won me over; perhaps I have become a better person as a result.

Unfortunately it also supports the age-old thesis that Germans are lacking on the spontaneity front and the negative image of mechanical, Teutonic super-efficiency gains further credence, fanning the flames of anybody wishing to sell us the ultimate German stereotype. This was precisely not my intention, but try as I may to avoid encouraging such tedious stereotypes, I still needed to give an honest assessment on how the "average German" approaches life, and the words "sensible", "rational", "goal-oriented" entered my brain early on and refused to go away. This is not prejudice: experience and observation has taught me that these adjectives must be applied to Germans - and in the meantime to me, too. This hints at how thorough my assimilation process has been.

I would still like to think, however, that the big Scouse heart and mischievous sense of bolshie anarchy given to me as a birthright fights back when the Teutonic sense of reason threatens to slow me up. But as German culture has changed over the years, a more relaxed approach to life has also made itself more evident, rendering the cliché of the robotic German obsolete anyway. This "improvement" in German behaviour patterns has also contributed in no small way in bringing me to my second conclusion: Germany is, all things considered, a better place to live in than Britain. There, I've said it. When I started writing the book, I was half convinced; as I write this final chapter I am fully convinced. Gulp.

Despite such unpatriotic statements, I have few feelings of guilt; I love Liverpool, but not Essen. I prefer to live in Essen, but need the warm hugs of Liverpool on a regular basis. I long for the pristine toilets of an Essen pub, but also miss the heart-warming chat with the Liverpool barmaid in the pub whose toilets an average German would only enter with full protective clothing and a bottle of Lidl's strongest disinfectant. In other words, German hygiene is wonderful (and something you appreciate more and more as the years go by), but man does not live on hygiene alone. Dietmar ,"Didi", Hamann, the German ex-footballer who spent a number of years as a Liverpool player in the nineties, explains this concept of hygiene in more detail when talking about football management in his 2012 book, *My love affair with Liverpool.* He calls hygiene factors basic German concepts such as working conditions, pay, status and security (Hamann 2012 cf. 229-230). These are the building bricks which, he argues, Germans expect as a solid, starting point and which must be in place before anything else is achieved; in addition, he argues that Germans are very good at providing such building bricks. They are perhaps not so good, he goes on to admit, at nurturing the sort of personal, motivational factors which British football managers excel at, such as giving recognition of the work you do through praise and kind words. He would seem to be arguing here (and generally in the book) that Germans provide the concrete items to motivate while the Britons offer the more indefinable relationship-based motivational factors.

Hamann would therefore seem to be pointing to the fact that things in German society are the real goals while the feelings in that society play a subordinate role. To put this concept into an even smaller nutshell we could use the opposing concepts of head versus heart. I am aware that we are now starting to take a minimalist approach to describing how life is in Germany, but as a general summary as we reach the end of the book I believe the approach serves a useful purpose. Whilst it would be unfair to reduce the difference between Germany and Britain to the head/heart or thinking/feeling split, there is certainly some truth in it. And if I compared Germany with my own home town, a city teeming with people living on raw emotion and impulsive urges, I would say there is a lot of truth in it. And if you were to do an extensive survey among citizens in Germany originating from Southern climes on what they believe is the main difference between them and Germans, you might well hear the following statement a lot: "Germans think, we feel".

When Hamann refers to his own difficulties getting used to life in Britain, he says the following: "Of course the legendary German efficiency was a major difference, too. Some people think that this is something of a myth, but I can assure you it isn't. From a very early age we are immersed in a culture that values orderliness, tidiness and control. You only have to walk through a German city to see it with your own eyes...inevitably this attitude seeps into everything we do". (Hamann 2012: 81) He is hitting the nail fairly and squarely on the head here and explaining probably one of the most important differences between Britons and Germans: when a German does something, he does it properly, or not at all. In contrast, our attention to detail and desire for only the best is often sadly lacking. This creates a more relaxed atmosphere, but leads, for example, to untidy towns, unkempt buildings and - we are back to the hygiene concept again now – below standard toilets. The easy-going approach to life makes things less stressful, but can lead to complacency.

That word was constantly on the lips of the taxi driver driving me to Liverpool John Lennon Airport at an unearthly hour last week after I told him I lived in Germany. Complacency was the one thing not afflicting Germans, he explained. They were always ready to learn, especially from other cultures, he continued. "Unlike us", I murmured. "Exactly", he replied. I was hardly expecting a Scouse taxi driver to be offering me valuable input for the final chapter of my book at 4.30 in the morning, but, just like Didi Hamann, he was summing up things very succinctly. If Germans did begin to suffer from complacency, it probably would be the only thing standing in the way of Germany remaining the most economically successful country in Europe (if not the world); it might also prevent them from recognizing and solving some of the problems discussed in Chapter 7.

There is, of course, also the danger that consumerist satiation, too much of a good thing, too high expectations and a general drift towards decadence could one day start to nibble away at the Germans' appetite for perfection and undermine their very successful system. Other challenges, as described in Chapters 6 and 7, such as completing East-West and foreign integration, the widening gap between rich and poor and squaring the circle of maintaining an effective social system with the backdrop of falling birth-rates and increasing life expectancy also remain stubbornly on the "to do" list. I feel confident, however, that the tuned-into-reality German mindset will prevent things from backsliding too far. External developments are, of course, notoriously more difficult to predict and the interdependency of globalised economies poses further threats which may spoil the German party; but if you were a betting man, your bet would still normally be on the German horse.

There is a price to pay for everything and the uncomfortable German stone in the easy-going Englishman's shoe is the degree of formalization that still guides the behaviour patterns of many Germans and the look of uneasy tension that often seems to accompany them. I can't speak for the other 100,000 Brits residing in this country, but for the sake of my own sanity I regularly feel the need to shout out to various Germans in my vicinity pithy pieces of advice such as: "For Christ's sake, relax/smile/take it easy!" I never do, of course, and comfort myself with the truism that if they didn't do it that way, Germany very probably would not be the place it is.

By the same token, Dietmar Hamann surely has moments when he feels like growling out insults in German - or in his case Bavarian - to disorganised, sloppy Brits whose performances fall below the norm his German mindset feels it can tolerate. By all accounts, however, he has been happily resident in Britain for many years now, which proves that Germans can indeed live without the high aspirations inherent in their own culture. Indeed, this lack of aspiration could be the very thing that originally attracted him to the place and still keeps him there to this day. I must ask him the next time I see him; I will report back in the second edition of this book.

Germany – a figment of somebody else's imagination?

For many observers, Germany remains an artificial construct: a country

229

whose borders were artificially fixed by the Four Powers at Yalta and Potsdam at the end of the war and carved into two to represent two diametrically opposed super power blocks in the Cold War years and separated by hundreds of miles of wall and barbed wire for almost 30 years during the existence of the Federal Republic of Germany (FRG) and the German Democratic Republic (GDR). The FRG had only a provisional capital city (and a rather provincial one – Bonn) up until 1992. Many such observers claim that the USA were never going to allow West Germany to fail economically in the fifties when the Cold War was raging most fiercely; the communist push for hegemony by the Soviet Union was quite simply too much of a threat. Recently uncovered documents reveal that the USA was doing everything in its power to spare Germany any sort of reparation payments in the fifties - West Germany was the last bastion of freedom and the way was to be clear for its continued economic development and to quell any doubts in Europeans' minds that capitalism was not the superior system. Harold Macmillan, British prime minister in the late fifties and early sixties, made no bones about his feelings on West Germany's position and put it plainly enough, in a combination of anti-German churlishness and envy, when he summed up the two countries' post-war situations thus: "Of course, if we (Britain) succeeded in losing two world wars, wrote off all our debts – instead of having nearly £30 million in debts - got rid of all our foreign obligations, and kept no forces overseas, then we might be as rich as the Germans" (Judt 2005: 354). On the same page, Saul Padover reminds us: "It's a terrifying thought that, in long range terms, the Germans may have won the war after all". "Terrifying" is the important word in this sentence, because Germans have, amongst other things, been attempting to do two things since 1945: working hard to forget the "terrifying" times and creating social peace and stability to prevent a repeat of the 33 to 45 horror show. Secondly, they are equally determined to convince their neighbours that there is no longer anything "terrifying" about them or their intentions.

Their efforts have consequently resulted in further artificiality in the sense that Germans, in contrast to the citizens of any other country in the world, have eschewed virtually any feelings of patriotism since 1945. Germans will quickly point out that it is an artificiality they are happy to live with – the consequences of extreme patriotism, they will argue, were the horrors of the Third Reich. They will also make it plain that what happened during those years gives them little to feel patriotic about anyway. The patriotism modern Germans are most wary of is the one the German poet Heinrich Heine spoke about over a hundred and seventy years ago, when he compared the German version to the French one: "We (Germans)", he wrote, "were ordered to be patriots and we became patriots, for we do everything our rulers order us to do. We must not think of this patriotism, however, as the same emotion which bears this name here in France. A Frenchman's means that his heart is warmed, and with this warmth it stretches and expands so that his love no longer embraces merely his closest relative, but all of France, the whole of the civilized world. A German's patriotism means that his heart contracts and shrinks like leather in the cold, and a German then hates everything foreign, no longer wants to become a citizen of the world, a European, but only a provincial German" (Judt 2005: 799).

I have chosen this fairly extensive Heine quotation here as everything contained in it which refers to Germany is the exact opposite of how modern Germans see their role in Europe and the world today. The French patriotism Heine refers to also defines how I believe most modern Germans would define "positive patriotism" which could indeed "embrace...the whole of the civilized world". If Germans were able to define their own identities in the spirit of this "positive patriotism", they would feel less inhibited about playing a more active role on the world stage. It is all a work in progress, but the fact that Heine's biting words bear little or no similarity to the reality of today's Germany gives genuine cause for optimism.

We should therefore hope that Germany can develop a new relationship with itself in which self-loathing no longer plays a role. Loving oneself, as all the best self-help books tell us, is the first step to being able to love others. Inversely, this would also facilitate the assimilation of citizens with a migration background as they would no longer be asked to love a country and people the "Bio Germans" themselves claim not to love.

Any book about a country, a nation or a people needs to be concerned with the question of identity and various attempts to answer this question are evident throughout the book. Germans wish to be seen as European, cosmopolitan, tolerant; they also seek solace and stability in their provincial or home-town roots; they are passionate democrats, environmentalists, travellers, hard-workers and much of the time perfectionists and seekers of high standards in all things. The label they have the biggest problem with is the German one.

The Brits, for example, are particularly fond of harking back to the past; for modern Germans it is the here, now and future that matters. One problem is that the rest of the world still hasn't got the message. How many times have I walked around the Olympic Stadium in Berlin with visitors and been asked the question: where did Hitler sit? (They are normally referring to the 1936 Olympic Games). In fact, it is the question that every other foreign visitor in that stadium is asking. It is an eternal topic which will never go away. The first twenty years after 1945 was spent working and re-building to forget. The time since then has been spent honing the successful, economic machine to new heights of efficiency and enjoying the best standard of living in the world – an equally effective way of moving on. But still the rest of the world wants to talk about the war. It is fact of life which will be around for a long time.

There is a rather goofy answer to the question "What is the German way of life?" and it echoes an off-the-cuff statement meant for Bill Clinton's campaign workers in the US Presidential election of 1992 when they asked for a main message to focus on during that campaign. "It's the economy, stupid", was the advice given and indeed, awareness of the economy and its importance for the country's political stability and future is upmost in anybody's mind in Germany. It was the strong economy which brought millions of foreigners and refugees here since the fifties and sixties, enabled successful German reunification and which allows Angela Merkel to call the shots at every European Summit meeting. It is, ultimately, the reason why I came here and am still here today.

This all sounds rather harsh on Germany and gives the impression that the country is one huge money-making machine with no heart and soul. That would be both inaccurate and unfair. Yes, a certain sober pragmatism has clearly taken root here, but I would not have survived 34 years on bread alone; or hygiene alone; or the trams running on time alone. Yes, people lead happy lives if those things are in place – and in this country they really are firmly in place - but we human beings need fellow human beings to live with, love with, laugh and cry with and sometimes have blazing rows and falling outs with. They have all been in ample supply in my time in Germany. Germans' honesty, reliability, generosity and determination to do things to the very best of their ability has always kept me in a permanent sense of admiration since my first days here as a hapless, scruffy Scouser. I have had my fair share of anti-German phases as phlegmatic, British carelessness has clashed with efficient German sobriety and obduracy. Many of these problems have been highlighted in various chapters of this book, but chapter 5 is the nearest I get to fuming about the place and its people. Other foreigners living here, however, might have a different tale to tell.

All my attempts to get to the bottom of the "German question" in this book will, hopefully, have shed some light on the matter. But national boundaries are becoming less important as peoples' lives worldwide become more and more similar. The influence of 16 million foreigners living in Germany has also changed the face of the nation beyond recognition. Individualism is as rife here as it is in many other countries; every human being leads a very individual life, made happy or sad by circumstances of their own making or by "the simple twists of fate" Dylan sang about all those years ago. National traits fly out of the window when individual human behaviour is determined by love and compassion or hate and envy. Despite the fact that Germans generally need more time than most before committing themselves to anything, and a fair supply of patience and perseverance is needed in your doings with them, I have found that love and compassion are indeed not found wanting and a general sense of fair play is one of their guiding principles. But as I have so often pointed out in the book, you just need to prove to the ever sceptical German that you are willing to go the extra mile before they get to the love and compassion compartment of their personalities.

I have now reached a stage of my life when I rarely think about the fact that I live in a foreign country. Certain passages of this book relate scenes and incidents when this was not yet the case; adapting to a foreign culture will always take time and involve setbacks. Regardless of cultural differences, however, most human beings wish to get on with other human beings and the tried and tested formula of treating people as you wish to be treated yourself remains a formula with the best chances of assimilation anywhere, including, of course, Germany.

As relationships develop, the culture in which they are developing plays an ever minor role anyway. Lovers, friends, colleagues, mother-in-laws, bosses and plumbers are no longer seen as Germans but as people who do all the things these people are supposed to do in any culture: mother-in-laws get on your nerves, plumbers never have time when your toilet explodes, lovers leave you and bosses screw you. Or perhaps they don't; but whatever they do, the fact that they are German becomes rather irrelevant. To employ the obvious truism, a good guy is a good guy and an arsehole is an arsehole, regardless of whether he comes from Hamburg, Harwich or Honolulu.

The people I have loved, liked, crossed swords with, got drunk with or done any other number of activities with since I was 22 just happen to have come from that stretch of land between Königsberg in the East, Kiel in the North, Aachen in the West and Constance in the South. They have been rough and ready Berliners, the more polished and refined Mindeners, hard-to-understand, earthy Mannheimers, easy-going Ruhr area people, hesitant but well-meaning East Germans and more spontaneous, lively Rhinelanders, to generalize and name but a few of the regional characters I have shared paths with over the last thirty years or so. And that is not mentioning any number of fellow Brits, Americans and other nationalities who have been following similar paths in search of employment, love or fortune (or all three). I am the man I am now as a result of events, encounters, relationships in the country I have been attempting to portray in the past two hundred pages or so. Things could have been worse.

My universal dedication at the beginning of this book is to the "*Trümmerfrauen*", the women holding the fort in the wrecked towns in the final days of World War 2 and who displayed a huge act of optimism by picking up spades to begin the seemingly impossible job of restoring order and hope in the annihilated Germany of May 1945 - somebody had to start again at a moment when everything seemed lost forever. They did and we should remain eternally grateful to them for making those crucial first steps towards re-building the Germany we see (and I live in) today.

From those heaps of rubble right across Germany, hope did spring, and those who survived the horrors looked to the future with a grim determination to survive, forget and strive for things their own generation had lost. Those born shortly after "Zero hour" grew up through the miracle of a reconstructed Germany, followed by those who were born either just before or after me. That generation was by then living a life completely different to mine as I ploughed a variety of formative furrows in the crumbling, former Second Port of the Empire on the banks of the River Mersey, a place so far removed from the bristling, prosperous towns emerging in the New Germany that people in Liverpool regularly asked themselves who had actually won the war. Liverpool and Germany were (and still are) different worlds, but no matter how different they were, they were about to meet head on as the seventies drew to a close and one particular Liverpool lad took the route many Liverpool lads had taken before him – the route out of the place.

At the end of the day, life is about people and your relationships with them and since 1979 my own particular world has been predominantly a world of relationships with Germans in Germany. My personal dedication at the end of this book is therefore to every German I have ever met since I arrived here - it's never been a waste of time.

Stop press

Any book which concerns itself with current affairs can become dated quickly; changing personal circumstances also need to be pointed out. This "Stop press" section is an attempt to point out some of these changes since I started writing the book a couple of years ago. I include them here as last minute updates before the book goes to print in early summer 2014

Chapters 1 and 8:

I rightly praise the work of the „Trümmerfrauen" in the time immediately after the Second World War in the historical survey of Chapter 1 and indeed dedicate the book to them in Chapter 8. Since then, Dr.Claudia Hiepel from the Department of History has referred me to latest research findings which indicate that the contribution of the "Trümmerfrauen" in the re-building of the country may have been overvalued and over-dramatized. More sinisterly, their super-human efforts would also seem to have been misused by certain right-wing factions in Germany to promulgate certain ideas linked to Aryan superiority. I have not had time to follow up the references Claudia has directed me to in this connection, but clearly recent research findings have thrown up (and, of course, will continue to throw up) new points of discussion on this subject. Whilst accepting this and making the reader aware of such new findings, I still believe that the work of the "Trümmerfrauen" should never be forgotten; they were there getting their hands dirty when there were very few people left around to rescue anything left worth rescuing. The losses and hardship they had endured in six years of war and the resilience they showed in shrugging off such deprivation and taking the very first steps to making Germany the place it is today is, in my opinion, still worthy of our respect and gratitude.

Chapters 1 and 7:

Following the federal election on 22 September, 2013, a new government came into being on December 13, 2013 when a Grand CDU-SPD Coalition was formed, headed by Angela Merkel as Federal Chancellor. According to the Coalition Agreement a minimum wage is to be introduced in most sectors of the German economy by 2015, a lack I criticized in both chapters.

Chapter 2:

I praised German football commentaries for not using a second commentator on live TV coverage of football matches. To my horror, yesterday's live match (Liverpool vs. Chelsea) on German Sky Sport (27 April 2014) featured a second commentator for the first time in living memory. I can only hope that it is a temporary editorial experiment.

Chapter 4:

Whilst writing the book I broke my record for the length of time lived in one German town. The previous record was set up in Berlin (10 years and six months). At the time of writing (May 2014) I have been living in Essen for 10 years and 7 months.

Chapter 7:

- In the trial in Munich against right-wing (NSU) extremists, who allegedly murdered ten Turkish citizens residing in Germany, no verdict has yet been reached (May 2014).

- No escalation of the problems caused by an exhibition created by English Undergraduates at the University of Duisburg-Essen has been observed.

- No similar books in the style of *"Deutschland schafft sich ab"* and *"Neukölln ist überall"* have since appeared in Germany, although the topic of integration is still discussed regularly in the media.

- I spotted my Bosnian neighbour using a vacuum cleaner the other day and would therefore like to revise my comments on his commitment to housework.

- No terrorist outrages have been committed in the name of anything people purport to believe in since I wrote Chapter 7. Long may this remain so.

Neil Deane, Essen, May, 2014

Bilbliography

Ardagh, John, *Germany and the Germans* (London: Hamish Hamilton, 1987)

Boyes, Roger, *A year in the Scheiße* (Chichester: Summersdale, 2006)

Broder, Henryk M., *Kritik der reinen Toleranz* (Berlin: Pantheon Verlag, 2009)

Buschkowsky, Heinz, *Neukölln ist überall* (Berlin: Ullstein Verlage, 2012)

Donald, Ben, *Springtime for Germany – or how I learned to love Lederhosen* (London: Little, Brown, 2007)

Dorn, Thea, and Wagner, Richard, *Die deutsche Seele* (Munich: Knaus Verlag, 2011)

Dylan, Bob, *Chronicles, Volume one* (London: Simon and Schuster, 2004)

Edinger, Lewis. J, Nacos, Brigitte. L, *From Bonn to Berlin – German politics in transition* (New York: Columbia University Press,1998)

Fulbrook, Mary, *Anatomy of a dictatorship - inside the GDR 1949 - 1989* (New York: Oxford University Press, 1997)

Hamann, Dietmar, *My love affair with Liverpool* (London: Headline Publishing Group, 2012)

Jones, Owen, *Chavs - The demonization of the working class* (New York: Verso, 2011)

Judt, Tony, *Postwar – A history of Europe since 1945* (London: William Heinemann, 2005)

Kaufmann, Tobias, and Tempel, Sylke *Die Tagesschau. Das große Deutschlandbuch* (Berlin: Rowohlt, 2012)

Sarrazin, Thilo, *Deutschland schafft sich ab* (Munich: Deutsche Verlags-Anstalt, 2010)

Watson, Alan, *The Germans – who are they now?* (London: Methuen, 1992)

Watson, Peter, *The German genius* (London: Simon & Schuster, 2010)

Welsch, Wolfgang (1999): Transculturality: The puzzling forms of Cultures Today. In: Featherstone, Mike/Lash, Scott (eds.): *Spaces of Culture. City, Nation, World.* London: Sage, 194-213

Winterson, Jeanette, *Why be happy when you could be normal?* (London: Vantage, 2012)

Thanks

A number of family members, friends and colleagues answered my pleas for help at various stages in the writing of this book. I would therefore like to sincerely thank them for their feedback and help. Dr. Stefan Müller from the History Department of the University of Duisburg-Essen cast critical glances over Chapter 1 and drew my attention to a couple of aspects which needed further depth and fine-tuning. Likewise his colleague, Dr. Claudia Hiepel.

Dr. Hannes Krauss (ex University Duisburg-Essen) also added valuable comments on this chapter, especially with regard to the literature overview. Hannes was a great motivator throughout and generally gave me the impression that I was producing something worthwhile.

Paul Newcomb, that famous Spurs fan (we all have our problems), confirmed I was on the right track in Chapters 2, 3 and 5, and even showed the offending chapters to German colleagues at the *Klett Verlag* in Stuttgart who reassured me that I would not be receiving any death threats any time soon from outraged Germans as a result of my ideas.

I also benefitted greatly from the needle sharp brain of my cousin, Brian A Lowrey, for the first two chapters. There is a lot to be said for the analytical, structured approach of a retired engineer. And being a Scouser, he'll do anything for a free drink. And nothing escaped the eagle eye of Mike Harrington in Chapter 4. This hirsute and multi-facetted Lancastrian, a resident of Essen's neighbouring town, Duisburg, helped knock it into shape in fine style.

Prof. Dr. Birte Bös, hailing from Rostock and our resident "*Ossie*" in the Department of Anglophone Studies in Essen, was the obvious candidate for the job of checking over Chapter 6, which she did with great gusto, claiming I had painted the picture of the pre and post 1989 East Germany in a balanced and accurate way. An American colleague at the university here, Christian Hunt, also gave his views on the same chapter and gave it a general "thumbs-up", along with Dr. Daniel Gordon , senior lecturer in Modern European History at the University of Edge Hill, in Ormskirk, GB.

My old buddy from the Berlin days, that erudite and dyed in the wool *"Germanist"* and Welshman, David Ladd, did a magnificent job on Chapter 7, happily improving and embellishing whenever he saw the chance. Once a teacher, always a teacher, his glee at pointing out syntactic and stylistic faux pas was evident at every stroke of his busy and well-meaning red pen.

When the final manuscript was ready I still had the nagging feeling that a professional pair of eyes needed to be recruited for one final look at the whole project. I contacted an editorial colleague from my time at the *Cornelsen Verlag* in Berlin, Jim Austin (another Scouser), who voluntarily abstained from more pleasurable senior citizen activities for a week or two to offer his valuable services. I believe he ironed out any remaining misdemeanours in the manuscript. A massive portion of thanks has to go out to him. Any remaining mistakes in this book are, of course, down to me.

My students who kept asking me how the book was coming along also kept me going; their insistence that I had to see it through to the end was a big motivating factor. A number of students with a migration background (particularly Turkish ones) also showed great moral support and provided much useful information as to how they and their families experienced life in Germany. Many of my assertions in Chapter 7 would not have been possible without their input. As I have already mentioned, everybody I have encountered in Germany since 1978 have inspired, helped and molded me and ultimately made this book possible. I thank you all.

Unser Buchbonus – Das digitale Extra zur Printausgabe.

Ab jetzt werden unsere Bücher flexibel. Im Buchbonus finden neugierige Leser noch mehr und aktualisierte Inhalte zum Buch: neue Kapitel, Literaturlisten, Tabellen, Bilder, Videos, Audiodateien und anderes. Damit das Buch nicht zu Ende ist, wenn Sie es aus der Hand legen.

Sie können den Bonuscode mit Ihrem Smartphone einlesen oder den Code direkt eingeben.
http://www.book-on-demand.de/autoren/buchbonus

C1wuog7BZG

ISBN: 978-3-86386-713-3

book-on-demand ... Die Chance für neue Autoren!

Besuchen Sie uns im Internet unter www.book-on-demand.de
und unter www.facebook.com/bookondemand

Neil Deane

Rocky passages

surviving 40 years of life with music

Preis: 12,99 Euro

Pro BUSINESS Verlag
1. Auflage 2011
Deutsch
248 Seiten, Taschenbuch, 148 mm x 210 mm

ISBN: 978-3-86386-060-8

Anybody harbouring the sneaking suspicion that "we are what we hear" will surely feel at home in Neil Deane's highly- personalized account of how rock music moved in with him at the end of the Beatles' era and refused to move out again. It made anarchy-bound Liverpool of the 70s a veritable demi-paradise, helped him survive various challenges in pre- and post- 1989 Germany and even made light of new millennium crises and general mid-life paranoia. Lists pertaining to several facets of his collection of 600 CDs, reflections on the live concert experience and pithy yet revealing philosophizing about the pivotal role music plays in our lives all combine to celebrate a 40-year journey many music lovers will recognise from their own "rocky passages".